Go Beyond stress
Twelve Self-Hypnotic Stress-Buster Sessions

Gary Edward Haymes, CMA, RH
Registered Certified Hypnotherapist

Sterling Paperbacks

Table of Contents

INTRODUCTION 5

The 12 Self-Hypnotic Sessions

Self-Hypnotic Session #1
Stress Management: An Optimistic, Powerful Positive Mental Attitude 32

Self-Hypnotic Session #2
Anxiety, Panic Attacks, Self-Obsessive Worry, Remorse Rumination & Overcoming Clinical Depression 73

Self-Hypnotic Session #3
Anti-Alcoholic & Illegal Drug Use 102

Self-Hypnosis Session #4
Marital Harmony/Sexuality & Lust 120

Self-Hypnotic Session #5
Palliative Care for You 140

Self-Hypnotic Session #6
Living with a Permanent Illness or Disability 158

Self-Hypnotic Session # 7
Public Speaking Enhancement 170

Self-Hypnotic Session #8
   Anti-Cigarette Smoking/Tobacco 187

Self-Hypnotic Session #9
   Problem Solving & Creativity 208

Self-Hypnotic Session #10
   Career Dissatisfaction—Motivation for Change 223

Self-Hypnotic Session #11
   Spiritual Depth 237

Self-Hypnotic Session #12
   State of the Brain—Serenity 250

Dedication 261

STERLING PAPERBACKS
An imprint of
Sterling Publishers (P) Ltd.
A-59, Okhla Industrial Area, Phase-II,
New Delhi-110020.
Tel: 26387070, 26386209; Fax: 91-11-26383788
E-mail: sterlingpublishers@airtelmail.in
ghai@nde.vsnl.net.in
www.sterlingpublishers.com

Go Beyond Stress
© 2009 by Gary Edward Haymes
ISBN 978-81-207-4405-9

All rights are reserved.
No part of this publication may be reproduced, stored in a retrieval system or transmitted, in any form or by any means, mechanical, photocopying, recording or otherwise, without prior written permission of the original publisher.

Printed and Published by Sterling Publishers Pvt. Ltd., New Delhi-110 020.

INTRODUCTION

In order to determine if you have a need to go beyond stress, answer the following questions as True or False?

You are happy and joyful 30-35% of your days?
You like everyone have a voice, with a huge memory capacity in your head that is always talking to you. Is this a kind friendly speaker?
You never permit yourself to be in a state of overanxious intense irritation?
You can control an urge for an excessive drink of alcohol, an illegal drug fix, or igniting a chain cigarette smoking habit?
You are self-aware of yourself only 10% of your non-sleeping time, definitely not self-worrying 50% up to 90%. A time of compulsive obsessive-self concerned self-talk, plagued with remorseful ruminations over unpleasant memories, a feast of mental pointless self-pity?
You can handle life's sometimes drastic ups and downs then "even keel" to a mental balance when necessary?
You do not feel a deep, nameless anxiety? You are not inclined to see more of the dark side of life, rather than life's brightness?
You have never spent a near-sleepless night thinking of your personal Nightmare Alley? You never suffer unexpected panic attacks?
You are not living with a permanent serious physical disability?
You presently are not receiving palliative care?
You enjoy giving a public speech in front of a large crowd?
You do not have career dissatisfaction?
You do not suffer clinical depression, when living through discouraging circumstances?

You and your true love are presently not experiencing communication or marital difficulty?

You do not allow crushing, continual unsolved problems to rule your brain?

You are not living in a spiritual void that totally lacks a blessed calmness and experiencing few glimpses of true joy?

If your responses to the above questions are True, you do not need this book.

Mr. or Ms. Serenity, you are presently normal. Psychiatrists' studies reveal less than 20% of any population represent this state of normality.

You should read this book if your answers to any of the above questions are False.

Mr. or Ms. Anti-Serenity, the expectation of *Go Beyond Stress: 12 Self-Hypnotic Stress Buster Sessions* and the preconditioning programs are designed to assist your reasoning and behavior habits to "get on track." A physical and emotional time out to attain a permanent mental comfort zone.

The Sessions do not endeavor to dispense or prescribe for treating medical or psychological problems. If you are experiencing significant difficulties, experiencing compulsive obsessive stress, self-talk and worry cycles that create periodic depression, it is recommended that you consult an appropriate health practitioner.

Synopsis:

Behavior and addiction modification through self-hypnosis is the same as being hypnotized by a professional hypnotherapist. Nearly 98 percent of all people can easily place the subconscious (inner brain) into a self-induced hypnotic trance. Hypnosis is the state of brain everyone experiences shortly when awakening from sleep.

In England, Doctor James Braid documented hypnosis in 1843.

The term "hypnosis" is derived from the Greek work "hypnos" meaning sleep. Doctor Braid determined he had used the word "hypnosis" incorrectly, since a hypnotized person does not actually go to bedtime sleep.

The doctor tried to change the word to "monoideism." However, the word "hypnosis" had taken hold of the scientific community. The doctor's efforts to rectify the situation failed. Doctor Braid utilized self-hypnosis during 3000 major operations before anesthetic was invented in 1846. Doctor Braid determinations classified "Beta" as the level of complete consciousness; this is the level of thought you utilize the most when you are not asleep. The next level, the doctor identified is named "Alpha"; this is the subconscious mind, henceforth named: "the inner brain." The inner brain is the dwelling place of a powerful imagination. If you make a major mistake in any situation, you have the memory ability to recall this event a million times, for eternity. When an animal makes a mistake, it has left their memory in moments. Not so with humans, this recycling thinking can be healed and stopped during the Self-Hypnotic Sessions.

The Alpha area is what we will deal with in self-hypnosis. The Alpha level of thought is 95-100 percent efficient in concentration compared to Beta, which is less than 25% efficient. Self-hypnosis is simply a way of relaxing and setting aside the conscious mind while at the same time activating the (subconscious mind), inner brain's limitless imagination to implant self-improvement suggestions statements which are issued directly into your subconscious mind.

The power of empowering thought replacement enables the reader to act on these improvement images with ease and competency. This gateway will be opened providing the self-hypnotized individual does not over analyze the text instructions and merely accepts what is presented. Self-hypnosis is actually semantics, the use of positive, impeccable words. It is you, the subject who hypnotizes yourself.

No hypnotherapist is required. You will be able to hypnotize yourself. You will not need to stare at any image for three or more minutes to make your eyes tired, this is a delusion some hypnotist use. Your eyes would eventually become tired after staring steadily at any object.

During each Session you will be lead to close your eyes for a restoring resting pause, at certain intervals.

A mild, light trace that will cause no harm to the reader shall be utilized. A mild self-hypnotic trace much similar to the drowsiness you feel before dropping off to sleep. Calming sensations, which you will be able to duplicate at any time.

When you are self-hypnotized, you do not go to bedtime sleep unless your body or brain is physically tired. Auto-hypnosis leads you to believe you can achieve whatever you practically want; it never leads you to think you can't.

Self-hypnosis has proven to achieve numerous powerful remarkable benefits for individuals. Pathways, which can open a mental determination to assist a serious abuser, overcome an addiction.

The Self-Hypnotic Sessions open the inner brain's iron doors to an internal journey. The greatest gift you have received is your mind. The greatest loss is to return it unopened.

During this unique journey you will explore your fully exposed inner subconscious: which contains the powerful, imagination and memory powers of the inner brain.

During a Hypnotic Stress Buster Session, you will structure unique, positive, optimistic alterations to your inner brain's habits and thought making process which are generated from the inner brain's memories recall system.

You will be self-hypnotized during the 12 Hypnotic Stress-Buster Sessions. You shall eventually dissolve any doubt.

You will go through a gradual process of mental reasoning to arrive at the certainty of materialization.

Expect a transformation; know that you can anticipate and shall realize positive changes.

To go beyond stress requires comprehending stress and resulting anxieties creating an inner mine and body connection. This mind-body connection is very important. A tremendous amount of physical problems have psychological roots. Cold sores to terminal cancer are influenced by our emotion's reaction to negative events or thoughts. The majority of backaches are triggered by mental turmoil.

Often a physical complaint is rooted in mental processes that are not real but imaginary. There are many types of stress: acute stress, episodic acute stress, chronic stress, stress-reaction mode (a habit of continual anxiety thinking of past or current negative situations that is frequently an impostor), emotional, muscular traumatic and post-traumatic stress. An acute stress can begin when you lose your job, a death in the family, a divorce. Continuous acute stress reactions in the body cause anxiety and physical ailments to flare up.

Your mind can tumble into the stress, compulsive anxiety disorder creating a physical syndrome, which becomes habitual. Physical reactions to chronic stress may encompass heart palpitations, shortness of breath, chest tightness or pains, dizziness, hyperventilation, muscular aches, stomach ulcers or general body pain.

A minor symptom such as a headache or stomach acid should not be ignored since such ailments may be the early warning signals that your life is creeping out of control and you must address improving the management of stress or anxiety. Unmanaged stress and compulsive anxiety can actually destroy your life but stress can be the kiss of death or the spice of life.

The scars in your mind may be bigger and more hurtful than any scar on your body. Compulsive stress is to the human condition the same as tension is to the violin string, too little and the music is dull and raspy, too much and the music is shrill or the string snaps. The opposite of negative stress is positive wholesome stress as you may experience in a challenging job that is excellent exercise for your mind and body. Unwholesome anxiety creates high-level frustration; long-term unwholesome compulsive stress opens the door to physical ailments.

Self-hypnotized stress management allows you to be productive and feeling in absolute command of yourself in any fear-based situation. Successful treatment for stress may include medicine but more important is a need for a modification in a stream of continuous negative thoughts, emotions and unwanted feelings that can produce physical ailment.

Combined in each Self-Hypnosis Session are progressive muscular relaxation exercises along with directions for Hindu pranayama breath control.

Incorrect shallow breathing may be picking up barely sufficient oxygen for your lungs but not enough to spread the oxygen to your body's other organs and tissue where it is vitally needed. Shallow breathing causes your heart to beat faster and harder attempting to supply other organs and tissues with enough blood to satisfy unfilled oxygen needs. The average brain weights 2% of a body's weight but burns about 20% of a body's energy. It is therefore very important to understand the mechanism, which supplies these energies. Eating and breathing properly are necessary.

The imagination is a healing tool, like no other, in self-hypnosis you will be able to entirely defuse and relieve the perception of stress caused body pain.

Progressive muscular relaxation is a calming technique to reduce muscle tension that assists with body awareness.

There are potent, unconscious forces that are always at work within the inner brain. Self-hypnotism will alter and improve your conscious desires, habits, open unimagined creativity, reduce or eliminate compulsive stress and overanxiousness and lead you onto the pathway for personal improvements.

Self-hypnotism opens the door to your subconscious when conscious judgment is disarmed; this is when your self-belief systems are awakening to self-improvement possibilities. During self-hypnotism your will power and imagination may be placed in conflict, if so the power of your imagination will always dominate.

There is magic in your self-hypnotized positive imagination; magic that opens the door for permanent improvement.

The 12 Stress Buster Sessions will sooth your body and calm your mind. You will call upon your deepest healing resources and discover an ability to remain balanced within.

Prepare for a retreat to a quiet center that dwells within your inner brain. It will be a spine-tingling, uplifting experience.

This book contains no other human stories, such as Jane's Story; Dick's Story or the Author's story. Such self-help literature is usually unsubstantiated fiction. This book is not about your relationship with a mother, a father, or a friend.

This book is one hundred percent, about you. A "time out" to refocus on what is most important: "taking care of you."

This book is non-denominational and has no religious persuasions.

This definitely is not a religious preacher's book. There will be absolutely no religion or belief systems forthcoming. You can cram your brain with all the thousands of religions available, but still become compulsively stressed out or addicted to an unwanted habit. You can feel good spiritually but you can still join the distressed, anxious, panic attack, depressed membership carrying any religion's Bible. Some of the worst people on earth carry a religious Bible yet remain spiritually deprived.

In this book there will be no further quizzes attempting to analyze the state of your mind. You have already done this quiz. By reading this book's introduction, you became interested in continuing reading.

Many gimmicks flood the self-improvement market now. You must take this complete program seriously, although movie stars, world leaders, writers, and various doctors are briefly mentioned. These are well-known humans, living or dead, who have supplied knowledge during their time on earth.

Do not be alarmed; you will experience profound improvements utilizing your inner brain's imagination.

You will experience a positive mental overhaul you never believed could transpire. Once you learn to acknowledge the capabilities of self-hypnosis, you will be able to train yourself to prolong and deepen your knowledge. The deeper you go, your abilities become stronger.

Empowering positive replacement statements are extremely effective in the very lightest state of self-hypnosis, autosuggestion that is called hypnoidal.

You may be thinking: "This is all pie in the sky stuff?"

Doctor Peter Whorwell, a well-known USA gastroenterologist, does not concur. Doctor Whorwell states: After 20 years of research on IBS (irritable bowel syndrome), he found only hypnosis and proper diet alleviated the condition. The American Gastroenterological Association has accepted hypnotherapy as the best treatment for IBS since 1996.

You shall be enlightened on this delightful journey while ameliorating the blueprint of your inner brain thought process.

You will achieve a healthier, reconstructed inner dialogue, a positive optimistic thinking design.

You shall find a balance and steadiness within.

How does the self-hypnosis program work?

You will learn to store away negative past events, and the unwanted addictive pessimistic self-talk thoughts about the present or future. More intense concentration of the present and now will eventually become a habit. You will gain the intelligence that there is no future in the past. Upon completing the Sessions any unpleasantness of your past can become the forgotten past. What will become primarily important is what opportunities are offered in "the present and now." What is coming next is emphasized in the program, not what once was.

Pointless mental chatter is a preoccupation with the past or future concerns that are valueless. Your past and future experiences have no meaning or value in the "here and now."

Your motto shall be: "I can take any cannonball fire of problems, even disasters that arise. I can relax under fire. I can look tragedy in the eye and overcome it. The bigger the better to test me. I have the power in the face of any adversity to choose how I will react."

You will control or eliminate any conscious mental suggestions that may attempt to inform you otherwise.

Each of the 12 Self-Hypnotic Stress Buster Sessions, and the preconditioning program takes approximately 45-60 minutes; allow this time to be free. Enter each Session seriously with an open mind. This is not brain surgery, but to be successful, to not be serious leaves a margin for error.

You will be utilizing a multitude of different ideas, which have proven to be successful.

The Sessions comes from a variety of sources:

Psycholinguistics is a science that delves into the buried meanings and reasons for inner brain reactions to events and semantically used words. Optimistic verbal messages said privately can trigger thoughts and emotions that positively impact all of your body's system. The etymology use of words although unnoticed in living everyday life is highlighted in each Session.

Indian mysticism, Hinduism, the oldest religion in the world, provides each Self-Hypnotic Session with a variety of Hindu

Pranayama yoga deep breathing exercises. These ancient breathing techniques were developed and practiced in India thousands of years ago. Simply breathing correctly, concentrating only on your breath can help relieve anxiety more than you can ever imagine.

The Hindu word "yoga" is derived from the Sanskrit root "jey." It is related to the English word yoke. Yoga signifies a Hindu's union with the inner brain, divine consciousness awareness. Advanced Pranayama Hindu deep-breathing techniques allow invigorating energy to flow unimpeded through the body. By focusing on energizing breathing properly, you will be more at ease.

Pranayma Hindu breathing stimulates the energy vortexes connecting links in the mind and body. "Prana" means respiration, life force, vitality, energy, and strength. "Ayama" means stretch, extension, expansion, and regulation. The prolongation, restraint of breath can create the ultimate calmness. Prolongation of breath and its restrain is easily learned. It allows you to see things that may have escaped your notice when the memory or thought is viewed at normal speed. Exhaling slowly properly is like running a video in slow motion.

To attain additional information regarding Hindu Yoga, Pranayama Deep breathing combined with stretch exercises—most libraries carry excellent videotapes on this subject. An easily assessable videotape is *Yoga for Dummies*. If you have taken yoga classes, during the Sessions, you will gradually become acquainted with a more complete understanding of Pranayama Hindu yoga breathing. Proper breathing techniques short-circuits stressful anxiety and encourages the brain to produce alpha waves stimulating the production of endorphins a mood-lifting natural feel good brain chemical.

Progressive muscular relaxation is included in each Session, a program that addresses different specific areas within your body.

The goal of this book is not to make you a physical super person. The intent is to provide you with a super mind.

Buddhism is a religion that does not have a God but an acclaimed concentration of universal intelligent power that connects to the inner subconscious brain. Nirvana, a state of eternal bliss, is a Buddha's long-term goal. Richard Gere, the movie star who was in the film *David*, is a meditating Buddha.

He chants for an hour or so each morning. Well, at least Richard made this statement on the Jay Leno talk show. Chanting is not included in any Session.

Pschocybernetics was a worldwide best selling book of self-help, by Maxwell Multz, MD. Doctor Multz was a plastic surgeon who operated on soldiers and civilians who suffered with facial disfigurements, suffered during the Second World War.

He concluded that his magical plastic surgery talents repaired the outward appearance, but did not repair the inner brain of the sufferer. Attempting to solve this deficiency, the doctor wrote many informative books on how to use one's brain. Some of the doctor's theories are included in the Session #9: Problem Solving. Mr. Multz wrote successful books when hypnotism therapy was not popular. Consequently, Mr. Multz did not address self-hypnosis as a tool to overcome negative self-talk thinking patterns, nor did he attempt to overcome negative addictions.

Over 200 serious, negative addictions have been identified by medical science. Overeating or under-eating addictions are not addressed insofar as a physician's supervision is mandatory.

The unpopular attitude regarding hypnosis began changing in the 1950s when the movie actor Cary Grant was to be put to sleep during an operation to remove a large cyst from on his forehead. Mr. Grant would sleep for four or five hours after the operation. Mr. Grant decided to forgo losing this time and allowed no medicine whatsoever.

Instead, Mr. Grant self-hypnotized himself, went through the operation, and successfully had the cyst surgically removed. After his forehead was stitched, he leaped out of bed and went to the movie lot where he was scheduled to work all day.

This feat was reported in the international press. People began to wonder why the medical profession did not promote self-hypnotism. Hypnotism is presently popular for those who wish to stop smoking cigarettes. Session #8: Anti-Cigarette Smoking/Tobacco offers a permanent ceasing of smoking if you really have a sincere motivation to quit, the only way "cold-turkey." Other popular choices to quit smoking cigarettes: Chewing nicotine gum has a 2% cure rate. A nicotine patch has a 6% cure rate. Laser therapy has a 10% cure rate. Nicotine pills have only proven to make humans sick.

Session #8: Anti-Cigarette Smoking/Tobacco was created for you, if you're really serious and desire to permanently quit smoking cigarettes or tobacco products.

If you firmly do aspirate to stop smoking, you can self-hypnotize yourself to do so.

The addictions: Alcoholic & Illegal Drug and Cigarette/ Tobacco abuse are among the most rampant and most self-destroying addictions in the world (after the addictions of child abuse and racial prejudice), and are usually linked.

Achieving new knowledge is a journey; enjoy the trip. You are about to inaugurate on a mind-opening voyage. Soaring through any of your inner brain's blackest, dark clouds into the pure clear blue sky of white clouds.

THE BASICS: PRECONDITIONING PROGRAM PRIOR TO A SELF-HYPNOTISM SESSION

Allied soldiers during the two World Wars, and the Korean War graduated from basic battle training, a preconditioning program before setting out to combat evil minds hoping to take over control of the world. The wars killed 525 million people, many innocents.

You are going to war against any compulsive negative self-talk or unhealthy addictions your inner brain may presently be supporting and enjoying. Faulty reasoning channels may lie buried as negative time bombs in your inner subconscious brain.

The hidden part of the brain, the subconscious was discovered by the Viennese physician Sigmund Freud (1856–1939).

Doctor Freud established the practice of psychoanalysis as a way to uncover the hidden dimensions of human nature. Freud's method is based on free association, in which the patient lets their mind run free using words, to reveal its much larger unconscious workings.

To assure complete advantage of the Self-Hypnotic 12 Stress Buster Sessions, you must read the preconditioning training program prior to entering a Self-Hypnosis Session.

The preconditioning programs must be taken seriously because you are going to be transporting yourself into the brain war zone—the mighty imagination and memory powers of the inner brain. A preconditioning program of each 12 Self-Hypnotic Stress Buster Session is needed to amplify the inner brain's thoughts which will allow you to be contemplative enough to lower any mental barriers.

The Preconditioning Program for each Session enforces a chasm, an access to the inner brain's thoughts and memory banks. The subconscious inner brain develops its own decisions, its secret thoughts, or any secret disturbances. Gradual persuasion is necessary to attain conscious awareness of these areas. Upon completion of reading the preconditioning program, you shall be fully prepared to march forward, armed and ready into one of the following Self-Hypnotic Sessions:

Session #1: Stress Management, an Optimistic, Powerful, Positive Mental Attitude
Session #2: Anxiety, Panic Attacks, Self-Obsessive Worry, Remorse Rumination & Overcoming Clinical Depression
Session #3: Anti-Alcoholic & Illegal Drug Use
Session #4: Marital Harmony/Sexuality & Lust
Session #5: Palliative Care for You
Session #6: Living with a Permanent Illness or Disability
Session #7: Public Speaking Enhancement
Session #8: Anti-Cigarette Smoking/Tobacco
Session #9: Problem Solving & Creativity
Session #10: Career Dissatisfaction—Motivation for Change
Session #11: Spiritual Depth
Session #12: State of the Brain—Serenity

How, When and Where to Enter a Session

You will set aside a time (one hour) when you will not be disturbed to read the preconditioning program followed by a Self-Hypnotic Session. Assume a position that assures physical relaxation. Sit in a favorite comfortable chair or lying down is fine. A sitting or lying down position that usually stills and settles your mind. A quiet spot, perhaps, lying on a floor with your head under a pillow. Initially, you cannot be self-hypnotized if you are standing or doing any physical activity requiring conscious mental contemplation, for example driving a car.

There exists a slight possibility that you may fall asleep when completing a Self-Hypnotic Session. This is good, it merely indicates your brain, and body needs a rest.

Instructions prior to starting a Self-Hypnotic Therapy Session:

The reader can substitute his or her first name for the word "reader" in any Session.

You must go to the restroom before you start. Don't delay.

Do not chew gum. You could gag on the gum in self-hypnosis.

Turn off any clock alarms. Turn off your cell phone, pager. Shut-off your wristwatch alarm. No background television or music, your absolute full attention is mandatory.

Under self-hypnosis you may become drowsy, and sleepy, your head may lean to one side, to prevent injury remove large earrings.

So where do you use the knowledge to open the doors to your subconscious inner brain upon completion of a Session? Whenever you need it.

Your life is what your thoughts make you. Your life will always be what you make it.

Your life will be lived, arranged, and organized in a fully awake, spontaneous consciousness.

The Sessions have been designed to assist you to live a positive thinking, healthier, balanced life. A guide to enable the reader to help them self.

Enjoy the journey!

Preconditioning Program of Hypnotic Session #1: Stress Management, an Optimistic, Powerful, Positive Mental Attitude

Over the past twenty years, taking Valium, Prozac, Paxil, Vicodin, Xanax, Celexa, or whatever tranquilizer has become the socially acceptable way to cope when beset by an overwhelmed panicky or depressed mind. It is an artificial, but never permanent remedy to quiet the brain.

Our high tech generation is labeled the Age of Anxiety. Some humans say to themselves: "I cannot do anything about it!"

This "give up" rational of being overly stressed and compulsively anxious, overwhelmed with negativity is becoming a global plague.

The field of psychoneuroimmunology is the relationship between stress psychological influences on the nervous system, anxiety disorders of the mind and the immune system. The release of negative stress hormones has a negative cumulating effect on heart, blood vessels, and the entire physical system. A negative stressor can vary in duration and are classified in the normal human events as: major life changes, a catastrophe such as a giant earthquake. An unpleasant relationship with other people or simply normal daily hassles that occur. Stress often creates anxiety when dwelling on unhappy past events or anticipated future events. Simply said negative stress is everywhere and stress becomes anxiety, which is internalized fear.

Your journey through life is not supposed to be easy, if it were, life would be boring. You are destined to live through a variety of cats and dogs of disappointment, dissatisfaction, and illness. You, like all humans, are bound to feel confused, insecure and anxious. Happiness would lose its meaning if it were never tempered by sadness. You cannot always control your circumstances but you can master and monitor your thoughts. The joy, contentment and happiness you experience depend on the optimistic quality of your thoughts. By properly supervising your subconscious inner brain you can enjoy, survive and plow through any difficult time.

You can break an unwanted addiction or unlock negative self-talk cycles, trains of thought chains that rob you of thinking pleasurably.

Finally you can abandon the negative reasoning polluting your thoughts. The truly optimistic person, with a gift of laughter makes everyone feel great. Wherever you go, wherever you remain the results of your actions and words will follow you. You can change your interior dialogue from negative to positive, optimistic thoughts and attitudes to experience astonishing satisfaction. Emotions and moods are constantly alternating. Within mere minutes, you can be on guard to dispel any unexpected speeding train of gloomy unwanted thoughts. An unwanted thought stream of unneeded, no value, exaggerated negativity and the average brains thinks 50,000 thoughts a day. So let's analyze how you are doing: Start thinking of the word BINGO to yourself every time you have a negative thought. Try and count how many times you think BINGO during one day. Carry an index card and make a tick mark each time for each BINGO negative thought, circle a tick mark when you have a repeated negative thought, dwelling on a previous negative thought which is called rumination. Some negative thinking is healthy and needed but excessive negative thinking leads to mental negative addiction and eventually depression. Your brain creates a minimum of 15,000+ individual thoughts per day, depending on what you are engaged in during the day. Even when these thoughts are pleasant—an inner optimistic brain filter should patrol and organize the mental interior.

You will learn how to improve the way you think. Your mind should never be over critical to its own self. You can be quick to listen, remain quiet and still any chattering negative self-talk, and always be slow to speak.

You can discover how to let go of the undone. Seal tightly and close mental floodgates to lock out, people or situations that can never be altered. A permanent closure that will remain securely shut forever.

You will realize you cannot change numerous situations, so you will let go and move on. To do otherwise has absolutely no value; often nothing can ever be changed in many circumstances or other people. You can learn to conquer and endure such situations through surrender with empowering thought replacement statements. You can de-hypnotize your inner brain's imagination to accept which was never acceptable before.

Your mind is like a factory, its product is as good as the raw materials you put into it.

Thoughts are either the optimist (positive) or the pessimist (negative). The defining characteristic of pessimist is that they tend to believe bad events will last forever, eventually undermining everything they do, and it is never their own fault.

It is next to impossible to think positively about some people or any situation as long you continue to uphold a negative concept. The optimists, who are daily confronted with the dilemmas of every day life think about misfortune and upsetting situations in the opposite way as a negative person does.

Optimists believe defeat is just a detour, a temporary setback, defeat is not their fault, and the event was due to temporary circumstances. The optimist is unfazed by defeat. In a tight situation, an optimist is much like a racing jockey who sits chilly, firmly in a brave pose, while in tight quarters, saddled to a galloping thoroughbred horse. The racing jockey calmly waits. Always seeking a breakout path through galloping horses blocking, the pathway to be the leader of the pack. The optimist gets things done in the world, not the cynics, critics or pessimists.

An optimist is a challenger like the racing jockey waiting with the imagination power to try hard to get on the track to improvement.

The pessimist easily gives up. A pessimist is very easily anxious and often depressed over circumstances that does not go their way.

A pessimist on arriving home from a visit to the bank knows a hair appointment is scheduled a half an hour hence. The person then learns: "I overlooked receiving the $100.00 cash from the teller, now I have no money to pay the hair dresser!"

Desperately, the pessimist's negative thought patterns begin to set alarms. It takes at least twenty minutes to drive to the bank! There will be no place to park!

There will be a big line up in the bank! The teller may be on a lunch break! The teller may say: "I gave you the 100 dollars. I will have to talk to the bank manager! Where did I put the withdrawal slip! Was there one!"

In a mad rush a pessimist drives a speeding automobile to the bank, there are no parking places, the worried, anxiety filled mind, can see, so the pessimist parks in a bus stop.

After the pessimist gets the $100.00 from the teller, returning to the car, the pessimist is relieved, but nearly later for the hair appointment. The car has been given a parking ticket!

Under similar circumstances, an optimist drives their automobile at the allowed speed limit and thinks: "I will pick up the money on my way to my hair appointment."

The optimistic attitude takes the extra time to locate an open parking spot.

After getting the cash from the teller, while walking to the car, reconsiders: "Today is so sunny, after three days of rain. The weather forecast said it is supposed to rain tomorrow. I think I will cancel my hair appointment until tomorrow and enjoy this beautiful day at the beach."

Pessimistic prophecies are often self-fulfilling. The thought: "There is nothing I can do that will matter" prevents a pessimist from being action oriented. If you have a pessimistic habit of thinking you can transform mere setbacks into full-blown disasters.

Depression is the ultimate expression of pessimism. Clinical depression is addressed in Session #2. With positive, empowering thought replacement statements flowing from your inner brain, you can gain the optimistic capability to get up and fight. You can arise with an optimistically attitude each and every day to carry you away from anxiety and compulsive distress, to inspire hopefulness through survival, striving onward until thriving and eventually achieving success.

You no longer need be a prisoner of negative unwanted self-talk revolving on past events, present troubles, and fears of the future.

You can unlearn pessimism and acquire the skills of seeing any setback, either past or present, or pending, in an optimistically frame of mind.

Negative thinking is the destructive thoughts you say to yourself and how you respond to events when experiencing any setback that life deals to every human being.

You can maintain an optimistic attitude when responding to people or events that are bad or good.

You can combat any feelings of helplessness that ever settles into your mind. A sense of helplessness requires a subconscious inner brain editing adjustment, which can only be achieved through positive, optimistic thinking.

If you ever mull over past events or future possible occurrences you are a ruminator.

A negative ruminator relives past events or anticipates future expectations in terms of negativity and doom. A ruminator is a person with a powerful memory who permits the burdensome, endless flow of bubbling negativity to filter into the thinking mind. Such thoughts often are impostors and physical or mental diversion can send them fleeing. Become active and engaged in any worthwhile activity. Listening to your favorite music is an excellent distraction.

A pessimist person repeatedly listens to their brain's endless negativity list of how bad things are until they often become non-action oriented. By utilizing a positive stream of preset subconscious "inner brain" replacement thoughts, an episode of unwanted and unneeded negative stress, action-prohibiting fears can be stifled.

This Session will assist overcoming the sense of hopelessness and helplessness, which is often caused by negative thought rumination. A negative rolling snowball of thoughts can grow to gigantic proportions if negative thoughts are allowed to ceaselessly continue.

The sense of helplessness especially develops when a pessimist imagines on catastrophes. As one thread of a pessimist's life snaps, the whole fabric unravels. Extreme pessimism always promotes heavy anxiety and stress. A pessimist's prediction negative mental images turn a setback into a disaster; a disaster into a deluge of calamity often based on unfounded fear. Optimistic hope in itself is life-sustaining. An optimist may become helpless in one part of their lives yet walk stalwartly on in the others. When you are optimistic and not over stressed, you are appreciating reality the "here and now" precisely.

Relaxing and delaying action rather than immediately responding rashly to an upsetting person or event can become the normal conduct for you upon completion of Session #1. Feeding your body is a priority in life. What you fed your brain is equally important. Negative thoughts are added to the accumulators in your mental storage banks just as positive thoughts are. All your prior negative and positive experiences are buried in your inner brain's memory storage banks—but buried alive.

An unfortunate individual who has been fired from their 17th job will not merely dwell on the recently lost position, but the entire 17 losers. The accumulated data that is forever stored in your inner brain's accumulator memory banks creates the image you have of yourself.

An infection of the mind is just as real as an infection of the body.

Session #1 will mildly surprise you when you discover yourself thinking and acting positively different, automatically and spontaneously, without even trying.

Session #1 contains the power of empowering thought replacement statements that will be healthful mentality food. There is such a person who can be over-optimistic, not seeing the negatives of any circumstance. These individuals can overcome this unusual over-happy frame of the minds tendency upon completion of the Session #9: Problem Solving.

The optimist tends to keep a healthy morale. Optimists believe that bad events have specific causes, while good events will enhance everything they do.

Everyone wants an optimist to be his or her leader. A pessimist's life is not as pleasurable as it should be. When in a pessimistic, melancholy state, the pessimist is going through a mild version of mental discord named depression.

Session #1 will teach you how to change your mental response to any type of adversity. You shall cope with any setback much easier. You will not allow your thoughts to emphasis only the negative aspects. Pessimism is an asset to no one, especially for you.

Optimistically thinking is easy to maintain once you start. You can get into the habit of disputing negative beliefs to optimize internal dialogue. Your daily life will run much better and you will be the master of your own fate.

Forgiving some person, who has harmed you or perhaps killed a loved one, is a giant mountain of tough brainwork; presently there may be the mental response of dislike or hatred. To hate is a psychological illness. The art of forgetting but not forgiving is a rare gift.

The satisfaction of getting revenge is momentary. The glory of forgiveness lasts forever. Forgiveness is often one huge challenge, and yet that need must be met if you are to find a livable peace with any degree of happiness in your mind. You can make this happen. You can dissolve an unforgiving mountain of pain.

You can transform negative brain energy of dislike or possible hatred into the positive energy of a forgiving, positive mental attitude. To enjoy contentment, you must offer friendship to all, even to those who may not deserve.

During Session #1 you will be given an alternative imaginative assertive, positive attitude thought process for when you "start beating upon yourself" for whatever reason.

An optimistic, positive frame of mind is even associated with more successful erections and a decrease in erection failures and climaxes.

Not all stress is bad. Monitored stress can compel you to work hard and complete a difficult task.

Mature managed negative stress can become a normal part of your life. If humans did not sleep or rest, the stress of living twenty-four hours each day would cause destruction beyond imagination.

All animals and humans experience stress that cause anxiety and worrying times.

By turning to medication, alcohol, or illegal drugs to escape an uninterrupted stressed-out worry-some condition may temporarily relieve but never remove the triggering negative source flourishing in your subconscious inner brain.

When your brain falls down into negativity, you can run five miles attempting to escape from the brain's unwanted thoughts, but you will find the very same situation waiting for you when you arrive tired and exhausted. You can travel to the other side of the world—the inner brain's negativity will not disappear.

Being stressed out is often caused by an over striving, a constantly craving anxious behavior. Over striving causes brain confusion as if you were thinking through peanut butter. You may have an inner dialogue of "push harder, push harder," "go-go-go-go," an obsessive stress and anxiety of missing something or someone.

Session #1 will relieve nervous fatigue from, "push-push-go-go"; when you feel as if you are coming apart at the seams, strung out emotionally and restless. You will acquire the ability to call upon a refreshing pause, a melt down, and be able to retreat to a mental comfort zone within.

10% of your lifetime will be what happens to you. The remaining 90% are how your brain responds. The 90% can be negative or positive. A positive optimistic attitude makes life so much easier, always supplying a ready supply of adjusting positive mental statements to deal with the ordinary and extraordinary problems, which you can expect, to occasional confront you. An optimistic approach assists you to take everything that ever comes your way, as it comes and optimistically accept the consequences.

Optimism is contagious. You can create your own optimism, wherever you go, to whomever you meet.

The optimistic attitude and feeling induced through the auto-hypnotic empowering thought replacement method will not wear off.

An optimistic attitude will remain with you through any adverse periods. You will be able to combat some of the worst negative mental and physical events.

Unjustified anger is despicable and is more harmful to you than the injury it causes to others.

The opposite of extreme negative signals is a positive, optimistic, calm, but always on alert mind.

Science has proven that you use only 7% of your brain cells, and they multiply each day; an inexhaustible supply that never burns out, unless you do not eat and drink as normal people do.

It has been scientifically proven that Paleolithic (cave men and women) was endowed with the same size of brain as yours.

Life is so short—so why keep yourself so busy by spinning the negative windmills of your mind.

All life involves constant changes. When life no longer changes illness and death commences. When you stop changing you're through.

A happy brain requires happy circumstances. Human circumstances are not always happy.

True happiness is a fleeting emotion; it is the by-product of experiencing satisfaction in the current circumstances of your life. True happiness requires problems to be solved, some challenging situations that can be overcome with an optimistic attitude. An inner strength of acceptance to take whatever comes. You can be ready to meet any distress with action towards a solution. The events of living within a moment could wipe a happy smile off any face. An unexpected event can shatter all your dreams and hopes for the day or future days.

It is not true that only certain individuals have the inner strength that can glide one through stressful changing times.

It is not true you can either take stress and an attack of anxiety or you cannot.

You will no longer give haven to such nonsense in your conscious or subconscious brain. Your inner subconscious brain can be trained to turn towards being constantly courageously and optimistic. An inner brain so strong that nothing, absolutely no trouble can disturb your inner peace of mind.

You can exist in the "here and now," displaying your authentic presence, with an abundance of optimism each moment of every day. Each morning you can awaken imagining a Valhalla of powerful, optimist thoughts.

You can open your inner brain onto a new speedway of hope with an unfaltering belief that a positive optimistic attitude can be attained.

Why not the best? The best you have ever done is now whatever was last completed. The very best you can do, is yet to be completed.

Like a flue shot, the Self-Hypnotic Session #1 allows you to avoid negative brain flue by never allowing you to be overwhelmed by negative situations that may arise at any time.

You shall de-hypnotize yourself from negative, false attitudes, words, or actions.

A powerful optimistic, positive mental attitude is displayed by one who takes an ever-hopeful view of life and its events. An Optimistic Imaginative Mental Attitude does not indulge their brain's efforts in continual self-critical analysis.

An optimist mental attitude never plays Monday-morning quarterback to past activities; this is defeating negative self-criticism. An optimistic imaginative mental attitude is the key ingredient for living the life you desire. An optimistic imaginative mental attitude can turn wherever you are into a haven of hope despite terrible circumstances.

A negative attitude creates limitations and creative constipation. Your attitude reactions to other people or events should and can always be positive—optimistic, hopeful not gloomy—pessimistic.

Positive reactions give you imaginative creative ability, pessimistic reactions diminishes it. If you are a pessimist you may start thinking of excuses. I am a mess because of whoever abused me; I have had so many losses in this life I cannot deal with life anymore. Your optimistic desires are positive; your fears are negative. Desire is the remembrance of pleasure. Fear is the remembrance of pain.

Change and challenge are a certainty, you can run and hide or you can open your inner brain to empower an optimistic attitude; a path that will supply action filled with hope.

Inner brain transformation, through positive thought replacement therapy is a skill you will learn.

You can teach your mind to plunge forward with optimistic confidence in your ability to handle almost anything, a new journey, or calling. Often the most difficult situations we can imagine create the most incredible opportunities.

Even thinking back on any rotten times can be a tremendous source of optimistic motivation for the "here and now," if done positively. Every adversity contains the seed of an equivalent or greater benefit.

Intense negative emotional pain can develop into physical ailments: muscle tension, cramps, upset stomach, and general aches. The auto hypnosis in Session #1 includes a personal care program to disarm any body area affected by overanxious stressing. The harder you try to reduce or change emotionally caused body ailments by using your will power, the less chance you have of succeeding. This is why willing yourself to sleep or curbing an unwanted addiction can become impossible. Your will power resides in your conscious brain while the much incomparable capability of your imagination and memory resides in your inner brain.

Whenever the imagination and your will power are in conflict the imagination invariable wins. You may believe that beneath the surface of everyone's existence there is an ache that will not go away. A pain that cannot be ignored, disguised, or submerged by any torrent of activity or religion, a longing pain that will only disappear when you enter another existence.

Maybe, you have read or heard: "Nobody will ever tell you have made it, because you never reach a level of absolute true contentment until you are dead."

"You were born naked, wet and hungry and get slapped on your ass, and then things get worse."

"You are born, you worry, and you die."

Do not believe in any such hopeless, negative nonsense. You were created to enjoy this world, not the next one.

You can gain maturity. You have been endowed from birth with the seeds of every possibility and every life. Your time on earth will always be only what you optimistically decide to make of it.

Canadian Jim Carrey displayed assertiveness, optimistic persistence, and the ability to take risks and remain calm.

You may have laughed during the movie *The Mask*. Jim made millions of dollars and won an Oscar.

From extreme poverty in Toronto, Ontario, Jim had years of total rejection but he was always optimistic, over positive and determined. If Jim had listened to all the people that told him to find a day job, to give up, you would have never seen *The Mask*.

Elvis Presley displayed optimism when Nashville told him to "Pack it in."

The parents' negative opinions of both Jim and Elvis advised their young boys to give up on their chosen careers.

Our sense of belonging is enhanced when we know that we are important to more people than our immediate family. That is why we need optimistic friends in our lives. Friends are more likely than family to encourage and push you on.

A truly optimistic individual can appreciate the scenery during any of life's detours. Perhaps enjoy the sights during a trip to the hospital in an ambulance.

Mental denial can be protective. Deniers are never incapacitated by fear; they are less flustered by bad news. To deny a fear-provoking situation you may get into is like flirting and laughing at danger. The opposite of fear denial is to feel totally powerless to improve conditions and resign the mind to compulsive stress and anxiety and over worrying. Denial is available through your imagination. The art of positive denial is often sustaining for a true optimist. An optimist can endure and float through tough times.

Why not enjoy the tough times with a detachment attitude?

You can defuse the fear of negative, unwanted thoughts, by quieting your mind, stopping and blocking unwanted bubbles of compulsive unpleasant thinking. Substituting conscious creative empowering thought replacement therapy would let you know that you are your own master.

Positive imaginative replacement thoughts supplied by the subconscious inner brain will make you feel happier, stronger, calmer, safe, and loved.

The Self-Hypnotic Stress Buster Session #1 is like an old-fashioned exorcist, preventing, and then casting out the effects of negative self-talking thinking.

After completing the Self-Hypnotic Session #1, for those who wish to grow in optimism, there is the Optimist International Organization, founded June 19, 1919. The Optimist Organization has 3500 worldwide clubs, 115,000 members. Anyone can join regardless of race or worldly status. The purpose of the optimist clubs is to foster personal Optimism and self-improvement and help child in any way.

Six million children are served each year and $100,000,000 is raised to do so. Phone 1-800-500-8130. For more details visit the optimist Web site, www. Optimist.org.

The Optimist Creed

Promise Yourself:
To be so optimistic that nothing can disturb your peace of mind.
To talk health, happiness and prosperity to every person you meet.
To make all your friends feel that there is something in them.
To look at the sunny side of everything and make your optimism come true.
To think only of the best, to work only for the best and expect only the best.
To be just as enthusiastic about the success of other as you are about your own.
To forget the mistakes of the past and press onward to the greater achievements of the future.
To wear a cheerful countenance at all times and give every living creature you meet a smile.
To give so much attention to the improvement of you're self that you have no time to criticize others.
To be too large for worry, too noble for anger, too strong for fear, and too happy to permit the presence of trouble.

NOW: Prepare to Go into Self-Hypnotic Session #1

Remember:
Initially, self-hypnosis cannot be achieved standing. Sitting in a comfortable chair or lying down is fine. Self-hypnosis positive suggestions may require time to incubate. Self-hypnosis positive suggestions do not necessarily commence upon awakening—the inner brain will activate the suggestions—at its convenient.

During self-hypnosis, it is not necessary to close your eyes, except for the eye rest periods as detailed in the text. If you wish to close your eyes continually, have someone read the text to you. It will make no difference.

Each Session uses an entirely different induction into self-hypnosis, Pranayama Hindu breathing exercise, progressive muscular relaxation, and self-hypnotic trance techniques.

Several Sessions have a pause for you to add your special request, self-suggestions to your inner brain.

Self-Hypnotic Session #1
Stress Management
An Optimistic, Powerful
Positive Mental Attitude

Now, reader, make yourself as comfortable as possible. Incidentally, fifteen minutes of hypnotic trance relaxation is equal to two or three hours of a regular sleep. That is why you shall enjoy it so much. And it is so easy, once you know how; you can do it easily and effortlessly.

Relax your hands, allow each finger to relax. Calm yourself. Relax.

In a moment, close your eyes and say to yourself, very slowly, as many times as you wish: Relax, become loose, and relax. Reopen you eyes and continue with the text.

NOW, TAKE TWO VERY DEEP BREATHS.

ARE YOU READY? Big Breath, Now.

Disregard everything except the sound of your breathing.

Breathe in...H-O-L-D...IT...and...LET YOURSELF GO...EXHALE out any stress and tension.

Breathe in...H-O-L-D—IT!...and LET YOURSELF GO...EXHALE out any bad feeling.

You will continue to breathe EVENLY...AS YOU BREATHE *DEEPER AND DEEPER* STILL.

As you breathe—*Deeper and Deeper* still—You begin to feel a heaviness drowsiness entering all through you. Completely let yourself sink down more, relax—unwind and relax.

Allow your entire body to be as loose as a goose. Your eyelids are becoming very heavy...your head feels *very heavy and relaxed* as the heaviness begins to go forward towards your chest.

Breathe *deeper* and *deeper* still...Allow yourself to wind down, wind down, wind down, uncoil and relax.

This *heavy, tired, relaxed drowsiness* feeling goes right *through* your body.

Deep relaxation is entering your shoulders...Into your arms and hands...feel the tiredness seeping *through* your body...down to both legs and feet. Deep self-hypnotic sleep blankets your chest cavity, feel your heart is gently slowing down, calming down to a slower beat. It is good for your heart to slow down and rest as you go deeper and deeper still into self-hypnotic sleep. Your blood vessels are operating smoothly, relaxed and dilated. Your white blood cells are vigorous and plentiful assisting your immune system to function efficiently.

Breathing evenly and *deeply*—breathing deeper and *deeper* still Just let any tight muscles or tension uncoil and unwind as you sink downward into drowsiness.

You are going to count to ten and on the count of ten you will go into an even *deeper*—refreshing hypnotic sleep. As deep sleep seeps all over inside your body.

1-2...Your eyelids—experiencing a very heavy *feeling*—your head feeling heavier and heavier still.

In a little bit you will close your eyes, for as long as it pleases you Study the patterns that you visualize in the darkness. Open your eyes when you wish to continue with the text.

3-4...This comfortable, hypnotic *sleepy,* heavy *feeling* is spreading—down into your arms and hands—as you being to uncoil each muscle in your fingers.

As self-hypnotic drowsiness enters your mind and you don't have a care in the world. Your mind is like an empty space; it is truly quiet with little or no conscious awareness.

You feel so free...in deep, deep self-hypnotic sleep. Relax and calm the muscles in your temples. As you think about relaxing these muscles. The muscles will relax and be calmer.

5-6...Your whole body is completely *relaxing* as this sleepiness sinks deeper and deeper into your legs and feet, as you—breathe deeper and *deeper* still...Sinking down into a pleasant self-hypnotic sleep.

7-8...so *relaxed*, so comfortable, concentrating on...Deep relaxation—as you prepare for a *deep, refreshing self-hypnotic sleep,* go into hypnotic sleep—*now.*

9-10...and *down* you go—*deep asleep, Deep*...into this deep hypnotic, refreshing *sleep.* Breathing evenly and *deeply*—You go down—*deeper and deeper* into hypnotic sleep with every breath that you take.

Creep deeper, sinking into hypnotic Sleep...Now...

Imagine that you are lying on a six inch, newly poured bed of wet cement. You can feel the imprint as your entire body sinks deeper and deeper down into the cement.

You are entering an even deeper, self-hypnotic sleep with every breath that you take.

Now, you are going to count to ten once more, and. on the count of *ten* you will go more *deeply* into hypnotic relaxation, sinking even deeper down into the surrounding cement...Upon reaching *ten* you shall go more deeply into hypnotic sleep, more deeply than you are now...More deeply than you have ever been before.

1...2...3...4...5...Your eyelids are so *heavy* now, they feel so tired, but you allow both eyes to remain open to continue on with the text. Your eyes feel so very comfortable as you do...submitting.

Even deeper and deeper into drowsiness.

As you continue to focus on the text...allow your conscious mind to wander, which is quite normal, let it wander where ever. Thinking of anything.

It does not matter. Your inner brain is alert and relaxed and ready to proceed. Feel your hands; each finger is becoming warm and tingly. Breathe in deeply into your stomach. Imagine that your entire stomach is a huge sponge soaking up all the fresh oxygen you are breathing in. Now feel, imagine and visualize squeezing all that oxygen out of your spongy stomach. Experience the feelings of cool, calm and becoming more relaxed.

Your head is heavier and heavier still.
Your whole body is at ease, relaxing and calming.
Your shoulders, arms and hands, lungs, stomach, feet and ankles, right down to the tips of your toes are sinking into a peaceful calmness and relaxation.
Your legs and feet so *heavy* you feel as if your feet are glued down sinking deeply into the bed of cement. You are so very drowsy.
Breathing deeper and *deeper* still....6...7...8...9...10 and *down-n you go.*
Down and even deeper into hypnotic sleep with every deep breath you take.
Perfectly relaxed going so much *deeper* and *deeper* into hypnotic sleep all the time.
In order for you to relax even more, and go even deeper into a peaceful rest. I want you now to: Think...Imagine...Visualize in your mind's eye and feel that you are feeling pleasant and safe, going way down, drifting like a feather dropping into a long, deep never-ending, brightly lit tunnel, a tunnel of the deepest self-hypnotic calmness.
Imagine being a feather while you drift down this safe tunnel of peace and contentment, you are going to count backwards. Down from ten to zero.
Begin counting.
Ten to Zero, with each count, you will feel yourself sinking into the bottom of the well-lit tunnel of relaxing self-hypnotic. By the count of zero, you will be much deeper into self-hypnotic sleep than you are now, sinking lower than you have ever been before.
10...Deeper...
9...Deeper...drowsy relaxation covering your entire body and mind.
8...Drifting down the tunnel, dropping down, floating down.
7...Going Down...even Deeper...
6...Down to the tunnel's bottom, where a bed of restfulness awaits...
5...Calm and so very relaxed as you tumble lower and lower.
4...Feeling so comfortable cozies all over.

3...You know you are enjoying yourself on this adventure.

2...Uncoil and be loose all over...be calm...Almost down to the bottom of the tunnel.

1...ZERO...and down you go....Into self-hypnotic sleep now.

Know that from this moment onwards whenever the text instructs you "go into self-hypnotic sleep now" you shall go into a self-hypnotic sleep immediately, right away, very quickly and even deeper.

Quicker and deeper each and every time that the text says..."Go into self-hypnotic sleep now." There is much you must learn. Let us commence:

You are going to teach yourself to calm down completely while relaxing to relieve any anxiety, stress, and muscle tensions, aches and pains that you may have. You shall relax every fiber, every muscle in your body. A normal change is starting to take place although you may not realize the changes, but the rhythm of your breathing is changing. You are beginning to breathe slower and it is comfortable, your heartbeat is slowing down and your blood pressure is lower because you are calming down. Acknowledge the very pleasant tingling, calming sensation blanketing over your mind and body. Your body resembles a wet dish towel.

Allow your body to let go all over, feel and enjoy the loose as a goose, limp feeling blanketing each area of your body. You are relaxed completely throughout every fiber of your body, existence, relaxing physically, emotionally and mentally.

Let go all over...You want to be as loose as a goose. Feel the absence of any distress, stress or anxiety. You are calm, relaxed and you feel so good. Think to yourself: "Let relaxation go all over. Let relaxation go all over. Let relaxation go all over." Enjoy being a loose goose, feel this sensation spreading into each joint and bone.

In a moment, allow your eyelids to close over your eyes while speaking aloud, three times: "Let relaxation go all over. Let relaxation go all over. Let relaxation go all over."

Do this now, close your eyes, and return to the text to proceed when you know you are calming down.

Focus on your breathing. Take a normal breath. On the next breathe in through your nose imagine descending the oxygen deep down into your lower belly. Notice how your belly expands. Now breathe out through your mouth, if you prefer not to inhale through your nose and exhale through your mouth, switch to whatever mode of breathing is most comfortable. Now, take one normal breath. After exhaling take one slow, very deep breath down deep into the abdomen. Try alternating normal and deep breaths in the belly a few times. Notice the difference. Normal breathing is tight and constricted. Abdominal deep breathing is much more relaxing. Expand your belly when you inhale. Exhale slowly and when you do so, sigh. Practice abdominal breathing for as long as you enjoy it before proceeding.

Make certain after you inhale deeply then exhaust slowly, that there is only movements below in your belly just below the chest, beneath the ribs. As you inhale there will be movement of the stomach. When you exhale slowly the belly will have an inward movement. So inhaling and exhaling, inhaling as the breath comes in, exhaling slowly as the breath leaves your body, moving out. Inhale deeply as the breath comes in. Bring in that fresh air to a count of 1, then as you exhale, do it much slower. As slow as you can, perhaps you can make a slow exhale to the count of 4, 5 or 6. Slowness in exhaling provides a full oxygenation of your being. A slow exhale is very refreshing. There should be almost no movement of the ribs. There should only be a movement of the diaphragm when you exhale.

Visualize and Imagine mentally traveling through your entire body with each inhale and slow exhale of breath. Practice exhaling slowly for as long as you wish or until you can do this exercise with little effort.

Imagine the blanket of relaxation and calmness as it spreads from the top of your scalp. Feel this calmness sweeping through your facial muscles, your nose, cheeks and chin, moving up behind your neck and going behind your ears. The sensation of a calming drowsiness perception submerges and rushes down the back of your neck. Feel the warm current of relaxation flow into your shoulders, biceps, your upper arms, your forearms, then into each finger. Send a mental signal "let go" into your chest cavity, your heart. Now allow this current of warm relaxation to melt down through your pelvis, into your buttocks. Send this wonderful tingling sensation of relaxation through your spinal column, through your waist, and stomach muscles. The very heavy blanket of the deepest relaxation and calmness sweeps through all abdominal muscles, your hips and into your thighs. Numbness travels over your thighs surrounding your kneecaps, then spreading throughout both calf muscles of your legs. Feel the sensation entering into both ankles. The peaceful blanket of relaxation and absolute calmness moves advancing to the very tip of your toes. Your toes begin tingling.

Your entire body is drowsy, so drowsy, beautifully relaxed, calm, peaceful, loose and limp. You are like a raggedly Ann doll, and it feels so good. You shall remember the positive statements in every detail while you are in this self-hypnotic slumber.

"Go into self-hypnotic sleep now."

Imagine all the stress and anxiety in your body is exiting, flowing out, flowing out onto the floor and way from you, never to bother you again.

In a moment, close your eyes and notice the darkness close in as your eyelids drop. Keep you eyes closed and you will see patterns of light or specks of gray. At this time, it feels very good to rest your eyes.

Take as long as you wish for a few moments of eye rest in this state of calm and peacefulness, before continuing on with the text.

As you breathe in, feel yourself buried in the bed of wet cement, letting go of tension, letting go of any worries, not holding on to anything. Sink further into the wet cement. Be loose as a goose. As you sink deeper feel this looseness. You feel even calmer and so very relaxed. You are so buried in the cement that if you decided to stand up you would view your entire body's imprint, which you have dug and sunk into. You enjoy where you are, at this very moment in time.

Relaxation is the foundation for personal improvement; it affects your state of mind and inner tranquility. The blanket of calmness and relaxation shall enable you to cope with the tensions and stresses of everyday living.

You shall be able to adjust yourself to your environment, circumstances and even to those difficult individuals you or nothing will ever change. You shall be able to tolerate the persons, unpleasant memories, places, or things that used to disturb and annoy you. You can do everything better when you are relaxed, whether it be physical, mental or emotional.

Imagine relaxing the muscles of your tongue, so you won't say things you will be sorry for in the future. Choosing your spoken words impeccably can avoid many negative outcomes and alter situations to enthusiastic optimism. You are now going to have a power that will supply you with the courage and confidence you need to take the "T" out of "can't" and discover that you can.

Want it to happen; expect it to happen; and it shall happen.

Incidentally, it is quite natural for your conscious mind to wander during self-hypnosis.

Do not be concerned that you might be wasting your time when this happens. Your conscious mind's activities or state of boredom is irrelevant to self-hypnosis.

You seek the limitless powerhouse of your brain subconscious: the inner brain's brilliant imagination. "Remain Relax," "be calm," "relax even more," as you go deeper into self-hypnotic sleep now. As you do, think and feel that you are a raggedy Ann doll.

Imagine that your arms and legs are loose and floppy just like a raggedy Ann doll. Visualize that you are raggedy Ann in the sun. Feel the warmth of a hot summer's day sunshine.

You are now a giant raggedy Ann doll, and you are lying in the sun; all your limbs are nice and warm, but your head is lying in the shade and is comfortably cool. You are so relaxed and so warm. You feel great. You want to close your eyes for a short period of rest before resuming with the text. So close your eyes and return to the text whenever you begin getting tired of the very hot sunshine.

Relaxation and being calm is the groundwork for a Positive Optimistic Mental Attitude and reduction of physical stress aches and related pain.

Now, summon your Herculean imagination, the creative force that also is the storehouse of all your memories, your nightly dreams and dormant abilities.

Comfortably and resting in quiet relaxation, you shall now utilize your amazing imagination's capabilities.

Pretend, imagine or dream that you are visiting a peaceful and special place. Imagine this special place. You may wish to see yourself again on a beach on a warm, sunny day. Or perhaps, sitting in front of a blazing fireplace.

Perhaps, you wish to imagine yourself walking along a tree lined mountain path, focus your attention on the birds singing, the light dancing through the tree branches, the smell of pine, the greenness of the forest, a cool breeze as it touches your skin. Smell the odors in the air, visually imagine each aspect of the forest trail enjoy each sensation.

So allow your imagination to select a location to your liking. Imagine a location where you have been or know you will be relaxed in, feeling free and safe.

Locate this peaceful, special place.

A special place to your liking, it can be any place at all, as long as the location is relaxing.

You are there alone. There is no other person there to disturb you. This is the most peaceful place in the world for you.

Imagine yourself there.

Enjoy the relaxation and peaceful calmness flowing through you, a sense of well-being. You shall keep these positive sensations with you long after this Session is completed, for the rest of this day, the evening, and tomorrow. The sensations are growing stronger and stronger.

Each and every time that you choose to do this kind of relaxation you will be able to relax even more.

Regardless of the stress, distress, anxiety or tension that may surround your life in the "here and now." You will be able to adjust and return to this location because in your special place, you do remain at peace, calmer, more relaxed.

Allow any tension and stresses to bounce off and away from you. Just let them all go. Stress and tensions are of no value. Just allow any unpleasantness bounce off and away from you. The positive feeling will stay with you and grow stronger and stronger throughout every day as you continue to simply uncoil.

In a moment, close your eyes, merely drop your eyelids and say out loud: "Allow relaxation and calmness to come all over," repeat these words to yourself as many times as you wish before reopening your eyes to continue with the text.

Go into self-hypnotic sleep now.

Your inner mind is constantly spontaneously thinking and imagining. You have automatic thoughts all the time. Negative automatic thoughts, incessant dialogue carry the strongest most damaging emotional charges. In all mental activity you place prominence either on negative or the positive thought. Your negative self-talk often remains silent until you are ready to relax, have a good time or attempt to enjoy yourself. Suddenly, without warning your inner brain can become an uncreative focus of imagined self-sabotaging anxieties. The inner brain retains all the joyless, negative information you have accumulated since birth. In a mere second, the inner brain can open your memory banks and display whatever it wishes.

The inner brain retains the worst, most frightening, most embarrassing tidbits of your worst times on this earth. The inner brain can repeat the same unwanted memories, millions of times, over and over. The inner brain can become so pessimistically tyrannical that it may attempt to shout down the good positive thoughts. Your mind can listen to enemy voices, a walking encyclopedia of every self-defeating thought, every failure or weakness you have ever experienced. Negative thoughts tend to mushroom to become your inner enemy, your worst foe; you're very worst reality. Unwanted negativity thoughts filled with emotions coming to bug you.

From this moment onward when your constant inner conversation, conscious or unconscious becomes overwhelmingly negative, you shall now be armed with the best available mental artillery. You shall now have defensive powers that will recognize the specific way unwanted negative thoughts influence your mind.

You shall do combat with any unexpected attacks of negativity. While you are in self-hypnosis, you will plan a counterattack, a focused positive outlook, and a retort with a built in upbeat negative converter.

You will expand your world, your personality. You will literally blossom out as a flower coming into full bloom. You will smile more often and when you do your smile becomes contagious. Everywhere you go you will smile and you enjoy watching others smile back happily.

A mind strengthening time bomb of optimism you can throw at the destructive part of your unconscious flow of unwanted self-talk.

You shall never allow the inner enemy voices to gain the authority to get out of hand. The empowering thought replacement therapy, you are about to implant into your subconscious mind are not catch phrases, they are the bludgeoning positive imaginative images you shall use to fight any attack of mind chatter filled with negativity.

You can use this program at any time to feel good, rekindle joyful memories that make you smile.

The empowering thought replacement therapy, which you are about to enter, will be joy triggers, inaugurated to reinforce the good feelings about yourself. A joy trigger can also be a memory of any success, a family gathering, the receiving of good news, of winning a prize. Whatever it is that provides pleasure to your mind. Whatever provokes you to feel good about yourself. Joy triggers will become your anti-negative arsenals. You shall strengthen your inner mind thoughts until there is more praise than criticism, more growth than stagnation, a place to turn to when things go wrong in your life. No longer shall you be at the mercy of the rantings of the mental imposters, those negative enemy voices.

You will now deny each and every negative thought about yourself, your past, your present and your future. Become mindful of focusing your full attention on whatever is happening in the moment.

You shall absolutely deny being trapped in unwanted inner negative over self-critical automatic thoughts that your subconscious has had a heyday relentlessly monopolizing your mind. Make any self-talk the voice of a friend. Say to yourself: "I made a mistake but I can learn from it." Do not allow self-talk from an inner negative bully voice that may inaccurately have you think, "I screwed up again." Positive mental talk effects attitude and reactions to situations. You will now interject inner dialogue to augment negative debates, refute your vulnerable spots and encourage fair fighting, moving towards positive thoughts and actions. Henceforth, you shall refute and absolutely deny any attack of negative self-chatter by developing strengthening positive self-talk allies.

When outside unwanted pressure comes at you, a magic stress shield of beaming sunlight, which bars and disintegrates any unnecessary negative thoughts now surrounds you. The magic stress shield shall always protect and guard you from negative mental pressure of any shape or form. The magic stress shield shall protect you from unnecessary stress or muscular tension or any other negative unwanted self-talk chatter. The magic stress shield prevents outside event pressure from invading you with undue stress or strain.

Pressure bounces off and away from your magic stress shield, unwanted, unneeded stressful bad, negative thoughts, emotions and attitudes will bounces off and away. Let this happen, since such mental negative activity has no value whatsoever.

No matter where it comes from or who sends it, unwanted worry concerns just bounces off the magic stress shield and melts away.

Any unwanted, negative mental pressure bounces off and away.

You shall feel fine because the magic stress shield protects you all day and night from stress, tension, pressure or possible melancholy.

You go through your day feeling fine. You feel the magic stress shield bounce off and away any burdensome, heavy stress and anxiety that comes to strike you.

The more stress outside, the calmer you feel inside. Calm resides inside of you. You are a calm person and you are shielded from unwanted damaging stressful self-talk. You act in ways that make you feel good. Prepare now to follow a newly fashioned, optimistic inner brain roadway. Any turmoil thoughts in your conscious brain can be resolved now. A fresh stream of healthy images is preparing to commence pouring refreshing, peaceful relief into your mind and body, as you proceed.

A peaceful, contented state of mind that no amount of weight lifting or no pill on earth could provide.

You shall have a new response to unwanted mental stress filled self-talk. The worry cycle will finally be ceased.

You can forgive anyone or those who have hurt you, those who have harmed you, those who may have done damage to a loved one. Your magic stress shield will now protect you.

You know you can and shall forgive those who have done you harm or injured you or a loved one in any way shape or form. Hatred or holding a serious grudge or a dislike is a terrible, mind killing illness that never resolves anything, so permanently bury these ugly memories forever, right now. It is a great gift to give yourself, a releasing gift of forgetting forgiveness.

Stand strong behind your magic stress shield. Feel yourself calming and relaxing. Imagine of how you are creating yourself into a healthy, unstressed, never overanxious person. A magic stress shield has arisen to protect and guard you at all times.

The magic stress shield protector, which shall not permit you to react incorrectly from the pressure of unpleasant negative self-talk or situation. You will feel fine because the magic stress shield protects you at all times.

You shall go through each day feeling fine. You watch the stress bounce off and away. The more stress outside, the calmer you feel inside.

You are a calm person and you are protected and shielded against distress and unwanted negative self-talk. You act in ways that make you feel good. An optimistic response to any negative inclination will make you feel stronger, calm and free.

Imagine a happy, optimistic enthusiastic memory.

Any positive memory will be beneficial. Perhaps: the last time you were kissed, the last time you were feeling successful. Any positive thought will be fine, even an imaginative positive daydream will do.

In a moment, simply close your eyes and for as long as you wish. Visualize a personal pleasant happiness producing memory or dream. Remember that thought or memory when you return to the text.

Prepare to implant uplifting, inspiring nuggets of motivational empowering thought replacement therapy, brimming with optimism and hope. A therapeutic program, you shall be quite able to make an easy memory recall, at any time.

I shall think positive thoughts to enjoy today. I shall not think negative thoughts to destroy the day.

I shall trust my mind to relax and calm all tension within.

When I breathe correctly, my heartbeat is steady and regular. When I breathe deeply and exhale slowly my skin remains cool and dry. The muscles of my chest and throat become loose as a goose relaxed and calm.

I shall accept my body as it is.

I shall transcend sorrow, after a necessary brief period of grief.

I shall make new friends, but always keep the old ones; one is silver and the other gold.

Every cloud really does have a silver lining.

I am ready for new challenges; I am exciting and enjoy my own company.

I can learn from body ailments and pain.

When it is dark enough, I can see the stars.

I shall travel to the stars through difficulty.

I will achieve whatever I desire to be happy and feel content.

I shall forgive myself, simply let go of the negativity of the past. It is done and over. I cannot change one minute of the past neither can any deity. I can begin to let go of guilt and move forward.

I know that even when worst comes to worst. It won't be so bad.

I am full of life. I love life. I am so happy to be alive. People enjoy just being around me.

I shall not fight useless battles with anyone at any time. I will choose my battles wisely.

I know any negative ideas can be postponed. I can even deny negative self-talk.

I shall laugh rather than cry alone.

I can calm myself in a difficult situation; I can talk myself out of any panic-causing problem.

I shall do all things in peace. I shall know peace wherever I am. Peace is my decision.

"I am peace. Peace and I are one."

I know looking on the bright side of every event; it is worth more than a million dollars.

For the rest of this day, I am going to have lots of fun.

I shall not wait for my ship to come in. I shall row out and meet it.

I know the best things are achievable.

There are a lot of good things I have. I have talents. I know how to give genuine love and affection. I can be confident. I am a positive person. I shall always radiate good positive feelings to others and me.

Whatever comes my way, I shall never allow myself to be disheartened.

I shall prevent a spiraling sense of negativism from dominating how I feel, think, or respond to any other person.

I shall meet each challenge, one at a time crossing one bridge at a time.

I shall transcend and move beyond any situation. I know that I am an evolving, dynamic problem solver.

Nothing has to go right today for me to remain steady and calm.

I shall never be a captive, bound by any unwanted self-talk negative shackles.

I shall look up not down. I shall look out and not in.

I shall spend more time focusing on the positive achievements in my life. I shall always accentuate the positive. Every winner has scars, but they are healing over with forgetfulness.

I shall spend less time thinking negative self-talk. I can eliminate the negative.

I shall latch onto the affirmative optimistic moment and enjoy each second of the "here and now."

I love me. I am working to improve me, to be more optimistic and stronger. I accept me for what I am today. I shall feel more optimistic and stronger tomorrow and even more so tomorrow.

I will find more enjoyment in the present moment. The past, future no longer exists and is not worthwhile thinking about, only the now and present is the most important.

I realize that optimism means hope.

I realize I cannot purchase happiness. I shall no longer struggle with uncontrolled internal discontent. I discontinue any further negative self-talk or conversations within myself or with any other person.

I shall live by these new thoughts because my most profound need is peace of mind.

I shall empower myself to activate positive thoughts and positive actions. Any negative self-talk and reactions, can be eliminated.

I expect the unexpected, the unforeseen misfortunes or gains of living. Any sudden, unexpected twist of fate will only cause a temporary imbalance. I can and shall rebound.

I acknowledge and accept that not everything in life is controllable, things will not always happen the exact way I want them to. Nor will every person I meet always respond favorably to me. I can make sense out of any chaos, accept and rebound quickly. This is a skill I can attain.

Therefore, I can shift gears and move forward in a new direction when confronted by any unexpected obstacle or unpleasant person.

I shall visualize a vast range of possibilities available in any situation. My creative imagination can supply many different directions of how I can react in any situation.

Thinking about yesterdays and tomorrows achieves nothing; such thoughts have no value.

If everything has a purpose, someday I shall know it.

I remain too blessed to be over-stressed.

I shall look forward, not back. "Onward, again, never back," is my lifetime motto.

I shall look to who or where I can lend a hand. To comfort is all I seek.

Positive, optimistic stress motivates me to achieve what I desire while fueling my imaginative creative.

I realize that one day of stressful worry is more harmful than a week of hard labor.

I shall do everything that I can. I am not scared, although I realize it is all right to be scared.

I will develop and maintain perfect health in every part of my body and mind. I can eliminate unwanted negativity.

I shall remain strong, capable and proud of what I stand for.

I shall remain in the present, the precise reality of the "here and now."

I shall make an effort to bring my positive optimistic attitude every where I go.

I shall work toward improving my relationships with others.

I know that by letting go of baggage, the ruminations of my mind in the past or with worries of the future will allow me the freedom to be happy in the present moment.

I shall be very careful with my self-conversations. Each self-talk conversation shall be examined to eliminate any negativity.

I shall bring a positive, optimistic attitude wherever I go.

I shall always keep my guard up. I shall be on guard to:

Guard my thoughts; they become power.

Guard my words; they become events.

Guard my actions; they can become addictions.

Guard my habits; they become character.

Guard my character—it is I.

I shall never; never think about anything there is no good in thinking about.

I shall promise myself:

All challenging times can be weathered but I shall only fight the battles of one day, that leaves me with only today.

I know that if I add the burden of yesterday and tomorrow those two eternities. I will simply break down.

Onward again, I will journey ahead, but always just one day, and just one battle, one at a time.

I shall know that my past, whatever it was good bad or terrible does not dictate my future.

I shall never worry about yesterday or tomorrow.

I shall keep my thoughts in the moment of the day and never worry about what might happen.

I am always working towards improving myself.

All these optimistic suggestions are now deeply firmly and permanently implanted in the deepest reaches of your subconscious and they are now part of your entire being to be used automatically. Use your photographic memory of each and every word in the statements which will help you in all facets of your life.

In a moment, close your eyes, merely drop your eyelids and think: "I am peace. Peace and I are one." Repeat this statement as many times as you wish, then reopen your eyes and continue with the text.

Henceforth unwanted stress, anxiety or unwanted thoughts shall evaporate and be replaced with optimistic, action filled power suggestions within minutes.

Each of your days will be full of accomplishments and you shall be pleased with these accomplishments.

You shall feel good about yourself because you have implanted positive inner brain suggestion replacement thought therapy that shall make each of your days much more pleasing.

You will always remain calm and strong.

Be calm...quiet...tranquil...in calmness now, allow any past disturbing feelings that you have buried in your inner brain come to the surface. Examine those feelings. Secret disturbances, hidden thoughts, review each unwanted memories or looming fear that come emerging from your inner brain. Decide which ones you want to keep and which ones you want to discard. Keep the ones you need right now, and cast away the others.

Your mind shall never again ruminate or be over critical of any unpleasant memories or exaggerated future fears.

You shall never allow your mind do such carping, this is "beating up on yourself," which is unwanted and of no value whatsoever. It is all right for you to feel sad or melancholy sometimes. It is your way of being good to yourself. Melancholy reflections are a healing process. Occasionally, allow yourself to mourn or be sad when necessary.

However when you have completed the time of sadness, you shall always set yourself free. You are good to yourself and the time will soon be over for those feelings of sadness and you will be forever free from them. You shall be free because you can accept or discard negative self-talk, emotions or feelings. Release sad memories or thoughts of unpleasantness; allow each one to bounce away, such thoughts or memories can never help you in any way. Discard, and disown yourself of any unproductive negative continuous worry spiral. Disassociate yourself from the undone, and unchangeable. Forever you shall forget and tempt to forgive any other person or persons who have done you or a loved one some wrong.

Close the floodgates in your mind's memory bank to lock out people or situations, which can never be altered. A permanent closure, a true denial in your inner mind that shall last forever.

You will let go and move on, you shall surrender to an acceptance that previously was never acceptable. The emotional scars, no matter how aged, shall now commence healing. These past or future concerns, worries or doubts, unwanted thoughts will eventually vanish. These collections of mental wounds filled with anguish are yours, and you can let them come and go, come and let go. Visualize all this mental collection of hurts as a gigantic balloon floating away in the sky. Breathe in deeply as you imagine yourself waving good-bye to the mentally painful filled balloon, as it becomes a mere dot in the sky before vanishing beyond the clouds.

On your own desire release the unwanted mental baggage. Release the negative worry cycle this very minute. As you do so, continue to be calm and relaxed. Feel yourself relaxing with only good feelings. And think, whole and beautiful, and pleasant thoughts.

One of the best stress busters is humor. Recall a funny incident, any very pleasant humorous personal memory, or any joke you can remember. Concentrate on anything funny, take as long as you wish. Remember whatever has caused you to laugh.

Simply just let yourself enjoy. Allow yourself to laugh.

Enjoy feeling the corners of your mouth turn up. That's it! Just let yourself laugh.

Feel the chuckles erupting in your throat. Release a few hearty chuckles.

Do you feel the chuckles vibrating through your body? When you finish laughing, experience a sense of release. Laughing reduces the stress hormone cortisol, relaxes muscles and enhances proper respiration.

Retain that good feeling of well-being with you throughout this day as well as forever.

Now that stress and tension has left your body and mind, you shall proceed to remove the perhaps long time stresses, which is causing physical tension, aches or muscle cramps. Physical ailments that may have been induced from being compulsively stressed out and burdened by a paralyzing negative worry cycle.

"Go into hypnotic sleep now."

As you do, allow you whole body, except your face to submerge entirely beneath the wet cement.

You enjoy the feeling of being so deeply wrapped in the warm blanket of calm and total relaxation.

Imagine this thought: "I want to be 100% well...all over. In a moment, close your eyes and speak out loud for three times: I want to be 100% well...all over. I want to be 100% well...all over. I want to be 100% well...all over." Reopen your eyes when you are quite certain you now wish to fell that you can be 100% well all over.

If you feel any spot in your body that is tight or sore with tension, ache or pain, you should take this time to become aware of this condition and send it your love. Breathing in deeply, mentally point to this spot in your mind. Signal this tight spot to rest. Breathing out slowly, smile to this sensitive spot with a happy face expression. Send this cramped spot one more interior thought signal. Bursts of loving care.

Supply this delicate spot with your imagination's great tenderness and affection. Be aware that there are other parts of your body that remain strong and extremely healthy.

Allow these strong parts within your body to signal their strength and energy to the weak or tightly tense area. Feel the support, energy, and love of the rest of your body penetrating the weak spot, soothing and healing it.

Breathe in fully and affirm your own skill to heal.

Breathe out very slowly and let go of any stressor trigger areas in your body, an ache you may be holding in this tender spot.

Signal a love and relaxation thought, from your inner brain into any part of your body that you wish. Breathing in and breathing out slowly smile with love and confidence to any spot of your body that is not well. Breathing in, become aware of the whole of your body. Breathing out slowly, enjoy the sensation of your whole body now relaxed and calm. Smile to your entire body as you breathe in, and send your love and compassion to your entire body as you slowly breathe out. Feel all the cells in your entire body feeling good.

Be gratitude for all the cells in your whole body.

Concentrate on the gentle rise and fall of your tummy. Sense the calm and mindful energy you have generated all through your entire being. Repeat this program as often as your inner brain instructs you. Now again, concentrate on the most unique location in your mind, your mighty imagination.

Now just begin to imagine yourself standing tall, proud of who you are. You are fine. The way you look and act and think are fine. Positive thoughts contribute to making you the magnificent person you really are. Visualize yourself experiencing a new and healthy optimistic energy in your mind and body. Just reflect on all the positive aspects of yourself: your creativity, your intelligence, and your many talents. People see you as a good friend, a good worker.

They see you as a good person. Imagine yourself creating a positive influence with a perpetual optimistic enthusiastic filled attitude. You know you are a very worthwhile person. Just imagine yourself speaking to coworkers, family and friends, you are always very certain of your abilities.

You are certain of your accuracy, your talents, and your sex appeal. Your conversation with others is always easy. Words flow easily. People are interested in what you have to say. People notice you and regard you as a wonderful person. Just imagine projecting yourself in the most positive way, assertive and self-assured. From this moment forward, for each and every remaining day of your life you shall approach obstacles with these thoughts: "I can do it." "I have the energy." "I am just right for the job." "I can take charge of this." "I can solve this." You are confident, capable, and talented. You have sex appeal and are proud of it. You shall be successful. You shall be proud. You shall be in command of yourself in every single situation. You shall always be kind to yourself; you shall be especially kind to yourself. You no longer tolerate wasting precious time allowing huge hunks of your precious time for negative self-talk, emotions or feelings. You shall no longer tolerate valuable thinking time to be spent dwelling in fearful, negative thoughts of any nature, shape or form. Flood your mind with positive ideas, productive goals, and grand visions. Your dreams when you sleep will reflect only visions of happiness, joy, achievement, courage and strength.

Dreams created by your imagination that will propel you to eagerly look forward to future fun filled real life adventures. If and when any persistent troublesome negative thoughts strike, you shall evade these attacks by saying to yourself: "STOP!"

Allow yourself to float through any unwanted negative train of thoughts, or unpleasant mood while you begin finding your calm imaginative positive inner voice that proclaims all is well. Unhappy memories may continue to flow unceasing. Never attempt to stop these memories. These bad memories are the negative energy stored in the subconscious. Allow the subconscious to empty itself. The memories, perhaps ancient, restart the cycle of prior physical symptoms a condition of fear and anxiety, or panic; however now you can simply float through and relieve yourself of such thinking habit. At this time you require a time where any tired mind requires a mental break.

To cease this negative recycling reaction, for relief, do this:

Make this mental command loud and clear in your mind "STOP!"

Do this the moment any train of bad moods, stress, unwanted memories or any negative self-talk commences. You will be attempting to take control of your mind.

Afterwards, take a few seconds to observe around yourself. Summons your empowering thought replacement therapy.

See your surrounding as if you are encountering where you are for the first time. Release your concerns and realize the profound beauty of your physical existence. You will have brought yourself to the reality of the "here and now." Any rumination of unwanted, non-stopping self-talk shall "STOP!"

The "Stop" self-talk process is a technique to "Stop" a negativity trail of mind moods. However, when this trail of self-talk floats away, a vacuum of unwanted negative thoughts always tries to resume.

To avoid this happening, immediately move into an action oriented positive task or recall the confirmation of the appropriate positive therapy statements that have now been implanted into your inner brain.

Recall and know that you have a protector, the magic stress shield protector.

Immediately, inhale two deep breaths; with two very slow exhales. Afterwards, use the thumb's nail of either hand to press into the tip of your middle (third) finger.

The tip of the middle finger is an acupressure point that calms the nerves.

Press your thumb's nail into the middle finger. Doing so simultaneously shuts off the internal worry cycle and activates your inner brain to become proactive and calm.

Think to yourself, as often as you wish: Relax—I am as loose as a goose—relax—relax."

Then feel the sensation as the joints and bones in your body loosens.

Try this procedure again, get it down pat. Hold those two fingers together while inhaling two very deep breaths before exhaling very slowly.

Think the code words to yourself: "Stop!" "Relax." "I am loose as a goose." "Relax." "Relax."

This private activity does work, you'll see and believe.

Be pleased with your progress. Your mind has been directed onto a positive pathway that will only be beneficial. But a mental overhaul may not be enough. A public, personal image improvement is sometimes required. The image you present to the world could be old fashion, filled with negativity; old clothes that are loaded with gloomy memories that are obsolete. Imagine and see yourself looking into a dark dingy closet chock full of the clothes you have worn during perhaps discomforting times. Old worn out dated clothes and battered shoes. Unless you are lucky enough to change your entire wardrobe frequently, you may not need a personal imagine change. Everyone does now and then.

A new public personal image always upholsters an optimistic, enthusiastic attitude.

Pretend, imagine and visualize that you are going to be like Cinderella. A big thought but you want to do this. Take a last look at that dark closet, which is loaded over with the clothes and shoes and underwear you have worn for to many days, months, and years. It may be that the time has come to reprogram your public imagine. You will like being Cinderella. It is going to be a lot of fun; you may not need to do everything Cinderella is going to do. But you can pretend you would like to some day. You have to decide when.

Whatever you really want to do, is the important thing. So for a moment just imagine and believe you are going to play Cinderella.

Start by seeing yourself going to a large mall, the closest mall to wherever you live. You notice all the attractions, but you have one purpose in your mind: Purchasing a brand new personal image. So, see yourself making purchases in a sports store. You buy all the sports wear you need, a flashy bathing suit, workout clothes, running shoes. Now imagine you are proceeding to a suite store. After a careful selection you buy three new suits brimming with design and color that will make you feel rich and confident. The suits you buy may be navy, black, gray, whichever suits you purchase will be just perfect for the new you. You also buy some sexy underwear. Then you purchase other wearing apparel regular clothes and sweaters with fresh light colors, red, blue, crisp white and a dozen pair of different colored socks. It is a good thing you picked up a shopping cart. It is almost fully loaded. Now look for a name brand shoe store. You find one and after examining all the shoes in your size you purchase three pair, black brown and tan. You also buy an expensive pair of white tennis shoes. You also enter a hardware store to purchase some other items to brighten the dingy close at home. After you have purchased everything your heart desired in the way of a wardrobe you leave the mall and return home.

You are now standing in front of your old wardrobe closet, the same old images you have broadcast in your world for so long. Same old clothes, same old you. Let's start remaking Cinderella right now.

You purchased a box of large garbage bags, see yourself taking out the bags and packing the entire old wardrobe in the bags. Keep the clothes hanger; just lay them on the floor.

Among your purchases you bought some bright yellow paint and a paintbrush. Imagine that you are now painting the closet and with each stroke of the brush you begin filling the closet with the sunshine color. It does not take very long. Afterwards, you stand back to admire the shining brightness of the closet. Now the clothes need a comfortable foundation, on the floor. Among your purchases you bought a perfectly sized thick peach colored floor mat. You had this special mat cut perfectly so that a large portion extends out beyond the closet door. Imagine laying the peachy mat on the closet floor, it fits perfectly. Take your shoes and socks off. Imagine standing in your bare feel on the rug that extends beyond the close door. Notice how the luxurious thick strings of the rug caress your bare toes. So on to the easy part, visualize organizing your new wardrobe, piece by piece hanging and arranging the new imagines you purchased.

When you are finally satisfied with your new images and the eye-popping closet, you realize that this is only the beginning of a new you. A positive, optimistic, enthusiastic reprogrammed personal imagines change for betterment.

Your inner journey for this Session has now been completed.

In a moment, you will close your eyes to enjoy the restfulness. During this closed eye period, you will permanently seal this Session into your imagination's storage banks.

When you close your eyes imagine, visualize and see a brown bagel. Imagine a slowly spinning bagel. The bagel is spinning in a clockwise circle.

Without moving your head, when you close your eyes imagine that by using your nose you can spin slowly with the bagel mentally by tracing the bagel's circle clockwise six times. Yes, you shall trace the course of the spinning bagel six times with your nose without moving your head.

After you have completed six spins with your nose, the bagel shall slowly vanish.

When completed permit your eyes to rest for as long as you wish. Whenever you feel the urge to return to the text, do so—to be totally reawakened. Now close your eyes and see the spinning bagel.

The optimistic benefits of this Session will now be with you forever. You have attained an optimistic coping skill.

You shall now return to full consciousness to become wide-awake. Beginning a count from one to ten. From one to ten you shall begin coming back to full consciousness. You shall come back feeling refreshed as if you have had a delightful rest. Come back feeling alert and relaxed.

Begin to come back now.

One...Coming back. You shall now be free to forgive anyone you know who has done harm to you or a loved one.

Two...Your inner brain shall remember and bring each optimistic, positive statement with you.

Three...Coming up with fresh enthusiasm filled experiences.

Four...You feel fine, fantastic and great. You enjoyed being Cinderella.

Five...Imagining reprogramming your closet of clothes was fun.

Six...You enjoy the feelings of being completely relaxed and calm. Now coming up fully awake.

Seven...Your magic shield will always surround you to protect you from stress, anxiety, and negative, unwanted self-talk at all times.

Eight...You can now forgive those who hurt you or a loved one.

Nine...you feel great. You love yourself; you are optimistic and full of hope.

Ten...Wide-awake now, you feel fine and energized.

Feeling very good, right! Remember you have a magic stress·shield, you also have the private code. On either hand, touch your thumb's nail into the middle finger at, any time, any place.

A take two very deep breath with slow exhales while thinking to yourself: "STOP! Relax. I am loose as a goose. Relax...Relax."

Stretch and rise slowly.

Preconditioning Program of Self-Hypnotic-Session #2
Anxiety, Panic Attacks, Self-Obsessive Worry, Remorse
Rumination & Overcoming Clinical Depression

Since September 11, 2002, the world has been in the middle of an epidemic of depression. Depression is ten times more prevalent today than it was twenty-five years ago. This condition assaults women twice as often as men.

There are many modern day solutions to living in an overloaded stress and anxiety generation. The most popular remedy for overloaded stress, anxiety, panic attacks clinical depression and most of the brain problems are to have your physician prescribe you a daily anti-anxiety anti-panic attack, tranquilizer or an anti-depressant pill. This type of mood altering pill has become the world's most frequently prescribed drug. If you are lucky, the best of the world's pills may mask the problem but no amount of devoured pills will result in a lasting cure of the condition that created a troubled brain.

A ninety-three-year-old man was informed by his physician that he was going to live to be at least a hundred years old, he was in tremendous physical condition from his daily exercise and good diet. The elderly person stated he didn't want to. The man was immediately handed a prescription for a daily anti-depressant pill. Clinical depression now strikes a full decade earlier in life than it did a generation ago.

Psychoanalytic therapy seldom is successful in permanently curing clinical depression.

Psychoanalysts often state the victim brings depression or panic attacks upon themselves. "Psychosomatic" is the word in our doctor's vocabulary that means: "It is all in your head."

Self-hypnosis can develop reversal thought replacement positive visions, which act to dispel a panic attack and relieve depression.

Excessive anxiety, fear or nervousness cause stress emotions. Emotions should enrich your life, however overloaded emotions can be disruptive. Panic attacks result from acute anxiety stress emotions. Posttraumatic stress disorder, are usually repeated recalls of memories of terrible traumas which contained high levels of intense stress. Everyone experiences normal anxiety or panic during brief periods of nervousness or fear when faced with a difficult experience or person. Anxiety disorder is a close cousin to depression and the opposite of feeling elated. The physical reactions of excessive stress causing anxiety disorder can be: sweaty palms, heavy sweating on the face and chest, muscle tension, racing heart, flushed cheeks, skin rashes and lightheadedness. The mental reactionary symptoms are overestimate of danger, catastrophic thoughts, extreme nervousness, irritability, overanxious, panicky, and the fight or flee syndrome.

Scientists have identified the cause of Panic Attacks: the Stone Age "fight or flee" defense system installed in every human body. One overfearful, churning thought recording in your brain imposes your glands to release a rush of hormone adrenaline. Upon this adrenaline release, the physical reaction to the "fight or flee" syndrome arrives. The blood becomes super charged with oxygen as adrenaline is released with a cascade of other hormones that begin spreading through out the body. The chemical rush is metabolized in your body in less than three minutes.

A panic attack is similar to a physical and mental electrical flash. An attack originates from an overload of stress. The root of all stress is fear.

A full-blown panic attack normally lasts three minutes. A panic attack can be halted after three minutes. This following is the mental and physical activity that can be reversed through self-hypnosis.

A victim's heartbeat quickens to a rapid pace, continually rising just as an ancient ship was rowed quicker in time of a naval battle. The ship's drummer begins speeding up the rowing pace by loudly increasing the pounding on a large drum. This compelled the galley of rowers to row faster. The body's systems inaugurate similar speeding up into the state of high anxiety or tachycardia. Adrenaline speedily marshals huge streams of extra blood, calling up blood from the stomach to reinforce the battle muscles: shoulders, arms, and leg muscles. The entire body becomes tense preparing for battle.

Each muscle awaits the brain's fearful thought to materialize.

A stomach lacking blood automatically evaporates any appetite. Stomach cramps strike. By continuing obsessive stressful thinking, the mind and body move up the process with each added fearful thought. The brain begins drawing upon the body's other organs' blood reserves. Blood supplies commence traveling from all over the body, including the very ends of your fingers and toes. Your fingers and toes start to quiver as the blood continues to flow into to the battle muscles.

Hard as a rock, the battle muscles tighten and filled with blood. The body and brain are now stationed for battle with your motor running in high gear but with the brakes locked on. Until the brain's attack of fearful thoughts is released, all interior systems remains hyper, gearing up numerous internal alert systems. The mind utilizes eagle eyes watching and waiting for impending danger. The body's blood remains trapped in the muscles.

The blood has become abnormally displaced in your body, while the brain begins to send another terrifying signal: when the body moves about, it becomes dizzy.

Self-obsessing, overloaded stressful thinking, sometimes awful thoughts cause these reactions. Unwanted thoughts that may not even be rational. A dreadful series of unwanted thoughts that are continuously projecting imagines of the future or perhaps a negative real life experience from your past. A train of negative, unwanted brain thoughts often can appear immediately into your full awareness without warning.

If obsessive fearful unwanted stressful thinking is permitted to continue: the "fight or flee" physical condition can become locked in your body and mind. After an average of twenty-one days any mental continuing situation or any addiction becomes an ingrained habit. You may not want this to happen.

Your mind can be your best friend—or your worst enemy. The average brain creates 14,000 thoughts each day. The caliber of these 14,000 thoughts can make or break you. If the majority of these thoughts are based in the here and now, you definitely are a lucky individual. It is often useful to make a percentage list of how you expended your allotted average of 14,000 thoughts at the end of the day. Unwanted or negative thoughts or prior negative memories score against you—the percentage that you estimate where you were in the "here and now" even if negative situations arose, score for you. For example if you estimate that you were bored for 10% of the day that relates to 1400 negative thoughts. Give it a try you may be surprised how you are using the greatest computerized machine you will ever own—a human brain.

Self-Hypnotic Session #2: Anxiety, Panic Attacks, Self-Obsessive Worry, Remorse Rumination & Overcoming Clinical Depression session can unlock obsessive, overload stressful thinking and dispatch the blood back to where it should be normally stationed in your body. This Session can be called upon when your brain triggers obsessive thinking over a really fright or an irrational false alarm, which all brains do from time to time.

Festering excessive stressful worrying immobilizes. Depression is admitting that you hate yourself. You are not providing yourself with the thought instructions you need to love yourself.

Self-induced obsessive stress worrying can trigger frequent crying spells. Have you become a crybaby? Are you a wimp! Is crying a sign of weakness? No way, crying when emotionally distraught or under great stress can actually help restore the chemical balance in your body. Chemical analysis has proven that tears remove chemicals that build up during an emotionally stressful situation, tears actual assist in restoring the body's chemical balance. Tears flow from within the body, cleansing, refreshing, relaxing and carrying some part of the sadness. Tears release emotional pressure. Sometimes tears are the only express or release the body can call upon. Whenever the feeling to have a cry strikes, have a good cry; don't even try to avoid crying, it is healthy to have a good cry now and then. Young children and babies do all the time; don't they feel better afterwards?

If you are ever deeply depressed, small obstacles can seem like insurmountable barriers.

The mental state of depression is a feeling of sadness at its most terrible. You believe everything you touch turns to ashes. Depression is having no positive or hopeful feelings, with little energy to care. One of the major causes of depressive unhappiness is self-pity. To wallow in self-pity is to play the victim. A major barrier to relieve depression and becoming a genuinely happy person is preoccupation. Living in a world of one. A narcissist is a person having a love affair with oneself—but cannot stand the object of their affections. Everyone has bumps in life. Everyone goes through insecurity and mental pain.

You hold the keys to every depressive thought or fear your brain has ever created. From this Session you will you can learn to take whatever comes easily and your life will always be what you make it.

Most worry overload stresses which can cause depression are not matters of life or death, most are short-term setbacks, inconveniences, unmet expectations or deadlines.

Some measurements of stress, obsessive anxiety and depressed thinking are:
Will this matter next week? Next month? Next year?
What is in it for me if I get angry, upset, anxious, whatever?
What is actually the worst thing that can happen?
Will anyone die?
Life is conflict. Conflict means to be alive.

When unwanted stressful thoughts engulf you, each bubble of negativity must immediately be put into perspective. Fear will not run your life, you can move forward despite a temporary semi-insane, uncomfortable feeling.

Eventually you will realize the enormous amount of wasted time you have spent by causing self-inflicted negative overload stress in your mind.

In this Session, you will be able to relieve yourself of any internal voices of self-hate that may run through your mind while chipping away at your self-esteem and draining the contentment from your thoughts.

You can learn to accept whatever cards are dealt—then move onward.

Gaining positive self-acceptance is vital for your health, if you choose to feel good about yourself; your health will be improved.

Your always have the choice of attitude.

Exasperation, frustration and stressful worry do not have to be your constant mental companions.

Be thankfully that life comes to us in a series of ups and downs. In one hour of your life, you may experience, good, bad, terrible, terrific or tragic events.

You may be spending most of your time, killing yourself to make a living, always working to earn more money. You may have become a mere money machine. There are many more important things in life than money. What good is a million dollars in your bank account if your mentality is on poverty row?

The Jewish bible, the Talmud, states that at first a nasty habit (or nasty thought) enters our lives as an invited guest. Soon, before long it becomes a member of the family and ultimately ends up taking over the house.

The Talmud has the Hebrew word of "Shalem" which means wholeness, integrity, and being at peace with oneself.

The word is related to Shalom: meaning peace, but much more than only the absence of quarreling. Shalom means everything fitting together, nothing missing and nothing broken.

Shalom actually means no turmoil within body and mind. No quarreling or bickering between the thinking conscious brain and inner subconscious brain, two distinct sections of thought transmission.

The past times of your life good or bad are over. No one can go back and change prior events. Good or bad memories should only be consulted for self-motivation to assist you to make better behaviors or choices in the present and the future.

Tiger Woods, the terrific young golfer, admitted that he experiences fear, worry and stress with every single shot. Tiger has trained his subconscious mind to overcome the alarm, to calm down before taking a golf shot is part of his training.

Overcoming haunting memories and those devastating things you have done that may have been wrong, or what other people have done to you can be achieved.

Regarding any past behavior errors, you may have made, Willie Nelson, the singer says it nicely in a song titled: "Nothing I Can Do About it Now."

You shall recognize when something is over, the mental notification will be "It is over with"—the only consequential word is "Next."

Living in the "here and now" moment is: Do not pursue the past. Do not lose yourself in the future. The past no longer is. The future has not yet come. Looking deeply at life as it is, in the very "here and now" where you can dwell in stability and freedom.

Everyone and everything are quite temporary you know?

Consider the ruins of the ancient magnificent civilizations of Rome,

Inca, and the Aztec. Huge empires now scattered pieces of rock. Remind yourself: absolutely nothing should be taken so very serious, everything and everybody eventually turns to dust, ashes, worm food. Worms can eat you when you are dead, overloads of stress and depressive thinking can eat you when you are alive. So take some risks, actually act goofy now and then, do something quite foolish, take chances on people and everything else, this is the real fun of living.

Your mind resembles a mechanical machine primarily and original designed to be a survival apparatus. Controlling and limiting the amount of time spent on unwanted stressful thoughts can be hard-wired into the subconscious mind.

You do not need to continually stare in the rear mirror of memories stored in your subconscious inner brain. Never remain brooding in bed, trapped in a cycle of mental suffering.

Maybe you're overusing the brain's telescoping powers to imagine a future anticipatory event with horrible distorted images, which seldom materialize. Self-hypnosis can assist to banish these and other wasteful thinking habits and bring your fill concentration and attention into the "here and now." Your past is history; your future is a mystery.

The present is a gift. A real "present" of abundant time where you wish to display your entire mental and physical presence.

Obsessive depressive stressful thinking of any matter is a subconscious choice you inflict upon yourself. Such inner brain misdirection can become a persistent torment. A mental state of unfocused concentration, overanalyzing, especially the past and fearful anticipation of the future. You may use vivid imagination of anticipatory negative events that most often never come to be. Obsessive stressful worrying is a brain attack, which robs you of the "here and now."

Unwanted thoughts can drain your energy and creates mental havoc. If the mental chaos is allowed to be a continuous overload stress it may lead to a serious mental or physical disorder. Obsessive stress worry make you think: "I am going nuts!"

When you become perpetually stress out, inhibited, worrywarty, overanxious, your words begin stuttering over each other while your heart commences to begin beating wildly. These are symptoms that you are running the risk of a pending panic attack. 10% of North Americans have panic attacks, four or more attacks per month indicates panic disorder. A panic attack, although a normal reaction to fear can be a very frightening experience. An attack can come from nowhere. A panic attack can waken you from your sleep with a feeling of dread.

You make think you are having a heart attack because there may be chest pains, shortness of breath, neck or arm pain, upset stomach, lightheadedness, dizziness and a feeling of unknown fear. It may feel like a rubber band has been stretched too tightly around your head. A panic attack lasts three minutes. You can endure three minutes.

By issuing self-hypnotized inner brain visions from the hidden powers of the mind, panic attacks can be ceased.

You can be reinforced to utilize common sense, which is a reasonable balance approach to living that is grounded in reality and lived experiences. Common sense is saying and doing the right thing at the right time, inspired by the subconscious inner brain's perception of events.

Self-hypnotic suggestions can ignite into positive reactions that will have tremendous effect on the universal energy that surrounds you.

The suggestions work as magnets attracting everything from the type of people you meet to the types of opportunities that come your way.

What are you afraid of happening the most?

Remain in this thinking state of worry with the fear of that happening and eventually your inner brain can impose that dread on you. In Session #2, you can embrace what is most feared, opening a door to the infinite potential of the subconscious mind, a door that may previously been closed. A door when opened can establish communication at the deepest thinking level and assist in the development of an inner calming, self-mastery awareness. The journey will turn the boundless universe into an unspoken ally.

Behind sad eyes is there a heart-crushing, defeated brain? Is there no pinprick of light in that dark, gloomy place perhaps not even a twinkle of joy? The light and dark forces of your mind may require a re-balanced, turning the ups and downs into an even keel.

The only time you have to learn how to have your mind balanced is when you lose that balance.

The human brain is the most powerful machine on the world.

You can deal with your greatest machine's occasional breakdowns, without escaping to any substance, alcohol, or excess cigarette smoking.

Prepare now to follow a new trail. Newly fashioned roadways to combat excessive overloads of stressful panic attacks. Session #2 will sweep in and install a fresh stream of healthy images and thoughts, pouring refreshing calmness into your body and mind.

A calm and relaxed state of mind that no amount of weight lifting or no pill on earth can provide.

However, much like Tiger Wood's game of golf, life would become very monotonous and boring without the bunkers and hazards, no fun whatsoever.

If any situation or a person distresses you, the pain you suffer is due to your own estimate of the event or the person. During Session #2, you will gain the imagination positive visions capability to revoke any such feeling.

You may be faced with living the remainder of our life with a crippling disease, like Michael J. Fox who has been diagnosed with Parkinson's disease, a slow degenerative neurological condition.

Life is often far from sunshine and roses, but challenges and obstacles do subside. You too can learn to accept each obstacle as an opportunity to grow and learn. Trials are inevitable for all living creatures. Trials and troubles come your way to put the finishing touches on your life.

Frustration, being alone, heartbreak must pass your path at some time, nonetheless your primary goal should be to enjoy the "here and now." You cannot make the world go away, but you can learn to cope in your world by utilizing the wisdom and inner strength that dwells in your imagination.

Your inner brain houses the imagination where a mysterious source of light and power can be reached during self-hypnosis to impose a mastery of any unpleasant situation or addiction.

Up until now you may have just wanted to turn everything and everybody off; but you could not do so because no one told you how. Most anticipatory obsessive worry and anxiety is worse than the event itself. Stress worry thinking is often inevitable but any overreacting mental suffering is optional. Obsessive overload stress worry thinking and its accompanying mental turmoil may be the difference between what is and what you want it to be.

Obsessive stress worry, unwanted thoughts can come bombarding throughout any waking day, especially when you are relaxing.

"Hello—here I am again." Session #2 will assist you to disarm this unwanted mental tendency. Your mind was not originally designed to have suffering thoughts.

Rational fears have a solution, irrational fears do not. Numerous worldwide polls indicate that the third biggest fear of humans is that of losing their mind.

This popular concern is caused by over obsessive worry thinking, the root of acute stress, anxiety, and depression. Obsessive stress worry increases your breathing rate, causing over breathing, rapid heart beating and hyperventilation. Doctor Douglas Jacobs, a Harvard psychiatrist and director of Screening for Mental Health, states: "Depression is not a weakness of character but a biochemical self-inflicted negative disturbance in the brain interacting with the environment." Clinical depression has become one of the major illnesses in the world. Two-thirds of the affected fail to recognize their illness.

Excess stress and obsessive worry graduates into obsessive thinking of unwanted thoughts that triggers a panic attack.

Those who have endured a panic attack know it is a torturous experience accompanied by rapid heartbeats, sweating, shaking changing the balance of your body's level of carbon dioxide, oxygen, and adrenaline. If you are standing you are overcome by dizziness, faintness. Confusion consumes your brain. Your heart will start pounding in an out of normal rhythm, often causing real chest pains.

Since your immune system is in disorder, any illness can develop.

Unchecked anger is frequently an avenue of escape. Are you quick and able to remove your anger with forgiveness?

As well as the injured party?

An over forceful emotion of anger can damage others as well as you. When is the last time you lashed out with unwarranted anger: words or actions?

Positive assertive people are open-minded and contain their anger. Always appearing grown-up, never over angered over trifling inconveniences or disagreeable circumstances.

Anger release and internal calmness is taught in Session #2.

Authentic happiness may have become a longtime forgotten memory. You may feel you have been depressed for years. Your future seems irrelevant and only dismal. These are a few of the symptoms of clinical depression.

It is estimated that within five years of suffering an unending major depression, one-quarter of the inflicted contemplate suicide.

10 to 15 percent of new mothers suffer from a serious form of a sadness condition called postpartum depression.

The symptoms usually appear within a few months of the baby's birth and include deep sadness, frequent crying, inability to sleep, lethargy and irritability.

You can understand and measure the degree of any harboring depression by taking your emotional temperature, ask yourself: "Do I more than often feel sad and depressed inside?"

Your own brain daily broadcasts the state of either mild or major depression—Ask yourself: are the majority of your mind's thoughts, positive or negative?

Your mind may be addicted to awfuling. As soon as one upsetting problem becomes resolved, you become obsessed with replacing it with another, real or imagined. In Session #2 an attitude of nonattachment is recommended.

Cultivate an attitude of nonattachment, by rejecting of despairing from any an injury and the injury itself can disappear. Your mind may need to be primed just as a carburetor primes an engine. It is necessary to dissolve your problems before your problems dissolve you. Your subconscious can solve your problems, merely give it a chance and

remember you don't have problems, you have opportunities.
You can lessen your grip of a worrywart preoccupation. To lessen your engaging mind to establish a refreshing metamorphosis, the priority of living in the "here and now." A new mental avenue while gaining the ability to forget past hurts and accept the present.
Particular stress events have a potential degree of obsessive worry ratings.
The following list associates common distress events and the stress thinking degree reaction. The report has been compiled from medical surveys. Be aware of the level of stress and worry an average person can endure.

Living Events Where You Encounter:	Degree of Obsessive Worry & Stress:
Death of spouse	100
Divorce	73
Marital separation	65
Jail term	63
Death of a close family member	63
Personal injury or illness	53
Your true love's negative habits	50
Fired at work	47
Jilted by a true love	46
Retirement, no real worthwhile plans	45
Change in health	44
Pregnancy	39
Sex, marital & lust difficulties	37
Your boss at work, other superiors	35
Serious problems with your children	36
Business declining	36
Negative change in personal finances	36
Ongoing arguments—non-family	36
Death of longtime friend	36

Your children's behavior	35
Change in career	35
Boredom in marriage and lifestyle	35
Arguments with a true love	35
Lack of time, busy schedule	33
Unpaid bills, and no savings	32
Promotion or demotion at work	29
Children permanently leaving home	29
Family quarrels	28
Spouse stops working	25
Starting a new school	24
Negative changes in living conditions	24
Negative personal habits	23
Trouble at work	22
Major change at work, good or bad	21
Changing residence	20
Church or community activities	19
Negative change in social activities	16
Negative changes in sleeping habits	15
Negative change in eating habits	14
Vacation	13
Christmas	10
Minor violations of the law	8

When you are depressed you are wearing blinders, only focusing on self-concerns, which is like attempting to read in the darkness of midnight. Your perspective is out of order.

Action is the name of getting out of the depression game. Sitting and dwelling on apparent misfortunes and contemplating how bad life is. Isolation and loneliness compound the depressed one's unhappiness. Get out of the house; get out and mingle and talk with other people. Any activity is a great antidote to cure sitting around and worrying. You may be conditioned to focus only on what is wrong with you, something, which is lacking, and your faults, your mistakes and failures. You may be seeing only your shortcomings and have become permanently blind to your strengths.

This Session will focus on your strengths; you will disown any imagined shortcomings. Session #2 will create positive acceptable thought replacements and outlooks for the future that will bypass your conscious brain's natural resistance to change. Life is not change; you change. Life does not get better; you get better. Session #2 contains a magic power that will commence to program your inner brain to permanently erase a habitual overloaded depressing well-worn negative thinking path. A pathway engraved into your mind by so much travel along the same route.

Session #2 begins to develop an indifference attitude that always remains calm and keeps stress under control even during the harshest of circumstances.

You will throw away pitiful apathy thinking—you shall think and act boldly in any crisis.

A mature, super-brained person shows energy and resolve, balanced in mental power, no matter what events occur, recovery and acceptance can be achieved.

You will have the mental power to do so. You will not become passive in the face of danger and fear. You will not doubt yourself.

The worst obsessive overload distress event that can happen is failure through inaction.

In this Session you can learn how to compel your inner brain to inaugurate necessary actions. If panic attacks are striking, know that: you have a "magic anti-panic switch" within your inner brain. The switch can transform the worst to the best, or the best to the worst. During this Session, you will discover and master this mechanism, of the "magic anti-panic switch."

Your brain is either your best friend or worse enemy. Your brain is your best weapon or a self-destructive, pistol carrying bully. Some of the greatest wars you will ever be involved are battles that may be fought in your mind.

You can have absolute authority over your inner brain and think and act accordingly.

You will learn to give up brooding over the past—you can realize the best is yet to come. You are your greatest asset; there is literally nothing you cannot do.

You shall be able to accept the unpredictability of nature's way.

You may be constantly pursuing positions of power and prestige to demonstrate your competence or value.

You may need to feel good about yourself and are constantly seeking external success symbols, trophies, a new car and an array of new expensive suits every year.

Session #2 diminishes these egotistic negative attitudes which can be placed into the proper perspective.

In some cases of overloaded stressful striving can be traced to human boredom. Too much idle time and not enough interesting tasks to fill the day. An extended period of living with an oasis of endless free time. Free time that may not have any worthwhile or contenting purpose.

If you find one thing boring, you shall find everything boring. If you are bored, you're boring and bore others.

You may be a person who decides to engage in the act of being boring, it is not the world that is boring you, it is you who are boring the world.

Do not let boredom, a self constructed emotion drain the fun from any major time of your life. You can develop a low tolerance for being bored. Boredom can be diverted. Even if that bitter enemy shoots you down during extended periods of enforced idleness. You can arise. Physical movement is very important during unavoidable periods of boredom.

Birds are always flying, never bored. The birds do not take a day off and put their legs up. Birds never retire. Birds are never inactive for very long. Be like the Birds keep busy as you can.

Self-Hypnotic Session #2
Anxiety, Panic Attacks, Self-Obsessive Worry, Remorse Rumination & Overcoming Clinical Depression

Now, reader, take *a nice deep breath*, momentarily close your eyes and begin to enjoy the sensation of sinking downward. Down to a drowsy, restful and very calming experience.

Just think *about relaxing every muscle in your body* from the top of your head to the very tips of your toes. Just begin to "let it all go, let it all go, let it all go."

Begin to notice how very comfortable your body *is beginning to feel. Everywhere you are just relaxing...and letting it all go.* You are supported, so you can just let go and relax. Inhale and slowly exhale. Notice your breathing; notice the rhythm of your breathing and relax your breathing for a moment. Be aware of normal sounds around you. These sounds are unimportant, disregard them, whenever you hear noise outside it shall compel you to unwind even more. Exhale slowly, release any tension, any stress from any part of your body, and thought. Begin calming down now. Just let that stress go.

Another breathing exercise technique will be introduced.

Breathe in deeply to the count of 1. Send all this breath into your tummy, allow your tummy to fully expand, NOW HOLD IT! Hold this breath for as long as you can perhaps to a count of 3 or 4. Afterwards, exhale slowly. This procedure of holding oxygen in your tummy has many mental and physical benefits. So let's try it three times.

Breathe in, count of one, and inflate your tummy, fully rounded with breath. Hold it as long as you can before exhaling slowly. Breathe in, count of one, and enlarge your tummy, fully rounded with breath. Hold it as long as you can before exhaling slowly. Breathe in, count of one, and inflate your tummy, fully rounded with breath. Hold it as long as you can before slowly exhaling.

Imagine and feel any overloaded distressful thoughts streaming out of your mind, allow all unwanted thoughts to leave as you commence to *wind down, wind down, wind down, wind down. As you are uncoiling calmness and relaxation begins to expand.*

Wind down and "relax…relax…relax…"

Let all the muscles in your face relax especially your jaw, allow your teeth to part just a little bit and relax this area. This is a place where tension and stress gather so be sure to calm and relax your jaw. Feel that relaxation and calmness flowing down from your scalp as it enters on both temples. Relax and calm both temple muscles. As you think about relaxing and calming these muscles will respond relaxing and become calm. Feel yourself seeping deeper in drowsiness. Drift and float into a pool of the deepest level of total calmness and relaxation.

Continue to relax and allow the muscles across your forehead to calm entirely. Feel those muscles smooth out the wrinkles. Becalmed facial muscles, as rest settles into your eyes.

Feel and imagine your eyelids feeling so comfortable, but so heavy, so heavy, so relaxed but very comfortable. In a moment, you will be asked to close your eyes. You will allow your eyelids to drop down. When you do feel the sense of calming enter both eyes. Do not ask yourself any questions as you proceed. Do not try to analyze the text or try to figure everything out at once. Merely allow your mind to be free and go with the flow. There is not reason whatsoever to ever rush as you enter self-hypnosis. As a matter of fact, the slower you absorb the text often produces quicker and superior results.

When you do close your eyes, in your mind's eye imagine, and really visualize a large black truck tire. Now do not analyze this request, merely allow your mind to flow onward. Loosen and accept the text.

When you see the black truck tire, just imagine circling the truck tire clockwise four times by using your closed eyes. Afterwards imagine circling the truck's tire four time's anti-clock wise behind closed eyes.

Close your eyes now and do this calming eye exercise, before continuing with the text at your convenience.

Be aware of the muscles in the back of your neck and shoulders becoming tired. Imagine a very heavy weight has already been lifted off your shoulders and arms and you feel relieved, lighter and sleepier.

The sleepiness commences to move into your chest; your heart is gently slowing down to a pleasant, relaxed beat. It is very beneficial for your heart to rest as you go deeper to sleep. Each of the muscles in the back of your neck and both shoulders are free of any tightness. Feel the calmness spreading soothing repose down your back, down, down, to the lower part of your back as those muscles simply "let go" with every deep breath you inhale.

Feel your body drifting, floating, down deeper, down deeper, down deeper with ease. Let the muscles go, uncoiling and becoming calm, more and more drowsy.

Let go of each of the muscles in your shoulders. Send the calmness and relaxation spreading down thorough your arms, out to your very fingertips. Feel each finger loosen. Let your arms go limp. Both arms feel so heavy, so comfortable, warm and tingly.

You may notice a growing warmth sensation in the palms of your hands, and that's fine. Inhale deeply once again unwind to the calmness, uncoil your chest muscles. And as you exhale slowly, feel your tummy muscles in your stomach go to sleep, let these muscles go to rest. On the next deep inhale; soothe all of the muscles in your tummy. Just "let go," deep into a calm relaxation. Allow this peaceful feeling to spread down into the muscles in both your legs. Feel both legs become limp as the muscles in your legs as you sink deeper and deeper into hypnotic sleep. You may feel that you can barely lift either leg, both are so at ease. Feel the heaviness drifting right up your ankles and into the tips of your toes. Wiggle all your toes. Notice how very comfortable your body feels, just drifting and sinking deeper.

"Let go" so completely go that you want to go into hypnotic sleep rest, and you can feel the drowsiness coming. As you start drowsing, deeper and deeper imagine a beautiful staircase appears. Imagine and believe you see a large staircase, which has been awaiting your arrival at a luxurious, magnificent Las Vegas casino. Any Las Vegas hotel is an exciting place. You think you can actually hear the noisiness from the gambling room at the bottom the staircase. Are you ready to begin descending? Of course you are.

From the top of this magnificent staircase there are ten steps, and the steps lead you down into a very special, not a gambling room. The gambling room is vanishing now.

Where you land will be a very quiet peaceful place. In a moment, you will begin to imagine taking a safe and gentle *easy step by step down the hotel's staircase.* In a moment, you are going to count backwards from ten to one as you visualize and imagine moving downward one step at a time.

While you take the first step, feel your body become even sleepier as you begin moving downward.

Feel the incoming sensation of leisure and calm as you *drift and sink down, down each step, and become even sleepier.*

10...*relax even deeper.*

9...*down you go, into deep...deep....sleep.* Deeper into hypnotic asleep.

8...drowsy, tired all over your body and your head.

7...sleepy...let it all go. As you go into hypnotic sleep now.

6...deeper and deeper into hypnotic asleep.

5...your whole body is getting so calm.

4...*deeper you go.....Sink deeper into self-hypnotic sleep.*

3...so relaxed...relax...relax...relax. "Let go."

2...deeper, deeper, deeper, so comfortable.

1...*go into hypnotic sleep now. And down you go.*

You can do everything better when you are relaxed whether it be physical, mental or emotional. As you become more relaxed and experience less tense each day you will develop much more confidence in your ability to do whatever you should be able to do without fear of failure without fear of consequences without unnecessary anxiety and without uneasiness.

Summon your amazingly powerful endowment of imagination. You can imagine your personal surroundings, the spot you just arrived in. It can be any special place you choose. Perhaps, you would enjoy a beach or ocean on a sailing boat breathing in clean, fresh air, perhaps lying beside a mountain bubbling stream; or sitting on a lazy boy chair beside a roaring fireplace in a cozy northern inn on a freezing winter night. If you are having difficulty locating a special place, experiment with this location: imagine and visualize walking along a tree lined forest trail; focus your attention on the birds singing; the early morning light of the rising sun. Brightened rays of light begin dancing through the tree branches. Notice, the beautiful aroma of the surrounding tall pine trees; the greenness of the forest; as a cool breeze touches your skin which is warmed by growing heat of the summer day.

Any quiet relaxing place you prefer is perfectly fine. You make the choice.

Go there alone and see yourself pleasantly resting.

Now, reader, once and for all end all this anxious worry thinking which might just cause depression or panic attacks. Thinking stuff that is affecting your mind and body in ways that disturb and hurt you.

Let yourself drift and sink deeper and deeper...go into self-hypnotic sleep now...Drifting and tired...Drowsy and drifting. Seeping down. Sinking into deeper sleep.

In your special place, you feel safe, calm and very relaxed. You may be aware of those symptoms of experiencing panic attacks.

During a panic attack the body's speed up is natural and harmless. Perfectly natural responses that will never kill or permanently harm you, once you stop the process. You can, shall and will stop the mental and physical reactions. Nobody ever dies right away from overloaded stress or a panic attack. It is only the thinking so that makes you believe so. No physical examination can discover or permanently cure the cause. Only you can and shall in your inner brain's imagination.

You know when your heart starts to beat faster; it is merely a muscle reacting to fearful thinking. So think about your heart right now. Visualize your pulse rate as its vibrations begin to slow down, notch by notch until the pulse rate approaches a comfortable sensation of calmness. Notice your heart's beating rate beginning to slow down.

Negative obsessive depressive unwanted worry thoughts and fears of the past and future are unimportant. Such unwanted thoughts are unimportant to your well-being and good health. The "here and now" is where you shall center your concentration. You shall not allow your mind to be overcome with negative distressful thoughts.

Toss away the symptoms of negative thought overload. Overloaded imaginative negative stress is often the perception of danger or a reaction to changing circumstances that appear to be threatening. Inform your inner brain to transform what may have become a perennial funeral of negative thoughts into a parade of positive celebration.

Toss away any unwanted thought stresses creating depression or panic attacks.

Trust the wisdom and competence of your inner brain's imagination to direct and guide the way to the accomplishment of reducing or resolving the travails on which you ponder.

You know that all things are possible and you can do anything or be anything you want to be. You can achieve anything that you really want to. In a moment, you shall direct your inner mind's imagination to positively visualize seeing yourself as the person in control, the individual you always want to be.

A confident self-image where every day you feel wide-awake, more alert. You are energetic and will become much less easily tired, much less easily stressed out, less worrying or discouraged and so much less easily depressed. As a matter of fact, from now onwards, your subconscious will cause you to become over interested in whatever you are doing and whatever is going on around you. You will be so involved in whatever you doing that you will never allow yourself to believe you could be bored. You realize that boredom is nothing more than a form of the emotion of self-pity. You were not created to pity yourself. You will always challenge your thinking powers to learn or do more. When you quit learning, you are quitting on yourself. Always seek new challenges and changes of every nature.

Your mind will become distracted and detached from all concerns, except the present moment. You shall no longer need to think so very much about yourself. You will stop being wrapped up with concentration dwelling on self-worries and self-concerns.

Just let "it go"; no longer dwell upon unpleasant unwanted emotions or thoughts.

From every day from now on, your nerves shall become stronger and steadier. Your mind and body will signal the nerves that all is well. More composed, more placid, more tranquil. Each day you will become much less easily disturbed. Much less agitated, much less fearful, and much less apprehensive, and much less easily upset.

You will even be able to think more clearly to concentrate more easily. You will be able to give your whole and undivided attention to whatever you are doing to the complete exclusion of everything else. Your memory will improve and you will be able to observe people and events in their true perspective without magnifying any difficulties, without ever allowing the situation to get out of proportion in any way. From now on, every day you will become emotionally much calmer, more settled, much less easily disturbed. Day by day, you will start developing a positive calm personality.

You will begin to visualize yourself as a very worthwhile and a very capable person. Your self-esteem will grow day by day. Each day you will be much more confident of yourself and much more confident in your ability, to not only do what you have to do each day, but much more confident in your ability in what you really want to do. Without any fear of failure or consequences, without unnecessary anxiety or uneasiness, because of this assurance every day, you will feel more and more independent, more able to stickup for yourself to stand up on your own two feet. You can and will banish any uninvited, negative unwanted thoughts or emotions. To hold your own, no matter how difficult or no matter how trying that may become. You will always "hangith in there." You will cease any ruminating over the shortcomings and failures in your life. Instead you will remind yourself of your successes. You shall feel a greater feeling of well-being. More safety and security than you have felt for a long time and as you become more and more relaxed each day; so you will remain relaxed, calm and less tense when you are in the presence of any other person no matter if they be few or many. No matter if they be friends or strangers. No matter whether it may be at home, during work time, socializing, in all places of any sort. No matter what the occasion may be, you will be able to meet every person on equal terms. You will now feel at easy in any one else's presence, without the slightest feeling of inferiority without becoming self-conscious, with no concern of being embarrassed or confused.

Without making yourself feel conspicuous in any way. You shall become so deeply interested, deeply absorbed in what you are saying and doing that you shall concentrate entirely on doing whatever task you take on to the complete exclusion of everything else. Because of this you will remain perfectly relaxed, perfectly calm and self-confident; you will become much less conscious of yourself and your own feelings. You will consequently be able to talk and act quite freely without any concern in the slightest when meeting anyone. Even if you begin to over think about yourself, you shall automatically detach and automatically shift you attention back to what you are saying or what you are doing and you shall no longer experience the slightest nervousness, discomfort, uneasiness in any way. In fact, the moment you begin to speak all your nervousness, every single bit of tension shall disappear completely. And you shall feel more completely calm and relaxed, completely at ease, completely interested in what you are saying or doing. The presence of others will no longer bother you in the slightest. You shall never be upset, angry or conspicuous in any way. Your mind shall become so fully occupied with what you are saying or doing that you will no longer think of self-concerns in the slightest. You will no longer feel nervous, self-conscious or embarrassed. You shall always remain perfectly calm, confident, and self-assured. And so every time, every day in every way you are now becoming better and better all the time.

Those nasty ugly penetrating memories or dreads of the now or future, these unwanted thoughts, must now become thoughts you do not want to think about any longer. You no longer wish to live in the past. You will overcome by forgiving and letting go. There can be a closure whenever you wish. You shall be free of the past at last.

Bad unwanted self-discussions that are bothersome, valueless and unneeded. Concentrate on what you think would make you less discontent. Let this inner force go to work in your imagination with the ability to transform and erase any negative unwanted thoughts, which have disturbed you. Any social or emotional past embarrassments you have endured can now be released forever. The source of healing is in your inner brain's imagination, just let this powerful engine know what you really seek. Visualize, imagine and believe, as vivid and detailed as you possibly can make it. See the self-image you really want to possess. Wish strictly for yourself in this self-directing period. Wish for the image everything your heart realistically desires. In a moment, it would be a restful time to simply close your eyes. Simply drop your eyelids down and as you do so, think, imagine and believe that your personal wishes can and shall materialize. Return to the text upon a knowing that you should do so.

Now go deeper into hypnotic sleep. Just, "let go" just "be free at last." All the instructional suggestions you have given yourself will be effective because you want each of your inner desires to be realized. You hope for the imaginative improvements you are making to yourself. You hope for these improvements to commence taking place as soon as possible in your daily life. Whatever you imagined will come to be materialized. Your inner brain shall direct you towards your desired positive changes. Each time you practice this Session you will be getting better and better at it. As you get better and better at self-hypnosis, you go much deeper into self-hypnotic asleep. You shall be in more control of everything, your actions, your words, your emotions, your habits, and your thoughts. Continue to drift more deeply into relaxation and if any disturbing symptoms remain, you know they are unimportant and that you are medically safe. Your symptoms are natural. You are losing your fear of these symptoms of overloaded anxiety, depression or panic attacks. You are becoming stronger, more confident, more self-assured.

You will now learn how you can relax your body and mind whenever you feel fear or panic. You will start with breathing deeply and holding the oxygen in your tummy.

Restoring the balance of oxygen and carbon dioxide in your body will shut off the fuel of unwanted thoughts. This is the first step for reduction and dissipation.

Sink the inhaled air downward into your tummy. Deep down through the lowest part of your belly before slowly exhaling. Take another deep breath into your belly—hold it! Then slowly exhale all the used air. Taking slow deep exhaling breaths exercises regulates breathing. Once again, take a deeper breath into your belly, slowing down before letting the air escape.

Whenever you feel anxious begin taking slow, deep breaths into your tummy. Hold the breath in your tummy for as long as you comfortably can before a slow exhale. Take another deep breath reminding yourself that you can regulate and be an authority on the function of your body's breathing.

Whenever you are experiencing overload anxiousness, you can stop storing any resulting tension in your mind or body.

Imagine you have a magic "calm" box in your imagination, a switch that has two labels. "On-Panic" on the top of the switch and "Off-Calm" on the bottom of the switch. Visualize the magic "calm" box, right now in your imagination.

Henceforth, whenever a mental or event appears to be going out of control: Imagine the magical "calm" box and its switch. Notice that the switch under these circumstances the switch is up on the "On-Panic" position. Imagine and visualize seeing a hand pulling the switch down to "Off-Calm" position and say "Halt" to yourself. By doing this the situation can be defused and dissipate.

You will know that you are in charge as you continue to sink down deep breaths, holding the oxidation in you tummy for as long as you can before exhaling slowly. Afterwards, use the thumb's nail of either hand to press into the tip of your middle (third) finger. The tip of the middle finger is an acupressure point that calms the nerves. Doing so simultaneously shuts off the internal distress cycle and activates the inner brain to become proactive and have a positive visualization, while you repeat the following code statement, to yourself three times.

"Peace and I are one. I and peace are one."

"Peace and I are one. I and peace are one."
"Peace and I are one. I and peace are one."
This statement will automatically curb the flow of distressful thoughts. Your inner brain will commence replacing your thoughts with a positive imaginative visualization. You shall know that you are in charge. You now have the magic "calm" box and knowledge to "let go" of whatever is bugging you.

Afterwards, you should do a quick physical relaxation check. Check your shoulders and neck, letting your shoulder droop down, never up hugging your neck, this cause's extreme stress in your neck and head. Allow your shoulders to droop and drop. Check your jaw, letting your jaw hand loosely, very loosely. You will check your forehead, letting it become smooth, smooth and calm. You will check your tummy, letting each deep breath sink deeply down into your stomach. Each deep breath calms your heart, chest and stomach. Panic reactions will now be a feeling of the past. You know the worst thing you can do in a tight, rough, fearful situation is to panic. You no longer have to be overloaded with unwanted thoughts or emotions in any situation. Remember the code to operate your magic "calm" box. In the case of a panic attack the imagination's suggestions will not be activated until the average time of a three-minute attack completes the normal cycle. You can wait it out and soon, very soon, the attack will pass.

Despair is an attitude you may have experienced in the mind and body, it a periodic mental time of disasterizing and awfulizing. You shall never look at any of your life situations as hopeless. Your inner brain's imagination can always assume command, recognize your despair then move onward to produce positive productive imaginative visions and thoughts with knowledge of hope. Positive solutions to combat the negativity and hopelessness, which the mind may be creating, shall commence to dissolve.

Many people live their day without really concentrating on the present moment. Thoughts can become trapped in the past, near future or responsibilities or other subjects, not connected to the moment of now. You will always be mindful of the real moments of now. Being present in the present moment may require some meditation. Simply say to yourself: "I am right here, 100% devoted and interested in right now." Live and enjoy the present mini-real moments.

When you turn to positive visions, lights of hope blink on darkness will begin to vanish.

A needed realignment of the light and dark inner brain concentration can now be requested by whenever needed.

You are always in charge of your imagination. You have the ability to release stress busting positive visions from your own imagination. Return to the "here and now," step back your imagination can do this and know it shall be done.

To make very certain you have cleaned out your memory banks of unwanted thoughts an imaginary conducted cultural trip is needed. Return to those bad, nasty thoughts. Those unwanted disasters. Perhaps memories about failures, maybe numerous failures, everybody has some. Think about the problem people problems that you may be enduring or have had to endure that mentally upset you.

There seldom is a major revival of a bad, nasty soul. A truly rotten person yesterday, will be a rotten person today and every day of their life. This is a part of living that must be accepted. The unchangeable problem people and circumstances that every person has to grudging live with. The alternative is to spin the windmills in your mind wildly trying to change the unchangeable. Imagine and visualize any unwanted distress memories or thoughts. Perhaps unpleasant circumstances or people, who have injured, humiliated or rejected you or seriously upset you.

Your own behavior or conduct may be a problem person to another individual. Personal shame which may have been caused by your own inappropriate behavior and conduct.

So bring all yours out, vividly clear into your mind. Your big worries, big anxieties, big unwanted people, negative and depressing thoughts, the nightmares of your dreams, embarrassments, perhaps fits of suicidal boredom. Bring forward the aged, emotional scars of the unconscious and the conscious mind. Scars that cannot be doctored or medicated can now be cut out, eradicated, but first a scar must be healed permanently. Reveal your mental scars.

You do not want to drive into your future while constantly concentrating at the rear mirror. To achieve a mental clean out of mental wounds you will now take a tour of an art museum.

In a moment you will close your eyes. When you do, you will dwell on the mental injuries. If the list is short, count your blessings. Count each one mentally on your fingers. Stop counting when you reach about 300. Take as long as you need, this definitely is not a book to be speed-read. You do not want to cheat yourself.

With that said, in a few seconds close your eyes, mentally dive into your inner brain's memory bank, and see how many disturbing concerns, past or present you can count. The bad memory recalls will come and go swiftly.

When you have completed the list of mentally painful scars, return your eyes to the text to continue with this healing exploration.

Well, how many wounds did you count? If you captured a good catch that is good. Now, imagine seeing each different unwanted mental wound as a picture hanging in a huge ten-story brick building: The Museum of Ugly Art.

Perhaps your mental scars represent a variety of pictures that depict war, strife or anguish. Perhaps, you counted enough nasty items to fill the art museum's entire ten floors.

Imagine, believe and visualize observing each of your distressful pictures as paintings posted on the walls of the Ugly Art Museum.

Visualize that you are going are going to float by and go past each one of your pictures of unwanted art. You will simply float past these sad pictures. In a moment, close your eyes; do not return to the text until you have examined with a quick inspection centered on each picture of unwanted art that your imagination has created.

The collection of recall ugly art thoughts, self-concerned pictures that once viewed, you have seen enough of begin fading as you float by, fading...fading...fading. Going away. See these distasteful pictures fading like a light going out in the distance. Henceforth, you shall have a detached and acceptance attitude regarding whatever you have floated by in the Ugly Art Museum.

Always remain nonattached to that you do not wish to possess any longer.

Learn Willie Nelson's song: "Nothing I Can Do About it Now."

Instruct your inner brain to permanently file away your imagined works of ugly art along with each item's emotional attachment.

Accept the emotions of relief and be free at last. You have floated past; floated past, floated past all the pictures are now gone out of sight and out of your mind. The pictures have faded and vanished, meaningless and valueless, and no longer harmful in any way. The counted ugly pictures are now where they belong buried in the files of the museum.

A place you never have to visit again. Promise yourself, right now to never again think of those ugly pictures.

You will now sweep your mind clear of all the negative horrors you have been storing in your mental art museum. You will tune out of the unpleasant past. Turn off any negative images. Any unpleasant memories are diminishing as the memory bank of your subconscious mind cancels them out.

Simply be unattached and "let go," and be free at last. You are ready to face life squarely.

In the same way, reject any future injuries the same way, nonattachment and the injury itself will gradually float and fade away before disappearing altogether. You have added a rebalance to your mind's thinking in the "here and now" where your mind will be primarily engaged.

In a moment, close your eyes and call upon your imagination to reveal whatever creative positive knowledge or future actions should be contemplated for any further wished for improvements. This is a significant project, so take your time. Open your eyes and return to the text when you are completely satisfied that you fulfilled the mission.

These improvement visualizations are achievable and in time can be realized.

You can now expand self-centeredness thinking to a dimension of multi-centeredness thinking, with an attitude conversion from introversion to extroversion. The inner brain will gradually lead you onward to these improvements.

By using your code statement, "I am peace. Peace and I are one," you will not give in to any future emotional outburst of uncontrolled anger or thought bubbles of despair or fear of panic. With this code you shall become a person of sound common sense, saying and doing the right thing at the right time. You can accept whatever good or bad cards you are dealt in life. You have the courage to turn any lemon into lemonade. Your attitude towards distresses can now be permanently altered.

Never look at work or doing tasks, or helping others as an inconvenience or unpleasantness.

Never look down on those who do dirty manual work.

Never believe having lots of zeros after your bank balance is most necessary for a worthwhile life.

Never allow yourself to indulge in excessive idle time. Excessive idleness is the breeding ground for self-centering of the mind's mental turmoil.

Remember the little birds.

A bird never retires. A bird is always comfortably busy, forever active in bird tasks.

Distraction of any type of activity where you can get out of yourself is the ancient remedy for getting yourself out of the dumps. Physical exercise of any type is better than any tranquilizer.

Lay out a list of accomplishable tasks for every day, no matter how mundane. Do so and you can avoid becoming bored. Always schedule "fun" in your agenda.

You know that you can now calm down your mind.

Living "on the edge" is much more challenging than "living in a rut." You shall accept any challenge without running from your feelings or emotions. You accept whatever comes, without running. You shall float past anxiety, worry, and depression and panic, knowing it is a brief time and in a little while you will feel much better. You will float past without fighting. You float past disturbing thoughts or events with no fighting or resisting.

You know now, your negative thoughts and feelings are transient and always passing away. Any setback is a fresh chance to step forward.

You are hopeful and confident. You are able to cope in any tension or apprehensive panic-producing situation; you can relax and cope with any event, problem, or person and remain calm. You know that when a poisonous snake strikes it is better to suck the venom out rather than chase the snake. This is the same if you are ever bitten by a bull dog—it is not productive nor does it make any sense to try and take a bite out of the bull dog. Likewise be wise, any feeling or emotion of dislike or hatred towards any individual release this negativity, forgive and forget. You can be free at last.

Visualize yourself walking tall and straight, feel the strength in your step. You accept the future without concern because you are learning to cope well with panic, worries, overloaded anxieties and tense apprehension…

You can enter any situation whatsoever because you accept your feelings, you are the master of your feelings, emotions and thoughts, you can cope. You shall go wherever you want and you shall do whatever you want because you are confident in your abilities to cope. You can enter any situation and utilize your code statement will immediately supply renewed coping skills. You now have a pathway to cope and you feel the growing confidence in your abilities to cope. Simply "let go. Set yourself free."

Your unwanted thoughts, emotions, and feelings are gone left filed in the vaults of a forgotten museum. A location you never need to return to.

You are becoming stronger, very strong. You are much more confident. You are stronger and more confident because your inner brain has accepted and embraced your feelings, both painful and pleasurable, because both pass on.

Now just imagine that some time has passed, a day or two perhaps a week or a month. Project yourself in the near future. Project yourself a little into the future, it may be tomorrow, or the next day or next month, or you may see yourself perhaps, six months from now, not too far into the future, just a little into the near future.

Imagine and believe that you have made tremendous progress in the improvements you wished for.

Each day you are growing stronger, more confident, more self-assured. You are coping in any situation, regardless of how stressful. You have practiced these new techniques that have proven that you can halt a panic attack before it has a chance to even blossom. Your magic stress shield and protecting code has worked. The magic panic/calm machine has been turned "off" with your halting command: "Stop." The image of a rebalance personality is an optimistic, positive blueprint is gradually materializing. Each day you feel free and excited to be alive.

Contemplate on the image of the improved personality of the positively advanced person you hope to become, the new you which you invited into your imagination.

Bring this admirable image to the present moment. This self-image shall begin to manifest and materialize itself. The desired improvements you dreamed for will grow stronger and stronger. Each day you will be more at ease, much less easily worried, much less agitated, much less fearful and apprehensive and much less easily upset. You will see things in their true perspective without magnifying them and without allowing them to get out of proportion. Every day your feelings of well-being, safety and security will be greater than you have felt in a long time.

You will win.

You are the master of your own fate.

The feeling is wonderful.

Feel proud of yourself.

Reach out for your dreams with unlimited confidence.

You can do whatever needs to be done.

Imagine a smile is now spreading over your face.

You are no longer a chained prisoner to whatever bad has happened to you.

You no longer need to be wound up reliving bad times.

The future days of life will eventually become memories, good and bad. But you can cope with the bad stuff.

Imagine yourself in that peaceful, private comfortable place you like. And because your mind, thoughts and body are in your favorite resting place, your subconscious mind remains co-operative.

Reflect on the code statement and the powerful feelings of calm assurance it shall provide during your journey to realize the highest vision of personal improvement. Remind yourself:

You will make good decisions.

You take care of your health and well-being, you experience joy, happiness, and laughter. You embrace the good times as well as the bad times and treat yourself with compassion and understanding.

You allow friends and family to support you.

You feel better and better and better every day.

You are a valuable person.

You are loved and cared for.

You are smart and creative.

Focusing your awareness to imagining positive goals, achieving positive and healthy objectives, imagine a checklist of positive goals. Here are some suggestions but not necessarily what you prefer.

Your goal list could include enjoying a good night's sleep awakening refreshed in the morning, feeling hopeful and positive about every day and the future.

A goal that you wish to continue feeling relaxed and calm, feeling beautiful and strong, feeling productive.

A goal of taking pleasure in leisure activities, seeing friends, taking a walk, going out of the place of your residence to visit to any exciting event that would please you.

Contemplate on having achievable goals each and every day.

Visualize and concentrate on any further personal goals you may have. Take a pause from the text, close your eyes if you wish. See all the pluses you have and ignore any minuses. For a few moments, merely float into your dreams and desires.

When you return, recall the last time you experienced a really good belly laugh. A joke or experience the whole body felt. You laughed, feeling the full force of uninhibited joy.

Recall this time, you were really, happy, maybe you were so happy, you felt a little goofy.

Imagine yourself dancing with joy, jumping, laughing, and really feeling good.

Happy positive feelings will come.

If you are finding it difficult to experience joy, at this time, that's all right, as you practice this materialization of happiness and joy, you will expand the positive good feelings, more and more. A real good feeling of happiness will eventually materialize.

Add to these good feelings a hope to serve a useful purpose, benefiting everyone you meet. This materialization of giving joy to others, more than any other goal can bring pleasure to everyone you encounter.

Begin to visualize the manifestation of yourself into the present.

Bring the positive images, feelings and goals into the "here and now."

You always owned these positive feelings. All this good stuff has been inside of you all along, and all you needed to do was bring the good feelings forward and create the space in time. The materialization of your ambitions is being created for you, just let it happen.

Your imagination will do it by itself, because you have directed it to do so.

However, as your manifestation develops it may not look the same as you imagined. It may be better than you imagined, you will recognize your materialization coming to be, by how you feel each and every day, and expect to feel better and better each and every day. You shall feel more alive, motivated, jovial, and alert. Whenever you feel the need, dwell on the code statement: "I am peace. Peace and I are one."

The doors to your inner brain will now temporarily shut down to retain and remember all that has been provided.

Session #2 will now come to close. Your secret code and protector shall always be with you, forever. Repeat this Session, as often as you wish, each time you shall go deeper into the inner mind. On each completion you shall discover fresh bouquets of positive visualizations blooming.

Now awaken, coming up on the count of one to three.

1...coming up.
2...feeling fantastically refreshed.
3...wide awake...relaxed, worry free and very calm.

Preview of Session #3
Anti-Alcoholic & Illegal Drug Use

Can you drink alcohol only one day a week, or go four weeks without any of the currently illegal drugs? If these deprivations would not upset you, or cause the least personal hardship, then you may wish to excuse yourself from this Session. Congratulations, many people cannot get through the morning awakening without a "rush of booze or an illegal drug." Many cannot stuff their bodies with enough booze or one of the currently illegal drugs. Forsaking an addiction habit of any nature is tough work. However; any addiction can be licked! You will never say, "I shall stop my addiction forever." This self-hypnotic suggestion would always be unacceptable to the inner brain. You can say, "I will not drink or drug today."
Marijuana is considered by most addiction many well-known experts to be the gateway drug that leads to the use of harder drugs. The most popular illegal drugs are opiates such as heroin, opium, cocaine, and marijuana.
Medically prescribed barbiturates and amphetamines that are took in overdose quantities, just as illegal drugs can lead to a lifetime habit of dependence. The normal human tendency is to increase the dose as the drug lessens its powers. A habit which becomes an addiction that develops an emotional drive to dictate a continual drug need for mental satisfaction.
The imagination that dwells within the inner brain has greater cunning, much superior to any of the drugs or alcohol in the world.
Chronic alcoholism will be addressed, with illegal drug over abuse (or O.D., overdose) since both sicknesses are usually linked. Both addictions are a serious illness.
Have you ever felt you could do more with your life if you did not drink or take drugs?
Is abuse continually putting you close to danger and big trouble?
Never erroneously think that everyone loves or feels sorry for a drunk or drugged out person. Today's society despises over abusers. Abusers are classified as weaklings and big time losers.

If your brain needs a drink of alcohol before or after breakfast, you are an alcoholic. Alcohol affects each body different. If you have been a heavy drinker for years, and begin to experience one of life's downers, the powerful escapism attraction of alcohol can pull you over the line, with one big thump. Alcoholics and drug addicts usually fall down, unconscious onto the floor.

A large quantity of alcohol or a drug may provide a freeing semi-consciousness, a temporary relief from mental disturbances.

Alcohol is a depressant that allows temporary relief but worsens despairing the cycle of depression during a sober period. Numerous studies have confirmed that two thirds of alcoholics and drug abusers are suffering depression when approaching the climax cycle of an addiction habit.

Over indulgence may release you into a mental blackout where you don't know what you are doing. During a "blackout," you will have no memory of what you did or said, nonetheless your mind and body continue functioning. If you happen to harm some other person or encounter an accident, then a report brings in the police: A blacked out mind can say: "I don't remember," the legal judge won't care; he'll throw the book at you.

One may escape or avoid this tragedy, but the exploding hangover after your first sober thought, at the bottom of the alcohol or drug user's cycle will seal your brain with three days in the spasms of physical and mental agony. An agony that only a bullet can stop for three days. A dry out period can leave one in an emotional and physical wilderness. The addiction climax is when a hard core abuser realizes another drink of alcohol or drug fix is not the answer, but a curse. There is one permanent cure, everyone has heard of the person that literally drunk or drugged himself or herself to death.

They usually spend months slowly dying in a total yellow body, including eyeballs, while still devouring heaps of the habit that is poisoning their body. This is the very worse scenario.

Abusive illegal drug use can be a much more painful experience addiction habit to break than alcoholism. The majority of alcoholics are sober in seventy-two hours, if enough of their liver has survived.

For abusive drug abusers, recovery to any state of normalization may not occur for months, if enough of their brain has survived.

Recovering from both addictions at the same time takes the courage of a herd of lions. Millions of humans have, and so can any abuser. It may be the hardest thing the abuser ever has to do. But first an abuser must be compelled to realize they have touched the very bottom. It is the time when an abuser can no longer bear the circumstances caused by their addiction. An abuser must have or gain a sincere desire to "quit cold turkey"—one day at a time. There is no such thing as tapering off. It does not work with any addiction.

Upon the first stressful situation, the addiction is back, or worse into his or her habit.

There is absolutely no alternative but to "quit cold turkey—one day at a time."

The fantasy ship of the abuser's Eden has become etched with leaking holes.

Humans each have their different levels of reaching the addiction habit point of no return. Some abusers must literally drop into a skid row dump site. USA President Ford's wife, Betty Ford, endured a "family intervention" meeting to touch her embarrassing bottom.

Hitting a personal bottom is an event that makes the abuser realize they have crossed the line one time too many. The hitting bottom of addiction abuse accompanies a sense of despair, hopeless and helpless, perhaps with serious mental and physical problems.

Up until 1935, there was no effective treatment for an alcoholic. During this year, two fellow alcoholics started AA (Alcoholics Anonymous). Prior to that time an alcoholic or drug abuser was an outcast, a leper.

Mature, controlled drinking of alcohol is an excellent stress and problem reliever.

Controlled alcohol drinking is beneficial. Controlled drinking has been around for centuries, except in 1926 when the USA legalized fourteen years of alcohol prohibition. The prohibition law made it illegal to manufacture or sell alcohol. This unpopular law only caused the USA bigger problems.

Chronic consumption of alcohol prevents the proper entry and your body's use of nutrients. Alcohol abuse sabotages every major organ involved in the processing and distribution of nutrients.

This lack of nutrient is worsened since the thought of eating, instead of indulging in drinking any form of alcohol or drug abuse often becomes extremely unpleasant.

This condition usually results in a long-term loss of a healthy appetite. The majority of those in the final stage of alcoholism and drug abuse are rather skinny in comparison to the rest of the population.

Chronic alcoholism and drug abuse changes the biochemistry of the brain, developing negative alterations in behavior that are not usual responses to external events.

Alcoholism and drug abuse can be caused because of ongoing stress, rather than concern about specific events. Chronic alcoholic and drug abusers magnify insignificant events, blowing everything out of proportion. For whatever reason, alcohol and abusing drugs offers only short-lived relief. Overindulging is the powerful urge to over drug or/ and gulp alcohol that often must be achieved secretly.

The habit is activated daily when the coast is clear, or if you must, panhandle the cost of the next bottle or fix.

A primary need to drink alcohol or take illegal substances can evolve into an intense, nearly unavoidable, involuntary urge to over indulge…

Some addictions spend their lifetime feeding himself or herself into an alcoholic or drugged out haze to escape guilt, shame or failure that is already ancient history.

Nasty behavioral alterations occur: aggression, sudden anger, violent outbursts, crying, confusion, irritability, restlessness; the addiction reaction list is endless.

Sometimes abusing is an attempt to fill a void, masking a need to be something more than what a person is. Disassociating alcohol drinking and O.D. drugging is about isolation and self-medication.

"Alcoholism" is described as "frazzling nerves." Mentally alcoholism and drug abuse is a place of emotional and spiritual despair. Living in a brain with an endless pursuit for the next "rush" of alcohol or illegal drug.

Chronic abusers suffer from insomnia, the abuser usually drink or drug themselves to sleep.

Desperate brains can get hooked on anything containing a hint of alcohol or a drug: bottles of Listerine, perfume, even mascara which has a high content of alcohol.

Living as a dry drunk or clean drug addict becomes a tremendous struggle, but there are relief avenues open to the chronic abuser who sincerely wishes to "clean up their act."

The one day at a time without abuse, the foundation belief of an AA organization constitutes a series of valiant accomplishments.

For an abuser, who make their own decision to stop "cold turkey," reality never gets better. Problems do not suddenly disappear.

Abusers in recovery are in a temporary functioning insanity but the battle has been won by millions of people often through the free assistance of AA and detox (dry out centers) centers.

Absolute physical monitored isolation is recommended, as a minimum for the first seventy-two hours after "cold turkey quitting." The isolation period may include worse than ever a tremendous hangover that you may feel only a bullet can cure.

This is the "lockup" period; first, to make certain of survival with no access to your addiction dependence. The human body and mind often will commence negative reactions due to an unsatisfied craving habit. Heat attacks during the seventy-two hours after quitting cold turkey are frequent.

Withdrawal symptoms are similar to the long-term cigarette smoker, who "quits cold turkey," except the compulsion to relapse for the heavy alcohol or drug abuser is all consuming with severely more intense cravings and unimaginable physical and mental disturbances.

A booze brain or drug craving brain, once the decision is made to "quit cold turkey" allows no magical quick relieving normality of mind and body, usually for the two or three following months after "quitting cold turkey." During the recovery months, the brain's urge for one alcohol drink, or a quick drug fix—will be doing pushups, gaining added power, waiting patiently for the abuser to cave in.

As a deflated dragon in your brain, the unending urge will

strenuously ask or beg with you to indulge, just a little bit. One gulp of alcohol or drug fix that will revitalize the dragon and reverse to its full size. A return to the addiction habits of a dominated will power that demands a regain of the abuser's starving instinct burning in the mind. Usually, it is never the recovering abuser's train engine; the first alcoholic drinks or drug fixes that knocks the abuser off the track of non abusing.

It is the caboose: the touching of the very bottom once again—the last drink or drug that smashes the addict once again into the horrifying rocks of heavy addiction. If you cannot recall your final, last embarrassing drunk or drug out—you have not yet achieved the life-saving changing disaster point.

One relapse and the familiar brain fog returns. Along with a stronger, reinforced urge to resume the abusive behavior. Thirty percent of AA membership suffer relapses, even after attending meetings for many years. A record was set at 600 relapses for an AA Alcoholic member—the abuser finally stopped the cycle, when the liver gave out.

The Relapse Victims:
Once again, one drink of alcohol or one doze of a drug is never enough—a thousand gulps of alcohol or drug fixes is never enough.

A relapse recovery usually requires another striking bottom incident to restart the desire—to redo the full "quitting cold turkey" cycle.

It is for these Brave Hearts, the reforming relapse victims that this Session was prepared.

Alcohol and Illegal Drug Abuse Recovery—Relapse Prevention Strategies:
You shall find relief, an avenue to take for escape from the compulsion to relapse once again. You shall return to the one-minute, one-hour, one-day rejection of chronic alcohol drinking and illegal drug abuse.

Relapse triggers for prior chronic alcoholics and drug abusers include places, people, and activities such as smoking cigarettes and all event situations associated with your drinking and drug abusing habits of the past.

During the two or three months after "quitting cold turkey," expect intense negative emotions, bitchy moods, anger, self-pity, depression or being over stressed. Expect a tough time regardless of the treatment that is utilized.

During this period you can curb the urge to drink alcohol or do a drug fix by drinking numerous glasses of water. Drink lots of water during the seventy-two hour dry out period to cleanse the addiction from your organs and blood. Eat ice cream—the brain is chilled. Ice cream cools and calms the brain, easing the urge to abuse.

A dry drunk or clean drug abuser given ample time can have a disordered life come back together. Reconstructed relationships, reconciliation of marriage, family and friends. Lost careers can be restarted. Removal of a misty fog, which may dwelt in the brain.

A fog may have had you living in a perpetual mental state of being half-unconscious mentally, perhaps saying and doing things you normally, when sober would never do.

Always remember, the mighty urge for alcohol and drugging disappear after the first seventy-two hours after quitting "cold turkey." Self-hypnosis can assist tame the urge to relapse.

The addiction habit urge can be subdued, although even now the addiction urge may in blazing command, and being satisfied.

The subconscious inner brain's imagination and conscious brain's will power strangle hold on chronic abusers can be altered. The gripping claws of alcohol and illegal drug abuse digs deeper and tighter, squeezing its tentacles deeper and deeper into the mind. The urge to abuse demands to be continually fed what it craves, until the addiction literally throbs throughout your brain and body. Your will power is located in your conscious brain, but your imagination which is located in your inner brain is a gigantic compared to your will power. When you indulge in abuse your will power and imagination are good friends and love the idea. Using self-hypnosis, your imagination can be led to fall out of love with abusing or relapsing. You can gain the power to turn unfriendly against any thought of abusing. The inner brain's imagination of the abuser's can eventually become accustomed to non-abusing. The imagination can be instructed to monitor the weaker conscious will power.

A relapse recovery will involve every aspect of the abusers mental, physical and spiritual being.

With the passing of time and appropriate mental or physical diversion activities, the powerful urge compulsion to relapse will eventually gradually, lessen and after a rehabilitation self-imposed period of addiction rejection, the urge will become tamed before vanishing.

But never think that this combat will be easy on the nerves, regardless of treatment. Many abusers after a month of isolation rehabilitation are back into full blast in the next month because of inappropriate follow-up treatment.

An unexpected impulse, at any time to relapse to chronic alcohol drinking and illegal drugging is the compulsion you will have to contend for several months.

Compare this relapse impulse that comes from nowhere, to the cigarette smoker, who celebrated one year of not smoking. The smoker decided to test their willpower and smoked one cigarette. The next week the person was back to two packs of cigarettes a day.

This Session will suggest positive visions and suggestions to lead your brain's willpower to resist this relapse impulse temptation, one day at a time. The dry drunk or ex drug user abuser's imagination will eventually dominate the brain's thinking process while the tempting compulsion to relapse slowly fades.

This Session's subconscious therapy will assist you in the cold turkey struggle, if you truly desire to do so to gain sobriety and drug freedom.

After a bum finally sobers up, is he still a bum?

Breaking your abuser's habit is not all mean and bleak, hard and tough—there are some real extraordinary, good things that can come your way.

You may think not, in the beginning during the "cold turkey" trial period.

For the first time in a long time, the abuser gradually will be able to manage their affairs.

Your behaviors and actions will become socially acceptable.

Count the money you will be saving! There is never again going to be another expensive trip to the liquor store, no more bar hopping, no more pay outs to drug pushers.

Guard yourself closely—be aware—drug peddlers will give you any free drugs, only to gain back a steady customer.

Gain the freedom to go anywhere at any time, drive a car or a bike if you must.

Most important your "insensitivity" to other people's feeling, especially to those who love you will dissolve.

In addition to these wonderful improvements, you will regain a tremendous amount when you are fully sober for meaningful activity. Make each sober day a quality bonus time.

In a moment of impulse abuse urge weakness, when you are fighting the relapse cravings, always remember the alternative: the abuser's lifestyle and terror and troubles that you may have encountered. All addictions start and end with pain.

After reading this synopsis preview of this Session, you may have come to the conclusion that you or someone you care for has become a chronic alcohol or drug abuser.

You can phone your local AA (Alcoholics Anonymous) organization usually listed in your home town or city newspaper, or consult the yellow pages of a phone book for free assistance. If you cannot locate this association in your area you can mail a letter to AA requesting assistance.

Alcoholics Anonymous, Box 459, Grand Central Station, New York, NY 10017, USA.

Your request will receive a prompt reply from the AA world central office, referring you to the nearest AA group with a literature mail out. Are illegal drugs or alcohol are negatively affecting your "here and now"? If you or anyone you love or know desperately need immediate assistance? Phone 1-800-565-8603, open 24 hours a day, 7 days a week. Wives of an alcoholic can contact: Sobriety Inc. It was established in 1976, has self-help groups around the world. The address is PO Box 618, Quakertown, PA #18951-0618. The phone number is 1-215-536-8026; the web site is www.women-for sobriety.org.

If there are no AA associations nearby, or accessible, you will be invited to carry on a correspondence which will do much to insure your sobriety, or discontinuance of illegal drug abusing, no matter how isolated you may be.

Should you be the relative or friend of an alcoholic or drug user who shows no immediate interest in self-help, it is suggested that you write the Al-Anon Family Groups, Inc., Box 182, Madison Square Station, New York, NY #10010, USA.

How old is the addiction to alcohol? Over 4000 years the addiction was well established by the alcoholic causing the death of Alexander the Great, a Greek who was preparing to take over the command of the known world.

Written in the Bible's Proverbs (23:29:35)

> Who has woe? Who has sorrow?
> Who has Contentions? Who has Complaining?
> Who has wounds without cause?
> Who has yellows of eyes?
> Those who linger long over wine,
> It sparkles in the cup.
> It goes down smoothly;
> At the last, the wine bites like a serpent.
> And stings like a viper. Your eyes will see strange things,
> And your mind will utter perverse things.
> And you will be like one, who sleeps down in the middle of the sea,
> Or like one who sleeps on the top of the mast. they beat me, but
>   I did not know it.
> When I awake;
> Will I seek another drink?

Self-Hypnotic Session #3
Anti-Alcoholic & Illegal Drug Use

Dear reader, just settle down, soon you will be dwelling in a very mind pleasing location.

As you inhale, follow the breathing techniques you have learned in the previous Sessions. Now add another feature to these techniques. Simply put a spare pillow beneath the arch in your back, if it is not too uncomfortable. Of course, keep one pillow under your head. This will oxygenate your spine, waist, ribs, and the lower extremities. An energizing breath technique can balance the mind and body through the stilling and easy flow of the pure oxygen in your every breath. Give it a try.

Take a very deep breath, hold it, and exhale the used oxygen very slowly.

Once more, take a very deep breath, hold it momentarily, and then afterwards exhale the used oxygen very slowly.

Keep using this breathing technique during the Session, soon you will feel the beneficial effects.

"Let go," be calm and relaxed. Start going into self-hypnotic sleep now.

Just picture yourself lying on seashore. A nicely warmed sky is above you on this pleasant breezy summer afternoon. You are sunbathing alone.

Feel the soft, warm sand.

Observe the blue cloudless sky.

Visualize the warmth of the heated sun shining all over your body.

Allow the muscles of your body to go quite limp and slack.

First the muscles of your feet, and ankles.

Let them relax and be calmed. "Let go." Limp and slacken both ankles and both feet.

Move up to the muscles of your calves.

Let them go...limp and slack...allow them to be drowsy. Loose as a goose.

The calmness moves into the muscles of your thighs.

Let these parts uncoil, unwind and relax..."let go" your thighs become limp and slack.

Already you can sense a feeling of heaviness in your legs.

Allow both legs to go into self-hypnotic sleep now. Let every part of your lower body be calm and relaxed, completely while uncoiling and unwinding.

You may feel that you are becoming more and more drowsy.

Complete restfulness approaches while the mind is calming and quieting.

You are beginning to enjoy this very pleasant, relaxed, drowsy sensation.

The feeling of total relaxation is spreading upwards into your chest cavity.

The tummy muscles are relaxing. "Let go." Limp and slack way down inside each and every muscle and tissue of your tummy.

Uncoil, the muscles inside the chest, then feel the sensation of relaxation entering your back.

Just let all these muscles go limp and slack. Sink into self-hypnotic sleep now.

Feel the perceptive of heaviness in your body, as though your body wants to sink down deeper into the soft, warm sand on the beach shore.

Sink yourself comfortably way down into the sand, as this happens, you become drowsier.

Your eyelids are becoming heavier and heavier and your eyes are tiring.

Presently, both your eyelids will desire to temporarily close. As soon as you feel they want to close, just let them close. When the feeling approaches your eyelids will start moving down. When you close your eyelids observe the patterns that cover your eyelids, how relaxing these designs are, enjoy these visual sensations for as long you wish, before reopening refreshed eyes to continue with the text.

Every muscle in your body is still uncoiling, resting, relaxing being calmer still.

You can feel the heat of the summer sun on your body. A brilliant yellow sun hangs high in the blue sky. Observe these wonderful beach surroundings as you sink deeper into the beach's warm and soft sand.

Warm and comfortable, you are going into self-hypnotic sleep now. Feeling very drowsy and sleepy.

The sensation spreads into the shoulders and arms. Each muscle in both shoulders are turning limp and slack as you move deeper into self-hypnotic sleep.

Now permit all the muscles in your arms to "let go"…let them uncoil, unwind and go loose as a goose.

A feeling of heaviness covers both arms.

A pleasant feeling of relaxation is now spreading into your neck.

Let your neck muscles relax as you become even more calmed. Now, the muscles of your shoulders, "let go, just let go." Allow the neck and surrounding muscles to be completely at rest.

And as you do so, you become drowsier.

So tired that your eyes feel like being closed again.

Imagine and visualize a bright multi-colored spinning merry-go-round spinning and circling clockwise.

When you close your eyes for a brief rest let your eyes spin with the whirling merry-go-round. Upon following six spins of the merry-go-round, notice that the merry-go-round starts to move farther and farther away. Soon the merry-go-round will be moving so far off in the distance that it will become a mere dot in your vision. Take this eye close refreshment pause. Close both eyes to complete this eye relaxing exercise for as long as you feel it is good to do so. Forget the merry-go-round and continue with the text.

Summons a creative force, your forceful imagination, the storehouse of memories, dormant abilities, and skills beyond all knowledge; a place where unlimited hope abounds. Concentrate and visualize yourself enjoying the beach shore.

The temperature is suddenly becoming extremely hot on this summer afternoon. So hot that the sun is baking your entire body. You decide to stand up out of the sand and go exploring. Imagine that you discover a rowboat with oars tied to some rocks not far from the shore where you are standing. You notice the rowboat is drifting towards a cave in the rocks. The cave appears to be an open tunnel.

Visualize walking out in the water and getting into the rowboat. See yourself starting to paddle inside the cave. Once inside the cave, after a brief period of darkness, surprise the boat enters a lovely, sun lit grotto, similar to the Blue Grotto in Capri, Italy. There is a soft blue light beaming in from above. You look up to see a large space in the top of the grotto open to the sky above.

You observe huge ancient beautiful paintings on all the walls of the cave. A gallery of dazzling artwork is blazing in soft, vivid colors. You hear soft music in the background, a personal favorite melody from the good old days. The sound is a beautiful, joyful music that warms the heart with pleasant memories.

A lullaby, lulling you more deeply asleep.

After a full view of the artwork, the boat emerges out of the grotto coasting into bright sunshine outside. As the rowboat drifts along the shore, you see a field of lovely flowers in bloom, yellow sunflowers mixed with tall white lilies. Breathe in the fragrant, sweetly smelling colorful corsages.

The rowboat docks on the shoreline. You climb out of the rowboat to begin walking up a grassy hill to a rolling green grassed meadow. Ahead you see a huge tree and walk towards what appears to be an apple tree at the top of a hill on the meadow. Upon reaching the apple tree, you see a large red apple hanging easily in arm's reach. Pick the apple off the branch. Imagine a taking a bite of the apple. The apple's taste is very good and sweet. As you bite into the delicious apple, you glance around at the grass-covered meadow to observe a golden brick, pathway magically appearing. The sparkling pathway beckons you to move onward. After taking another bite of the apple, place in your back pocket. You walk forward onto the goldbricked road to see that the footpath leads up to an enchanting large pool, waving with bright clear blue water and there is a huge waterfall right in the middle of the pool.

You desire to go there. So you do. Approaching the pool you notice that colossal baking volcano rocks surround the miracle pool.

Warm vapors of steam are rising up from the water. A magic pond heated by volcano rocks. Carefully, you climb over a cliff to the edge of the pond. Instinctively, you reach your right hand down into the deep clear water. The hand in the pond enjoys being in the warm, crystal clear blue water. At the brim of the waterfalls there is a large rock ledge extending out from under the running stream of cascading water. The bright sun is shining brightly causing beads of perspiration to cover your wet face.

You are so hot that you decide to take all your clothes off and dive into the heated pool. Diving into the water you suddenly feel so refreshed and clean. You begin swimming to the waterfall's rock shelf. See yourself grabbing onto an embedded boulder while you pull yourself out of the pond you stand on the base of the rock beside the waterfall. In the next moment, you slowly take several side steps across the platform to stand under the waterfall. Your entire body is under the center of the cascading chute of life changing falling water. You enjoy drenching and soaking each of your cells, with the magical mighty power of the miracle Niagara of the water cataract.

Imagine and believe and know that the waterfall has magical powerful washing, cleansing powers. The dropping stream of magic water is cleansing away your every craving urge to drink alcohol in any way shape or form, along with the craving to take illegal drugs in any way, shape or form.

You shall never want to take these poisons again, illegal drugs or mind blowing and body destroying quantities of alcohol. You know what a mess your life has become from alcohol and illegal drugs. You sincerely regret and will apologize to anyone for any wrongs you caused and can now remember.

Believe this phenomenon, you are just in time to be cleansed by the fully cleansing, magical waterfall. You are now totally refreshed and cleaned out of all cravings and urges for alcohol and illegal drugs of any way, shape or form. Slowly you exit out of the miracle waterfalls. When you come forth from under the waterfalls, you notice two waterways that mysteriously branching out from the magical pond. At one end of one waterway is an exciting looking bay. There is a sign posted, you read the words on the sign: "Abuser's Bay." You see a yacht filled with familiar acquaintances, your drinking booze and smoking pot and taking other drugs pals. They are summoning you to come out to join them. "Everything is free, no charge. Anything you want and we got what you know you have always loved to devour, come on over with us," they tempt you. You did love alcohol and illegal drugs until you went under the magic waterfalls in the miracle pool. Your attention is distracted, you hear other noises in the adjacent waterway. A sign is posted on this waterway, "True Joy Lake." You see a barge containing your loved ones. Visualize them standing there. Whoever they may be.

Momentarily, in a few seconds close your eyes and concentrate on the people you like or love who are on the barge in "True Joy Lake." These people are also beckoning you to come and join them. Some of folks on the barge on True Joy Lake may not love you anymore because your alcoholic drinking and illegal drug abuses have caused them to lose respect for you.

If you see an empty barge, perhaps, your addictive behaviors have made everyone you love not want to know you anymore. The world is full of disowned, unloved people. If the barge on "True Joy Lake" you imagine is empty. Imagine and believe in, and reconstruct the fine person you were before you overdid your addiction. See this image of yourself as you were during this earlier time. You once enjoyed being that non-addicted individual. You can become that fine person again. You love your miraculous new washed and cleaned sober self and soon you will enjoy every minute of it. Think deep and think hard with your imagination.

In a moment you will close your eyes to concentrate and consider which waterway you really want to venture out into. Allow your temptations and desires to surface, all the offsetting negativity, and the resulting troubles of all kind that overdoing your addiction brought.

Think of your loved ones on the barge, who do not want you to drink or take illegal drugs, they want to love you as you once were. Take as long as you wish before opening both eyes returning to the text.

When you open your eyes you notice that a large, life-giving raft with an oar has drifted up beside you at the water's edge.

You are now faced with a profound spiritual and mental crisis, a two pronged challenge to your inner brain.

In your heart, which water way do you truly wish to paddle in...

After you walk out onto the raft your hands pick up the paddle. Deep within your imagination there is only one choice you have to make.

Do you wish to continue doing booze and drugs with your addicted pals?

Or do you wish for your body and mind to live a healthy, chemically dependent existence? You have dwelled a long time in "Abuser's Bay," certainly in the past your imagination and willpower did convince your mind that you enjoyed abusing alcoholic drinking and/or illegal drugs. But only now can things begin to seriously change.

If you are not truly hooked and sincerely desire to "stop your addiction forever, one day at a time," you can.

The addiction groove is like spending all your money and energy for items you really do not want, or have no value. Henceforth, your entire energy system shall be devoted to getting yourself better. All of your body's energy and every penny you spend shall be spent on getting only what you really want and need. You shall support a complete removal of energy expended or money wasted on things you do not want. The words "addict," "alcoholic," "drug addict," are all negative which indicate those who can not get enough of what they really despise.

You are no longer an "addict," never use these words: "addict," "alcoholic," "drug addict," or attributes to desecration your good name. Henceforth, you are a pure, natural healthy being.

Imagine and believe and remember being under the magic pond's waterfall. The magic washing enjoyed under the waterfalls can guard you against any possible relapse back into the addiction habit. Now are being moved to make a lifesaving and long-term happiness choice. Imagine paddling the raft out to the barge floating on: "True Peace

Lake." You experience a joyful relief as you do. When you arrive, you are quickly pulled out of the water with an extended arm of one of those who have always believed in a better you, the person you truly want to be.

In a few seconds, close both eyes, project your thoughts to travel a little bit into the future. Dwell on who or what person you meet on the "True Peace Lake" barge. See how everything can now change for the better. Value the privileged company of your loved ones and friends; lock in their embraces. Concentrate on the coming back to your real self. Close your eyes now and take as long as you wish before continuing with the text.

Never forget to revisit the miracle, magical pond. Its magic waterfall has many other benefits to bring you. To revisit this magical place all you have to do is merely press your thumbnail into the third finger of either hand, this is a nerve ending acupuncture point that brings relaxation to the mind. While doing this, take three deep breaths, and think or say to yourself: "I am free at last. I am free at last. I am free at last."

From now on, you will want to give up drinking and drugging altogether. Your desire and have determination to stop killing yourself. The desire to stop cold turkey will become so powerful it will eventually completely overwhelm any craving to drink or drug. Every day the relapse cravings shall become less and less, weaker and weaker, until in due time the craving will vanish completely. You will realize that alcohol and illegal drugs are poisons that can only kill you. Whenever you have an urge that you simply must have a drink or a drug you should suck on a hard candy, which you will carry with you at all times from now on, this will immediately assist in removing the urge to relapse. You now possess the power to stop a relapse. Just as you have the self-hypnotic power to relax every cell, muscle, bone and tissue in your body and mind, as you are now doing. You can stop drinking and drugging because you really want to do so.

Drink lots of water to wash the traces of your addiction out of the mind and body. The time has arrived to be awakened with new courage along with the strength to avoid a temptation to relapse.

Merely count forward from one to five to become fully awakened to be feeling very pleasant, self-assured of future success and relaxed.

1-2...You have found the capacity, the imaginative capacity to overcome your will power.

3...You are now free.

4...You shall remain free. One day at a time.

You are free and feeling great, healthy, pure and clean. You have gained new powerful hope.

Preconditioning Program of Session #4
Marital Harmony/Sexuality & Lust

If you are absolutely satisfied in your relationship with your true love, you may pass over this particular Session.

However, if you are experiencing an unsatisfactory sex life, endless conflict, excessive anger or even mild adversity with your true love, please read on.

Without a single doubt, a mutual loving mate enjoying a spectacular sex life is the world's best ever stress buster. Both self-hypnosis and sexual intercourse take place in an altered state of consciousness named "alpha-theta."

Good sex with a singular, loving partner is the world's best tranquilizer. The pleasure is free, always available and temporarily removes most traces of stress.

Rapt ecstasy during a sexual climax momentarily paralyzes before totally relaxing and calming your mind and the body muscles.

The stress antidote of making love is what our forefather; the Stone Age folk specialized in. They populated the world.

If you are not married, you can look forward to a gratifying sex life.

Only 100 years ago, the more children you had the better. This was insurance that the parents' farm would continue with prosperous crops or their children would get out to earn more money for the family at any early age. A large crop of children would earn money for their parents when old age prevented them from doing so. The majority of women were full-time mothers, they didn't need a lot of money. These aggressive women knew that money did not play the major part as it does in today's civilized jungle. The earlier times men and women lived only in the war of daily survival. Life was simpler then. Nobody needed a big house or automobile with a big mortgage attached to each. The goal was to merely survive day to day. The early folks didn't have to save up a fortune to make certain their children could attend the best university. A hundred years ago, getting through grade eight was considered being well educated.

This Session embodies erotic sexual enhancement hypnotherapy. This Session can be a marriage saver. Needed sexual adjustments and improvements modifications can be realized. Alterations, which often provide a fresh sizzle to, sexual, married life. A section of the hypnotic Session is dedicated to restore or enhance the imagination's powerful libido. What may now be buried in ashes, can arise again with the fresh vigor of the young. The most important organ that is required for achieving successful sex is the inner brain. With the co-operation of the inner brain and mutual sexual attraction you and your mate's sexual life will be intensified. Upon completion of Session #4, consider a roller coaster of a second honeymoon. You and your true love have earned a recess, some time out; a stress less time spent together ignoring any unresolved issues. Take at least one entire day to have some fun with your mate, this is why you picked your companion in the first place.

The emotions of true love have driven some humans mad with desire, inspired monuments, like the Taj Mahal in India, inspired paintings, songs and poetry, instigated wars. Practically all humans are happier with a true love than living alone. A true love is anyone you can share many happy experiences and help you deal with life's burdens.

Love: the search for true love and the pain of loving, is the subject of most songs, all soap operas, most movies and often broken-heart suicides.

The USA Census Bureau reports that nationally in less than 30 years, the "never married" number has doubled. The average age of those entering a first marriage is at a record high: age 25 for women, age 27 for men.

Are these trends a good or bad?

A titanic loss of family values developed in the 1980s when the divorce revolution started. Three out of five (60%) marriages were officially voided and statistically recorded in North America.

People are now waiting longer to marry, because they are willing to wait for the real thing.

Communal living with multiple partners has become as obsolete as the do-do bird. But during the 1970-1980s multiple partners almost became traditional.

Communal living was a reject of the obsolete Victorian courting regulations, anti-women, anti-birth control, anti-sex ideas, created by the countries pioneers.

Living common law with several partners before a first marriage was a remedy to cure loneliness and lust. Couples living together without marriage on the near horizon is no longer a fashionable lifestyle.

In today's generation the majority of the young adults desire to know their partners for at least one year or more. Most attempt to avoid intimate relations, before they make a lifetime commitment.

Marital adulthood, unconditional true love, is beginning to seep into the human brain. The statistics of divorce and separation are now in steep decline.

True love has turned out to be the real treasure of living.

True love has become more valuable than fame or fortune, or anything else this world has to offer.

The institution of marriage itself is changing, it is becoming less about security, financial gain and social status. It is about true love.

The current generation is not the first generation to marry for love, but today's young people are the first to wait to do so in such great numbers.

Today's generation wants a one time, permanent, soul mate. A special someone who is forever caring for mutual well-being and welfare.

True love is more important than sexual gratification and reproduction.

True love expressed primarily, but not exclusively in marriage and parenthood is the most accessible way we have of being genuinely and supremely important in another person's life. Your greatest blessings are derived from loving, not being loved.

True love gratifies a human's natural lusting, the sexual urge produced by the reproductive impulse. True love meets our need to matter, to be somebody's somebody.

There is a basic human need for a singular "lifeline," an intimacy. Your brain would be emotionally starved if you only dealt with strangers all day long.

You need someone in your life; a person who knows you thoroughly and sincerely cares about you.

You need to feel loved.

You need someone to tell you that you are special and irreplaceable. Someone who will tend to your needs and assist you in overcoming stress and fears, perhaps a fear that you are badly flawed, and no one else will love you.

You need someone to share your insecurities with, the way a mother does with her infant children.

You need to give love, to make a difference in one person's life. Like siblings you need the reassurance that somebody somewhere finds you adorable.

The need to matter, to make a difference in another person's life is a two-way street involving mutual nourishing, not just yours.

You marry for intimacy, to find someone who will care for you, in sickness and in health, in poverty or wealth, in joy or in pain.

You marry for sexual access, responding to strong, Stone Age desires natural and good healthy urges.

You join up with someone whose life will be different for having shared life with you.

You should often tell your true love, "You matter more to me than anyone else in the world."

Your true love will see you with a different mindset than all others. Your flaws will be recast as strengths, self-doubts removed by your true love's acceptance.

Marriage and parenthood gives you the promise of immortality. You realize that it is very few children who willingly sever spiritual and emotional bonds with their parents.

Your sense of belonging is enhanced when you know that you are important to someone other than your parents or friends.

True love assists and encourages you with each pleasant or unpleasant change in your life.

Your true love is the key to survival in a sometimes-unfriendly world.

True love must be strengthened beyond neediness and self-interest, it may die a thousand deaths before the union begins to rise like the phoenix, beyond worldliness.

Romance opens the door to true love, but it does not help you walk through it.

Difficult times shall be weathered with your true love.

A real, living breathing true love relationship is full of ambiguity, complexities, resentment, anger, compassion and often distrust.

Marriages fail because one or both partners are not receiving the love, affection and attention they crave. Sometimes, a marriage fails when one partner is frustrated in their need to give true love, to make that special difference in another person's life.

When sexual or emotional needs are ignored or unfulfilled, marital problems often develop: overt flirting with others, having affairs with others: adultery may occur.

Modern times list many famous men who went this route, but few women make headlines by doing so: Margaret Trudeau and Elizabeth Taylor. Senator Gary Hart, from Colorado, a top USA presidential candidate was caught doing monkey business, on a yacht with the same name. USA Presidents Kennedy and President Clinton also similarly endangered the security of their marriage vows.

The bond between you and your true love is sacred. If you dishonor your commitment, you destroy the relationship's foundation.

"Standing by your mate" is often merely the granting of approval of continued unacceptable behaviors. If your true love is incapable of being faithful to you now, what real hope is there for a relationship in the future?

It should not be that you only rely on one person to meet all of your emotional needs, to supply answers to all the problems. This may be putting more of a hardship on that one most intimate, true love relationship than it can bear. Adversity and conflict with your true love can be caused by many diversified situations, anxieties to earn more money, the feeling of rejection, over criticism, henpecking, back biting remarks, a never-ending boring yawn in your company, a dominating true love who refuses to let you out of their sight. The cause of problems one could experience with a true love is endless. Being love-starved destroys many unions. It is agonizing when one's heart is starving for love and does not get enough. Mutual love sharing is the foundation of any union with a partner. Love refreshments should be part of everyday life. Unexpected kisses, a compliment, the displaying of affection, which include physical intimacy: touching, holding, sitting close together and holding hands. This is what love is all about, this vital link has nothing to do with sex. Physical affection soothes and heals one's body and mind. Gratitude and appreciation: paying attention to your partner's needs and spoken words, a love letter, a thank-you, and saying "I love you" takes only minutes but create instant mini-real moments of bonding.

When the doldrums consumes a marriage, it takes a strong wind to get it going again.

Dark doldrums often develop during midlife during the so-called menopause periods. During the female menopause the entire brain becomes rewired with new thinking patterns, new insights, new ambitions. Males often experience a midlife change that can lead to previously unknown territories. The empty nest syndrome often occurs at the same time, with the finality of continual care giving to offspring. Suddenly, parents gain enormous free time while seeking to comprehend the mental and physical changes of menopause.

The interpretation of what is going wrong when adversity comes along in your marital life is how your subconscious inner brain's imagination will create your behavior responses and actions. When things go wrong in a marriage, whether you will give up or whether that you start to make things go right, is up to you.

Your true love relationship is turning unhealthy if you answer yes to any of these questions.

Are you continually preoccupied trying to please your true love at your own expense?

Is cuddling on the couch with your true love a rarity?

Do you depend on your true love to feel good, to redress any imbalance in yourself?

Do your moods alter according to your true love's moods?

Do you spend too much of your free time away from your true love?

Is your true love causing a diminishment in your sense of self-worth?

Do stupid, pettiness arguments, exaggerated little troubles, become "big deals," lasting days, maybe weeks?

Are private conversations with your true love becoming strained and filled with long silences?

Do you fear that making waves which will upset your true love?

Do you feel an obsessive desire to possess all your true love's affections in order to define yourself as worthwhile?

Are you and your true love enduring unpleasant emotional moods causing temporary disharmony—disconnecting for the wrong reasons?

Are you or your true love hiding or manipulating the truth? Are lies begetting more lies?

Are you or your true love existing in a "Messiah complex"—too big for their britches?

Are you treating your true love like an enemy, not an ally. A balancing act between attraction and attack. A team that is not always working together?

Have you allowed jealousy or possessiveness into your relationship. Have these emotional behavior habits grown into an over riding obsession?

Are you or your true love always making excuses for grossly disrespectful, rotten behavior?

Has sex attraction, formerly the high point of your relationship with your true love become boring or repugnant, or non-existent? Is your sex live going downhill fast?

Has your true love become cold, unaffectionate and uncaring? Is living with your true love, similar to living with a stranger? Is your greatest secret fear that your true love despises you? Do you fear that your true love will leave you, find another lover because your true love often says you are boring? You want to live in love not martyrdom. Do you often have an impulse, to jump out, to get away as fast as possible, from a stressful emotional and physical relationship with your true love?

For some, the time may have arrived to cut losses and permanently leave.

For others a mutual compromise along with a serious heart-to-heart negotiation, spending time with a couple therapist or a trusted wiser, older person often open communication avenues that have stubbornly remained shut.

Session #4 could amazingly turn the tide for improved compatibility. If nothing works, at least you will know that you gave it your best shot.

Session #4 will not touch upon abusive behavior. Abusive behavior can be physical, mentally or verbally insulting, belittling and over controlling.

Anyone can become a sexual or physical bully. Abuse can start with a slap and result in a murder. 25% of unions contain abuse and assault. Abuse can go on for decades. Abuse always gets worse. Nothing you can do or say will stop abusive behavior. Abusers usually cannot be stopped until it is too late.

If your marriage has deteriorated to chronic physical abuse, the police should be summoned. You may prefer not to do this, because children are or could become involved. It is a false motive that the family image must be perpetuated to relatives and community. The abuser is responsible for their actions, they are committing a crime. One last ditch solution, under these circumstances, where you truly wish to preserve the relationship, "is to remain continually silent" when there is a possibility of any type of abuse.

Abuse of a true love, putting children at risk, domestic violence, is a widely spread problem. Abuse is a major subject that cannot be properly expanded in this program. A small root of abuse was found underground and followed. The roots trail of abuse leads underground for hundreds of measured feet towards a giant oak tree.

The oak tree of abusive people is a subject of degradation. The author addresses this major human abuse conflict containment in the book titled: *Hope for Abused People: The 12 Self-Hypnotic Sessions.*

Lust:
Lust for another human is a natural inclination. It is a normal human reaction not a sin.

Has controlling the robust lust instincts become a problem?

Marriages fail for three major reasons, abuse, incompatibility, and infidelity.

Oscar winner Halle Berry was informed that her husband, Eric Benet who she has been married to for two year, had been unfaithful twelve times during the first year of marriage.

Eric has been in the news and is reported to be attending Sex Addicts Anonymous meetings.

USA President Carter is one of the few famous men to publicly state that he sometimes "goes in heat" with goggling eyes viewing the opposite sex, just as every normal human does.

To control that spontaneous "going into heat" feeling similar to believing one can direct all the winds of the world and all the waves in all the sea. It is not an addiction, it is merely the ancient, stone-age urge to conquer a new, fresh conquest.

A pretty hooker approached Paul Newman, the actor. This woman offered her services at no charge. Paul stated words that were well reported by the news media: "Why should I eat hamburger when I have steak at home."

You must make yourself content with what you have at home. This is the only physical sexuality that you are entitled to enjoy. You may have made a vow to do so in a marriage ceremony.

The consequences of doing otherwise, adultery, eventually results in a serious, complicated guilt complex mental problem.

Divorce and only divorce, will always be your main deterrent to maintain alertness of an impulse of a lust's desire to sample sexual wares other then your true love.

The governing impulse of sexual addiction signals a craving for meaning, purpose, and value. Discussions with other people, or your true love about "your heated lust periods" seldom reduce natural lust. However, hearing the immense problems that lust has caused other people may cause you be to be regretful and instill defensive attitudes in your imagination to walk away from the temptation to indulge.

Nothing can stop lusting, even castration doesn't stop lust's reaction in the brain.

The act of lusting can be brought under control but never relieved. Only the great fear of divorce firmly established in the subconscious inner brain's imagination can master and subdue an out of control urge of lust.

Everybody has flaws. Nobody ever married a perfect person. The ultimate question is: are the positive things that my partner offers me so worthwhile that I can put up with the flaws? Certain things will always be the way they are forever; compromise may be the only possibility.

Many movie stars who earn 30 or 40 million dollars a movie have little to fear of divorce, since a new attractive wife is for these stars is an endless supply. However many attend Sex Addicts Anonymous to reestablish some form of domestic harmony in their lives.

Divorce to the average person means financial disaster, perhaps permanent loss of children, and restrictions that make remarriage to a replacement true love very difficult.

"There is nothing either good or bad, but thinking so makes it so."
—*Hamlet*, act 11, scene ii, William Shakespeare

Self-Hypnosis Session #4
Marital Harmony/Sexuality & Lust

Dear reader, let us begin, take any position except standing that makes you completely comfortable.

The deep breathing progressive program introduced in the previous Sessions will have a further addition. Locate another spare pillow, the heaviest pillow you have and place it under the curve in your back. Have a pillow under your head and a pillow under your back. Your inhales will now be more contoured throughout the effected organs. Did you know that through deep breathing you not only release mental and emotional stress, but also eliminates 80 percent of your body toxins? Let's begin by taking a very deep belly breath, inhaling slowly, feel your belly expanding as you count to ten. Visualize that you are inhaling hope and new possibilities. Exhale slowly through your mouth, as you release this breath, imagine exhaling what is old, untrue, tired and not serving you well.

Continue breathing this way. Consciously, take three deep breaths of air along with the text.

Ready—One, inhale one long breath sending it down as deep as you can. Hold the inhaled breath down in the depths of your stomach as long as you can, then very slowly exhale the unwanted air.

Two, inhale one long breath as deep as you can. Hold the inhaled breath down in the depths of your stomach as long as you can, then very slowly exhale the used air.

Three, inhale one long breath as deep as you can. Hold the inhaled breath down in the depths of your stomach as long as you can, then very slowly exhale.

Good, continue breathing in this mode throughout the Session. Now uncoil and relax.

Think about your feet.

Count back from 3 to 0 with each number you count down let your feet go, completely limp. Like a puppet that has had its strings cut. Ready: Three...Two...One...Zero.

Now notice that relaxed feeling move up to your ankles. Your ankles do not have to support you now so you can "let go" uncouple and relax.

As you uncoil and unwind let each muscle in your feet to merely go limp like a raggedly Ann doll. Your knees feel smooth and relaxed let them uncoil and be limp. Deeper relaxation and drowsiness moves into your thigh muscles, your thighs unravel as they sink and collapse into deep rest.

Your pelvis is lose and relaxed, your rear end is warm and comfortable, deep self-hypnotic sleep is moving up into your tummy, As you go deeper, asleep. Deep relaxation, even deep sleep moves slowly into your arms, your forearms. The calmness moves into both arms spreading a warm relaxation. The elbows become loose, the wrist and fingers become limp.

Deep self-hypnotic sleep is moving into the chest cavity, as the heart gently slows down. It is good for the heart to rest as you go into self-hypnotic sleep now. Your breathing is changing, becoming slower and deeper, drowsiness gently announces that the chest is resting.

Deep relaxation is sinking downward as self-hypnotic sleep moves into the lower back spreading down to the bottom of your backbone. All those muscles down there are becoming soft and mushy. Remove any stress and tension out of your lower back. Self-Hypnotic sleep covers the backbone, now into both shoulder blades, throughout all the shoulder muscles. A mellow feeling travels from the shoulders and into your collarbone. Allow any tight muscles to release any tension, uncoil and unwind as you go into rest. "Relax. Calm down. Relax."

Deep self-hypnotic sleep is entering up the neck and behind the ears. Relax all those little tenants back there. These spots become soft and relaxed, you release tension from the neck by letting it go limp into a peaceful slumber.

Deep sleep moves up the back of the head right threw the very top of the scalp. A feeling of repose enters on the forehead.

The forehead becomes smooth and relaxed as your eyebrows lower just a fraction and deep sleep moves into your eyes. In a few seconds, close both eyes to permit a rest period as long as you feel necessary. Reopen your eyes when you are refreshed and ready to continue with the text. Imagine and believe you are uncoiling and relaxing each muscle in your body.

Deep sleep moves up into the facial muscles. Your face becomes sleepy and soft all over, your nose, cheeks, lips and chin going deeper into rest. Your mouth is becoming quite dry when you swallow. Deep sleep moves inside the mouth, your jaw becomes heavy and lazy, your tongue is soft and rested, take pressure off the teeth by lowering your jaw downward. Self-Hypnotic sleep is every where inside your body.

Your mind and body are calm and at ease, carefree. Everything inside of you works perfectly and automatically as you go into self-hypnotic sleep now.

Your breathing is smooth, relaxed and normal as you drift even lower. You haven't a care in the world. You feel secure in self-hypnotic sleep.

Now use your imagination. Pretend, feel and see yourself at the top of the foot of a twisting hardwood stained stairway with a sturdy handrail for you to hang onto, you are well supported. There are twenty steps from the top to the bottom. With each step down you can go at least 100 times deeper into self-hypnotic sleep.

When you step off the last step, you will be standing on the floor of the first level. This will be an opportunity to enter deeper into self-hypnotic sleep.

And so it is as you step off with the left foot going down from the 20th step to the nineteenth step, you feel yourself become more drowsy commencing to go much deeper into self-hypnotic sleep.

Visualize yourself going down each hardwood step as you countdown:
18...17...16...15...14...13...12...11...10...9...
Going way down, deeper into self-hypnotic sleep...

8...7...6...5...4...3...2...1...
It was a long walk down. You have reached the floor of a hallway. You need a little rest. So lie down on the floor enjoy the luxurious self-hypnotic sleep. Continue to focus on the text. Now search for stress, cramps, tension any where in your body. Search for any tight spot in your body. Start with your head and work down.

If you locate any stress send a get well feeling to that spot touch the spot with love. Send a cheer up a mental signal to that spot from your mind. As you do so, allow any spot of tension to simply go limp. Allow any stressed spot to completely relax. See if you can locate a stressed spot anywhere within. Touch any sore spot with a mind thought of love. Permit that area to go limp as any tightness leaves your body.

Allow the mind to roam through the body looking for stress tension to be released. Take as long as you wish.

Flow some calm and relaxation into the face. Send this sensation down the neck and into both upper shoulders. Send this sensation through your tummy and chest, middle and lower back, the entire torso. Gently explore all these areas in your mind.

Continue searching for soreness. Become limp like a raggedy Ann doll. Move into your pelvis and legs now. See what is there. Go into your feet, they are warm, comfy and sleepy. When you read "go into deep hypnotic sleep now" you sink much faster asleep. A thousand times more asleep, even more than you are now, deep into self-hypnotic sleep. The text will now address your imagination within the subconscious inner brain. Your inner brain is open to positive imaginative improvement suggestions and enjoys receiving them. You want to have healthy feelings regarding your marital relationship, sexual feelings and drive. Now mobilize the magnificent, mighty imagination.

Visualize yourself back at the hallway at the bottom of the long spiraling staircase.

Stand up and look around.

See that you are inside of some house, any house, will do. You are standing in the hallway of this house and you notice a sign at the end of the hallway: "The House of Love." You also notice that there are several doors in this hallway. Behind each door is a special "love" room. When you enter a room you will go, at least a thousand times deeper into self-hypnotic sleep.

Walking along, the first door you encounter is marked, "Harmony Theater." Step in and close the door behind you. You have entered a theater room with a big huge wide, cinescope screen; there is only one seat in front of the screen.

Imagine sitting down in the solitary seat. On the armrest you smell popcorn, you see and smell a bag of hot buttered popcorn. You can start to eat the popcorn, and in the other holder on the opposite arm of the chair, is a container of diet Pepsi. Eat and drink these delights for your enjoyment during the presentation.

The spotlights above dimmer out as the show commences on the giant screen in vivid color.

My goodness, the scene is you meeting your true love for the first time. Imagine how you felt that day. Didn't you feel unbelievably great at that time? You found the treasure and the love of your lifetime. The person that you had searched everywhere for a very long time. For the first time, you feel absolutely complete and joyful. You are having so much fun, reliving exciting day, as these early memories appear one after another onto the screen. You hear the words being exchanged, your true love and yourself enjoying each and every moment you were together. Back then you wanted to meet your true love every day, all day long. You even got a little jealous if your love when out to some exciting place without you. Of course, you always had some minor arguments, maybe even verbal fights. All humans do this it is part of our nature. We would be mere automated robots if we didn't. Right now, recollect one of the first times you did have a rather serious argument with your true love. Look there it is on the screen. It certainly appears like it's all over between you two. Maybe—but no maybe about it. A little later, it was all forgotten, there you two are getting married. There it is, you're wedding day up on the screen.

You both look lovely. Wasn't that one of the best and most nervous days of your life. Now you are leaving your wedding party full of good cheer ready to depart on the honeymoon night. Think about that night.

Recall the immediate memories that followed. You couldn't believe life could ever be so pleasant. You won the love of your life. Think of those times for as long as you wish. In a few seconds, close your eyes and remember these spectacular early days for as long as you wish, before proceeding with the text.

At that time, you would have taken on the whole world for your true love. You were the happiest you could ever be.

If your true love were not alive, you won't want to live. You lived and breathed to be with your true love. Recall happier than every moments of contentment that a billion dollars could not purchase. Despite whatever has occurred or changed since those times. You will always wish for the memory of these golden days to be reinforced and engraved forever into your inner brain's active memory bank. The early day of true love shall always be at your access to your conscious mind regardless of the circumstances, good or bad. To return and relive these merry memories to mind at any time, take three deep breaths while pressing the thumb and third finger of either hand while thinking: "Lifeline. Lifeline. Lifeline."

Remembrances of early-married joy will especially come blasting into your conscious mind when any unavoidable lust accidentally appears in your realm. The condition, a rush of raging lust in some unfortunates can occur frequently. You made a vow to remain faithful, you never wanted to commit adultery, with no ifs and or buts.

If you break this sacred vow, think of the horrible times that often develop. Your true love may divorce you, and take away most of your treasures and most of your paycheck. The very least you can expect is for your true love to be very upset, jealous and secretly try to get even maybe behind your back.

You never want neither of these events to happen. When you are alone with your true love, as soon as possible. Smile and say: "I am the luckiest person in the world to have you."

Restoring any disharmony within your marriage must always become the first priority. Agree that you will always protect and cherish your true love.

Now stand up and walk out of the theatre room. See yourself closing the door behind you as you exit. Imagine and see yourself walking down the hall to the next door marked: "Restricted." Enter the room and close the door behind you.

This is a very comfortable dimly lit place. In the middle of the room is a king-sized bed with opened sheets under a rolled back pink blanket. You feel the pillow at the top of the bed. You realize that the pillow is filled with feathers and is very soft. You decide to lie down on the inviting bed. After lying down you decide to pull the blankets up to your chest. Your imagination may now be wondering what is so restricted in here.

This word "restricted" may open sexual feelings and thoughts you may have never experienced or imagined before.

"Restricted" may be a new experience for some. The positive incentive of this room is to improve and enhance your marital sexual drive. There is absolutely nothing better than sex to keep you sane and happy while reducing stress. Sex is good exercise for the heart, the lungs, the muscles and especially the mind. Sexual intercourse is profound relaxation. The greatest benefit comes from loving, not being loved. You will always think about pleasing your partner. Do not think about yourself. Do not ask yourself or your partner how you are doing. Concentrate on pleasing your partner. After you please your partner you will feel happy. After sex you will share a reinforced strong feeling of emotional intimacy with your true love.

You inner brain's imagination erotic desires and sexual abilities will be increased to such a high degree that you will become very pleased and active regarding your sexuality.

You can become the robust, sexy person you were always meant to be. The sexual part of your imagination can spring up every time it is appropriate and natural. You and your mate truly desire this sexual betterment to materialize.

Begin to think about your sexual abilities, realize that in the past, you may have felt you had to perform well sexually in order to feel sexy. Perhaps you never felt adequate or positive about yourself. Know now that performing is no longer important, you no longer have a need to think of perform during sexual encounters. Sexual activity to you has nothing to do with performance. In fact, performance takes the fun and enjoyment out of loving sex for you. You will now resolve to never to have sex or think about sex as being a performance or a chore. You have a tremendous desire for good, healthy and safe sex. But you have no desire to be put into a situation that calls for you to perform sex without returned love.

Loving and sex is something that comes to you naturally. It is never a duty you feel obligated to perform. You have no one to impress sexually, especially yourself.

You realize you are a healthy natural human and your desire for good sex comes from a need to give to another all your deepest loving feelings and to have those feelings returned.

See, feel and hear yourself in youthful sexually situations, prior to meeting your true love. Recall each and every early feeling of sexuality or circumstances the time in your life that may have preceded meeting and courting your true love.

There is no guilt attached or associated with the recalling of these perhaps ancient memories. These memories are for your privately enjoyment. Enjoyed memories should never truly be forgotten.

In a few seconds close both of your eyes and concentrate on these exhilarating, sincerely enjoyed sexuality moments of youthful loving times.

Return your eyes to the text when you receive a feeling that you must.

As you imagined these early days of sexuality, you may have had a feeling of being absolutely free during performance, an awakening that you never really noticed before. Henceforth, you will not give a single thought about sexual performance. What you deeply enjoy is the natural human response that comes up from inside.

You are going to start loving your partner with all that you have. The huge potent loving and sexual feelings you possess. The way you respond to normal urges is far more than adequate. Thrilling sexual feelings are marvelous. You shall be a natural lover without performance on your mind. You actually shall perform as never before. Intimate exchanges and sexual intimacy arrives naturally without a thought. Giving and receiving sexual love comes natural and effortless to you. Some may call it erotic. It is. It is a holy blessed and given erotic pleasure.

Loving sex is the most exciting and stress busting event your mind and body can ever experience. You know this and you believe it. Sex is part of your very nature, your personality. You positively enjoy being a healthy, naturally sexy person. Adopt the attitude that you do not care of how good or bad you are when you are involved in loving sex. In fact, the more you think about how well you are performing the more impossible it becomes to concern yourself with performing. You always find yourself in a natural state of passion while having loving gratifying sex, far above any concern about performance. You realize that you are partly responsible for your partner's satisfaction or climax.

Primarily, you enjoy sex for yourself. To express your mind's deepest feelings at a physical sexual level is absolutely a normal human emotion.

Realize your body is fine just the way it is.

Try to figure out what your partner really wants and try your best to grant the wish.

Talk freely with your partner about sex. Communicate what you like and what you do not like. Feel at ease talking about sex. Take the time during loving sex to engage each of the five senses, there is never any need to rush. You are wide open to pleasure. During loving sex you are relaxed, uninhibited, totally at ease and never self-conscious. Any impulse to be frigid or irritated, annoyed will roll away like water off of a duck's back. You will become invulnerable to any such negative thoughts during sexual encounters.

The memories of your early sexuality dim and vanish as you pull the blanket and sheet down off your body. See yourself rising up from the bed then walking out of the room. Remember to close the door behind you.

See yourself strolling down the hall to the next door. The door has a painted red sign marked: "XXX Rated."

Perhaps, you have never been to one of these pornography pits of wild, unleashed passion. Don't get all concerned. In this imaginary location, no stranger will be there. No one except your true love.

Besides you and your true love have already dwelled in this location, in your imaginations, minds and bodies.

Imagine and visualize yourself opening the door marked "XXX Rated," enter the room and close the door behind you. Once again you locate a comfortable ready made king sized bed in the middle of the room. You can now go at least one thousand times deeper into self-hypnotic sleep. As you do so, imagine your mate magically appearing. Your true love is reclining nude in the middle of the bed. Imagine approaching the bed while you start disrobing yourself of any clothes you are wearing. Imagine yourself being nude.

See, hear and feel the presence of your partner. Lock into your mate's embrace, as you lay yourself down on the bed. In a few moments, just let down both eyelids, for as long as you wish to look even deeper into your imagination.

You should be suitably rested, reopen both eyes to clearly visualize yourself and your mate having sex. Visualize, feel and hear yourself actually loving and being loved.

Enjoy sharing sexual affection, to your chosen mate, your true lover.

The first thing you notice is the expression of love on your true love's face. Notice the warm happiness that automatically appears upon your lover's face. You are both existing in a state of anticipation and ecstasy. You enjoy sharing your deepest expression of sexual love. Your true love is extremely responsive to you sexually. Your partner is sexually hot and wants you. Your partner is turned on with your sexual thoughts and the words you say. By the way, your true love and yourself look and feel fantastic. It feels good and natural to be sexually hot. You don't want to analyze sex. You simply must have sex. Getting sexy is easy it is automatic. You feel overwhelming passion in your genitals arising with explosive feelings and sexual emotions.

Your body is throbbing and thrusting. It feels so good to thrust and thrust. You feel forceful and alive. You feel a warm glow. Your skin is hot and excited by touch. It excites your lover and your love is responding. You feel close to your lover. The excitement is building. You cannot pull it back. You feel a deep rapid throbbing growing inside.

Your sexuality is passionate and exciting. It turns you on sexually to see your lover respond to your sexual urges.

You enjoy initiating any sexual activity with your partner. You have no problem being sexually aggressive with your special one. It turns you on to do so, you feel safe to let everything fly. You are sexually alive. See and feel yourself acting out any hidden unfulfilled secret sexual desires and your lover automatically supports your desires. You excite your partner because your partner does not know what you are going to do next. You take pleasure exposing and acting out your deepest fantasies. You do this with your body and spoken words. You are not concerned with your partner's approval or disapproval, you both have absolute sexual freedom to act out and enjoy even the wildest of fantasies. You always have permission to do whatever makes both of you feel good. You always encourage your partner to do the same. You are uninhibited and can act verbally and physically receiving mutual love during sexual intercourse.

You are beginning to climax. You are exploding deep inside.

You feel hot spurts of passion rumbling within you.

Your mind moves into paralyze as your entire body moves rhythmically.

In you imagination, you need and want to climax. Finally, the sexy feeling rumble into a tremendous explosion.

You feel absolutely fantastic. You feel as if you are on top of the world, sexy and alive.

You desire more of the sexual excitement, but a cooling, most calming relaxation overcomes each of you. Cling together for as long as you wish. You and your true love truly enjoy these times more than any other. You both look forward to doing quite often.

Your exploring nature comes to the surround of the imagination and arouses you to full awareness of the room you are in. You stand and dress, and as you do so, you observe that your mate has fallen into a peaceful slumber. Quietly guide yourself out of this room. Close the door behind you as you leave. Visualize yourself going down the hallway to the next closed door which displays a blue painted sign: "Reality Room." See yourself eagerly opening this door. Step inside after closing the door behind you. A prepared queen sized bed is in the middle of a brightly-lit room. The bed beckons you to lie down. When you have done so, call upon your magnificent imagination. Open the receptive doors of the inner brain to consider these suggestions.

Some day, perhaps sooner than you wish to face, you or your loved one is going to be sitting beside the deathbed of the other, grasping a frail, clammy dying hand. You will look at each other through tearful eyes during those aching, final hours. Happy, pleasant memories will flood through your grieving minds in a raging torrent. On the last day you spend with your true love on this earth, you will sincerely realize that all those "big deal" disputes and arguments, you both created, for what these hassles really were—absolutely nothing!

When this terrifying moment in time arrives, you would never let any former hostilities over shadow the shared, unbelievable sweet awesome memories that you both shared together. With the knowledge of this unavoidable coming day, you shall often tell your true love, "You matter more to me than anyone else in the world."

In the future take the time to recall the early days of true love, the early days of love memory recalls you viewed in the Harmony Theater. These memories can always return to your conscious mind regardless of the circumstances, good or bad. Do remember that to bring these merry memories to mind at any place or time, You simply have to press the thumb into the third finger of either hand while inhaling deeply for three breath and saying or thinking: "Lifeline. Lifeline. Lifeline."

Soon you will be alone with your true love, Smile and say: "I am the luckiest person on the world to have you."

Restoring any partnership disharmony whatsoever will now become the first priority. You will always protect and cherish your true love.

Now your tour of the "House of Love" is complete. Return to any of the rooms in this house as frequently as you wish.

The time has come to awaken. To be alive with a fresh zeal to regain and fully appreciate the beautiful memories and experiences you have enjoyed. Intimate memories that have always dwelt within your imagination.

Coming up now, to the count of 5. To be fully awake.
1-2-3…You know sex is good. You and your mate enjoy mutual passion for everything. You both particularly cherish family and friends.
4…Your true love needs you. Your mate and yourself both possess a warm sunny disposition that attracts good-hearted people.
5…Wide-awake now. Live on "the present and now."

**Preconditioning Program of the Self-Hypnotic Session #5
Palliative Care for You**

The word terminal means "the end." It is a very negative word, perhaps the meanest word in the world. The Nazi's Jewish death squad Einsatzgruppen, of 5000 dedicated German men and women swept through a conquered Russia, town by town.

The squad of Jewish killers issued 48 daily report copies to Nazi superiors and the leaders of German industry. The reports bragged of their evil achievement: "August 15, 1941: Town of Estonia, terminated: 3244 Jews, 2987 Jewesses. Higher termination rates expected during remainder of the week."

The word termination is usually used inappropriately for the word "incurable." Nonetheless, humans have survived decades with a multitude of incurable diseases.

Remissions of many diseases often occur when least expected. All fatal diseases usually have their gathered statistics. Your physician may have told you have a 25% chance of surviving an incurable illness. Amazingly, the survival statistic changes as time passes and various treatments are attempted. You do not want to succumb to the percentage game until you are almost 100% certain of death within days or weeks. Loss of hope and heart is the worsted disease. You must never give up on yourself, your survival percentage may contain an opportunity to entitle your decease day to be vastly postponed.

You must think or say, "I'm just going to keep going until I can not go any further."

The daily irritations of life do not go away when an incurable illness strikes, kids still have to be fed, cars get in crashes, and earthquakes do not cease. Life's problems may even be exacerbated. Nothing stops; in addition one has to cope with a continual sense of despair over a painful incurable disease. As always during life, fear creates more fear, so never allow fear to enter your conscious thoughts.

Despair is not necessarily a negative condition preceding the upcoming event of predicted death. Serious illness often develops a fresh ethereal dimension.

Despair in this situation is a resource to call upon spiritual resources and healing powers within the subconscious, the inner brain.

You can limit the gut wrenching hours you live with the fact you believe you are dying. Despite debilitating pain peace of mind and hope can be achieved.

Sometimes there may be no reprieve. In such situations, there can be no further denial, only acceptance. You may be in the final chapter of your life. Often, there is more to life than a final part.

Your dying will end the story of your time on earth.

In irreversible cases, you must make a major decision. How do you prefer to spend the little time left on your meter? When your ambitious expectations for life are reduced to zero, without warning everything is bound to be different.

Perhaps, everything and every person you meet should be more meaningful and loving.

An enormous beautiful and indomitable weeping willow tree, brimming with hanging green vines of leaves on its branches has existed for centuries.

Other similar trees were cut down before their roots could expand. Other trees were stricken by a flash of lightning during a thunderstorm. Some trees were torn up from the ground to build a subdivision of houses.

Eventually each weeping willow tree will come to the end of its time.

The final bloom of leaves will fall to the group, leaving a few solitary leaves throughout the tree's age withered branches. Singularly each remaining green leaf will drop. The final harvest of leaves will in due time fall onto the ground.

Picture each of leaf of green leaving the willow tree, one by one. The falling leaves which represent the last days you shall be alive on earth. Let each green leaf represent a moment of happiness filled with as much joy as possible. The withered decaying brown leaves on the ground represent the past.

Henry David Thoreau in a letter to Ralph Waldo Emerson, in 1842 wrote: "Every blade in the field. Every green leaf on a tree, lays down its life in its season as beautifully as it was taken up."

You have had your brief time on the stage of your living time on earth. The appointed time for you to depart leaves only a short period of time.

Death some times arrives unannounced. Your final time on earth and the assortment of accompanying moods may include uncontrollable emotional swings. Some time will be good days. Some time will be bad days, crying streaks could erupt like a sunny summer's day rainstorm. Bad days, with temporary reversible depression, venting a growing anger, are actually your best days—your brain is beginning to initiate the work of protecting the body, preparing for the final journey. Some time will be healing days.

You feel yourself shutting down.

Body pain may often be a raging fire. Medication is like rain soothing the burning flames. Always take your medicine as instructed.

Circumstances may require that you have the following Self-Hypnotic Session read to you.

A pacification of mind and body will help you endure any burning pain that often follow chemotherapy, radiation and other radical medical treatments.

You must control the time that you may wish to wallow in sad moments. You will not lie down staring endlessly at the ceiling while ruminating about the past, present, and whatever future. You must avoid forever the regretful thought of "if only" events that the expected scarce remaining time will never allow to be materialized.

This Self-Hypnotic Session was created to assist you to discover a helpful perspective. You should try to channel anxiety and stress into a sanctuary of peaceful emotional balance.

This Session was designed for only one purpose: to help the remainder of your life to be better.

For everything under the sun—there is a reason. Just maybe, you were directed to read this particular Self-Hypnotic Session.

You disbelief in religion or your belief in a religion is eternal. Either way you desire a hopeful heart that never takes a dive.

You can share love with those close to you for the final time. To leave a memory of authenticated love in the hearts of those who you cherish should become a priority.

You can depart from your earthly existence secure in the respect and love of your loved ones.

You want to be remembered with loving, grateful hearts because during final chapter of your time, you made yourself cheerful, warm and kind.

You want to be remembered for:

Your kindness over your accomplishments;

Your generosity over your riches;

Your help to others learn from your own successes.

As you approach your final days, you will sleep a lot. You may turn inward, gathering whatever religious strength you may have maintained for the upcoming event, the transition.

Gradually, your interest and intuition in the material world begins to disappear. Still there may be time enough to add a few laugh lines. You still may have time to share, to pass your best memories and thoughts to family members and friends. Such opportunities must not be put off.

Your final spoken words are now a first-rate responsibility. You can speak your last words with no hint of sadness. The very last thing you want to do is leave a concluding negative impression with anyone, even yourself. You want to leave an inspiring model: a brave spirit to the very bitter end, who always was in good cheer. The very last thing you really want to be near you is a sad, crying, family member or friend. You will inform each visitor, to not discuss your illness. You have limited time to be with your loved ones. You wish to cherish each and every moment. Demand that there be no crying or sadness while in your presence.

Your remaining time is power, the power of living time. Do not allow yourself to feel impotent.

With some individuals you may contemplate unusual productive endeavors. You may wish to say, "I love you," "I am sorry," "forgive me," or the hardest, "I forgive you."

For some, this may be hard stuff to do.

To survive the final times, you may have to fake happiness. Always, attempt a big smile for each person you encounter. You should project yourself as being brave and unafraid to all people, especially those you love.

Concentrating, complaining and being cranky about your worsening physical illness is not good medicine.

Consciously, try not saying the word: "cancer," or any name of an illness. Never speak of death in every conversation. Merely, refer to these negative illness words as a "problem."

You can be in the "here and now," living in each single moment as much as possible.

You can say to those that you love these final words: "I love you all. My time has come. I have enjoyed a full life. I am ready and prepared to go."

Letting go is vital, do not cling to what is being taken from you, something you never really owned. You always hoped for a long life but you also never really wanted to grow old.

You always knew no life on earth is guaranteed for long-term. In the long-term, everyone is a temporary visitor.

Continuing your life at all cost is never a worthwhile goal.

The grasp you have on the remaining time of your life is no longer in your hands. Forbid yourself to try and grab onto one more minute of time. "All my possessions, for one more minute of life," is a selfish meaningless plead.

Despite every attempted cure to save you. The rattle of death will commence in your throat.

Your family will be making phone calls:

"Come quick. The time has come!"
Much like the lottery balls that drop a number. Unbelievably terrible, your ball's number has dropped.
A cheerful atheist may think: "It has come. The end of everything." Nothing is so deeply human normal as the search for a meaning of life.
Every person's life is a mystery. You can decide how to treasure the time remaining.
The writer T.S. Eliot wrote: "What we call the beginning is often the end. And to make an end is to make a beginning."
The pits and peak experiences you may encounter can bring on exasperation, frustration, and regret. The hope of this Session is to assist you in the dealing with these unpleasant companions.
An imposed stagnation must not become settled in your mind: Thinking only about yourself can become a negative habit: "How do I feel today? What pains have I got today? Who calls me, who ignores me?"
Part of being ill is endless boredom. All humans suffer from periods of boredom, especially when illness is tedium of day-to-day repetitive routines; a person often becomes to feel imprisoned. Is life not a hundred times too short for you to bore yourself? Age brings no exemption from boredom. No one is too old to try something new and interesting. Do not permit yourself to be bored to death. Interest lies, not in the activity, but in the mind of the participant. In this affluent society, the world is your oyster. Within reason, you can do whatever entertains and occupies your mind. The mind can be set free to play upon enormous interesting subjects. When your mind is occupied in any activity of interest you become more alert, more truly alive and every aspect of your life becomes richer and fuller. Unoccupied leisure, perfect idleness is delightful and beneficial in small doses. But in large amounts idleness is a hellish torture. Leisure time frittered away in idleness degenerates into monumental boredom. Leisure time must be filled with some satisfying mental occupation. It matters little what the activity is.
This Session includes reinforcement to avoid self-disgust, stagnation and boredom and detachment from regrets.

A slowly worsening illness and treatment is very intimidating and medically complex. There are special retreat hospitals for the dying a hospice, which originated in the Middle Ages by religious orders. Such hospitals do not try to cure you until you die. A Hospice usually has an understanding, especially trained staff that consoles and comfort. Much like Mother Theresa achieved for the dying during her lifetime. You should be aided until death arrives. In a regular hospital: "Nothing more can be done," is most often the last resort. A hospice does not do medical things to prolong life. At hospice care centers machines, such as artificial lungs are never used. In some hospitals the incurable and dying may become pawns to be manipulated, some times solely for profit.

As your health worsens—you should consider a hospice residence. This is a wise alternative, if you cannot be properly treated in your home.

Pending death should not become the source of unending discouragement. Rather you can think positively, optimistically, make any limited time to be a new-sprung stimulus to live your remaining time in fulfillment.

The saying "slow down and smell the roses" contains much wisdom. The living in the real mini-real moments of time is often something the approximated 200-250,000 people who will die today and each and every day around the world may not have achieved. Some missed this opportunity because they were always in a rush. A rush to the next minute, event or hoped for goal. The hurry up disease can turn what should be a relaxing pastime into stressfulness. The opposite of the hurry up disease is a fully attentive mindfulness where one focuses entirely on what is happening in the moment. Increased pleasure in a relaxing pastime can be restored.

The hurry up disease is when:

I was in a rush to finish high school and start college.

And then I was in a rush to finish college and start working.

And then I was in a rush to marry and have children.

And then I was in a rush for my children to grow up and find their way.

And then I was in a rush to retire.
And now, I am dying but strangely I am no longer in a rush.
Do not cry because the ending of your life on earth is approaching. Try to smile, because it happened. When if you are smiling the whole world smiles with you. Cry and you cry alone. Unfortunately, life's concluding journey often does not speedy deliver you up to the last breaths.

"Of all the wonders that I yet have heard,
It seems to me most strange that humans have so much fear;
Seeing that death, is a necessary end,
Will come when its time arrives."
—William Shakespeare (from *Julius Caesar*)

Leaving the following message has helped many others whose time did arrive.

I have passed on,
Please do not stand at my grave and weep,
I am not there. I do not sleep.
I am the thousand winds that blow.
I am the diamond that glints on the snow.
I am the gentle autumn's rain,
When you awaken in the morning following my leaving, please do not cry.
I am the swift uprising rush of the chirping birds in flight,
I am the soft star that shines at night,
Please do not stand at my grave and cry.
I am not there.
In your heart, I will never die.

Self-Hypnotic Session #5
Palliative Care for You

Dear reader, sit in a comfortable chair or try lying down on a carpet or in a bed. In a moment close both eyes, to notice all the sensations that occur when you begin to be at ease. See the patterns of spots of gray that blend with light on your closed eyelids. Reopen your eyes one at a time to prepare for body relaxation. Notice the sensation of breath as you in hale and exhale. The differences between the air when you exhale as your lungs warm the breath. When you exhale, each time you exhale think of the word calm, if you have to move during the Session don't worry it just doesn't matter one little bit.

Notice your breath again as you inhale effortless, no purpose whatsoever in your breath. Merely notice your breath, notice within your body, the way you breathe the gentle rise and fall of your chest. As you breathe in, hold that breath as you exhale slowly out. Breathe in, and breathe out slowly. Breathe in, and breathe out slowly. Breathe in, and again breathe out slowly. Be aware of that after these breaths feel the movement in your chest as you breathe there. To commence relaxation throughout your body you will set the stage by breathing calmly. Your body is a walking chemical factory, the mind is a factory its product as good as the raw materials you put into it. The three primary products in the body's factory are oxygen, proper food and drink. Unacceptable brain functions can occur if the brain is not oxygenated appropriately. An energizing breath function can balance the mind and body through the stilling and easy deep breath flows along during the circulation of the oxygen you breath. Half the problem during being stressed out, perhaps unable to concentrate normally is that many do not breathe deeply enough to supply the brain with sufficient oxygen. When stress strikes humans have a tendency to hold the breath or only breathe in a shallow way, using only the top part of the lungs. In order to deepen your breathing and get oxygen all the way up into the brain you need to supply the brain with an oxygen hit. The expansion of circulation of inhaled breath can be achieved. Try this breathing exercise. After breathing in imagine drawing a circle from your head down to your feet.

Breathe out while mentally tracing the other half of the circle from your feet to your head. With each new breath imagine a larger circle until it expands bigger into an oval shape. With each deep inhaled breath imagine drawing the large oval circle around your head and feet. Exhale slowly as you complete the oval from your feet to your head. Practice this circulation breathing exercise several times.

Relaxation is the platform to introduce complete access of the inner brain. Notice the sensations in your feet, and as the sensations in your feet become clear and clearer in your mind, relax both feet and let go without movement or effort. Feel your feet go limp and "relax, relax, relax." Notice and let go, noticing and letting go.

Both calf muscles notice them uncoil and unwind releasing any tension that might be there. Calm both thighs let go of any tension in your legs just let go, relax and be calmed.

Flood the muscles of your legs with relaxation. Allow yourself to commence to go into deep self-hypnotic sleep now. Send a mental message to your buttress, notice and let go. Your lower back, you can release and calm any strained spots you feel in the back.

Notice you can calm your tummy the area where tension and stress likes to accumulate and grow, and may cause your stomach to fell upset. Notice any strain in either of your hands. Simply let go of any tension in both hands as you continue breathing in deeply and exhausting slowly while imagining an oval circle of air movement surround the outside of your body. Notice your chest; notice the gentle rise and fall of your chest as you breathe smoothly. The movements in your chest, as the ribs contract and expand easily, no effort, no deliberate thought of breathing. Your neck, notice the muscles at the back of your neck. It is in the neck tension and stress has a habit of accumulating a tightness that can cause your neck to ache relentlessness. Release any stress and anxiety in the neck, allow your neck to go limp, drowsy. Any tension and just let it go, let it flow out and away. Notice then letting going. As you do, you now approach another of the worse accumulators of stress and tension, your throat. When stress come tumbling out this area, you may begin slurring the words you speak, or use words that march over each other. There are many sensations of stress in the throat, dry voice, speaking to quickly, too loud, or allowing harmful words. Your throat is going to be absolutely, magnificently relaxed, and you will be able to do this any time you wish. Proceed to relax your throat. To accomplish this program a short break will be beneficial.

In a moment, you shall close both your eyes and contemplate on a large shining bright white light. The white image you will imagine will be in the shape of an eight-pointed star. The star vibrates twisting brightly. Pretend the bright white star is located in your throat. Close both eyes and see this vision for as long as you wish before returning to the text.

Turn all your attention to your throat, the whole region of your throat. Notice any spots of tension or stress in your throat let it go. Merely release any tight spot and let it go limp. Most important are the muscles of in the mouth. Your jaw muscles, the tongue, let your jaw and tongue to be smoothed and relaxed. Relaxed and calm, make certain that there is a space between your upper and lower teeth. Use your tongue to assure that you have a slight space between your teeth. The jaw muscles let go, relax. Totally uncoil and calm your jaw.

It is very important that your jaw muscles tongue, lips are completely relaxed. Let go of any tension or stress that is there. Your cheeks let them become very light, smooth and relaxed. Your eyelids are heavy with sleep, very heavy, let them be totally relaxed. In a moment, you shall close both your eyes for as long as you wish. Reopen your eyes when you are prepared to continue.

Notice your scalp, notice and be aware that you can relax your scalp. If your mind wanders, this is all right. If you notice your mind is wondering come back, come back to the text and allow the program to guide your attention. Again the scalp, the scalp is relaxed and free of any stress and tension. Your forehead is smooth, both cheeks are lightly drowsy, and relaxed. Lips slightly opened and completely relaxed. Your jaw muscles are tired with sleep with teeth slightly apart, if this is comfortable.

Your chin, the back of both shoulders, let your shoulders be completely relaxed.

The feelings of pleasant heaviness with warmth and relaxation floods into your biceps, your upper arms, your forearms hands fingers, the back of both your hands allow them to relax. Imagine each part of your body, notice and let go into a deep self-hypnotic sleep now.

Your back, spine, shoulder blades and lower back, your chest again. Belly, buttress, thighs, knees calves and feet are all calmed and relaxed. Notice the feelings in your hands once more there is no tension whatsoever in your hands. Notice the feeling in your right hand, and each of the fingers of the right hand. Momentarily the relaxation feelings spread deeper into the feelings of your right hand. The sensations in both hands become clearer and clearer in your mind. Be calmer as thought waves are signals passed from your inner brain to your right hand. Your mental signal of relaxation now touches the fingers of each hand. The tummy signals deep self-hypnotic sleep. The entire tummy is relaxed. Allow inhaled air to expand your stomach. With each breath coming in send the oxygen downward to circle around the brim of your fully expanded stomach. Exhale slowly in the opposite direction. Turn your attention to your left hand. It is relaxed. Notice each finger of the left hand. Count them mentally.

One Finger...going down deeper into self-hypnotic sleep now.
Two Finger...your body is drowsy, limp and tired...
Third Finger...your mind is very calm...
Fourth Finger..."relax...calm...relax."
Fifth Finger...down you go into self-hypnotic sleep now.

Momentarily, close your eyes and notice the grayish patterns against your closed eyelids. Notice the specks of blinking light spots. Take as long as you wish for this eye rest before returning to the text.

Notice any sounds around you. Be aware of any sounds around you. For a few seconds just listen. Notice the temperature of your hands, be aware of the temperature of your hands and your feet. Notice the temperature of your feet and be aware of the heaviness in your legs, the perception of heaviness. Experience the growing tiredness in both your legs your arms, notice the heaviness in your shoulders. Add to this experience the noticing of sight, sound, temperature and weight. Review the feelings as they pass in and out your mind. Observe these thoughts for a few moments, notice these thoughts. Notice your breath. Always notice your breath, noticing the smoothness of your breath, the flow of air as you inhale smoothly and effortlessly. Hold the air before exhaling the smooth and easy current of life giving oxygen. Each breath time you exhale, inhale and exhale instill your code word "calm, calm, calm." You shall remember your code words by taking several deep breaths while pinching your thumbnail and third finger of either hand, any time you so wish. The third finger is an acupuncture spot for release of nervousness. Whiles doing so say or think the code words: "calm...calm...calm." This practice will allow you a much deeper, state of awareness. Now or any time and all these great feeling of absolute calm and relaxation will return into your mind and body.

Notice all the sensations circling your stomach with each inhale. As you pull air in, deeply through your nose and out through your mouth, just be aware. This awareness is important, Your mouth, jaw, tongue, lips are so fully and completely relaxed.

You are enjoying this state of calmness, as if your entire body was completely wrapped in a blanket of relaxation. You remain awake, clear minded, calm and aware. Inhaling calmly as you exhale slowly. You enjoy a total alert state of consciousness, your mind is detached to observe all these sensations and all the mechanics of movement caused merely by breathing. For it is the breath that produces the voice and your awareness of the air that produces the calm, relaxed voice in its flow of calm, relaxing words spoken. Normal inhaling and exhaling is a continuous smooth rhythm and at the end of the exhalation there can be a pause that is natural and will come in time and is perfectly natural.

In normal breathing do not hold a breath after you inhale. When you hold the breath after inhalation there is a stop valve and when you continue you may be aware of a click. Breathing exercises strengthen normal breathing.

To make certain that you remain in a calm state—mentally travel through your body, signaling a deeper calmness and relaxation. Notice the awareness of deep relaxation and calmness in your feet, ankles, calf muscles, knees thighs rear end, stomach, lower back belly chest, shoulder, shoulder blades spine, both shoulders, upper arms, and fore arms. A deeper restfulness enters your neck throat, chin, lips tongue, jaw forehead cheeks, and scalp. Think: "calm, calm, calm." Thinking or saying the word "calm" releases a signal of calm throughout. Relaxation and being calm is the foundation of all improvement, optimistic positive mental and physical improvements.

Sink deeper and deeper into the drowsiness state of "go into self-hypnotic sleep now." At this time, if there is any spot in your body that is sick or in pain, you should take this time to become aware of this condition and send it your love. Breathing in, allow this spot to rest, and breathing out, smile to it with a facial express and an inner calm signal which supplies great tenderness and affection. Be aware that there are other parts of your body that remain strong and extremely healthy. Allow these strong parts within your body to signal their strength and energy to any weak or sick parts. Feel the support, energy, and love of the rest of your body, as the strong spots flow penetrating strength to the weak spots, with soothing relaxation and healing.

When breathing out let go of the toxins including worries or distress you may be holding. Breathing in and out, smile with love and confidence to those sore spots of your body that do not feel well. Breathing in, become aware of the whole of your body becoming heavier drooping and sinking downward. Breathing out, enjoy the sensation of your whole body being heavy and drooping down. Smile to your entire body as you breathe in, and send your love and compassion to your entire body as you breathe out. Feel all the cells in your entire body smiling joyfully with you. Feel gratitude for all the cells in your whole body. Return to the gentle rise and fall of your tummy. Practice to carry the calm and mindful healing energy you have generated with love, return to this text as often as you desire.

Let's summon that very unique dwelling with in your mind, a very special place. The place where all wishes and desires are possible. The place that is the storehouse of your lifetime of accumulated memories. The place where your lifetime of nightly dreams, dormant hopes and latent abilities is permanently stored. The greatest possess you will ever possess, the creative force of your inner brain's imagination.

Suspend any disbelief.

Imagine, believe, think and visualize a giant clock, with large fluorescent numbers one to twelve. You are seeing the magical clock of life.

The clock reads a second before one o'clock. The large clock begins to chime on the hour of one. Notice that your name is appearing in glittering letters right in the middle of the huge clock. Your first name is engraved in sliver appears before being followed by your last name which is engraved in gold.

The hour one indicates the very moment you were born. There is a time a place for everything under the sun and your exact moment of birth just arrived. Recall your earliest memories of arriving on earth. Recollections, good or bad as far back as your memory permits. Be with a loved one, the first human who immediately enters your remembrances. Shortly you will pause to close both your eyes, take as long as you wish remembering the first memory of being a baby or a child with a loved one. Enjoy these recollections. Reopen your eyes to continue with the text whenever you feel comfortable to do so.

Concentrate on your earliest memories. See yourself as child playing with other children. Select early childhood friends, the one or ones who first enter your memory.

Momentarily take another pause to rest your eyes. Take as long as you wish reviewing the memory file or files, you have rekindled from the memory vaults of your mind. Enjoy these pleasant memories before rejoining the text. Open both eyes whenever you feel compelled to return to the magical clock of life.

The lighted hour one on the large clock has vanished. A shining, sparkling diamond replaces the number one on the clock.

Two chimes announce the hour of two on the clock. The hour two ignites into a bright yellow. This indicates a time when you where a teenager perhaps going to school, or where ever you where. You are now going to recall teenage remembrances. Concentrate on your teenager years. Again you will pause to close and refresh your eyes. Take the opportunity to gaze at these teenage memories for as long as you wish. Reopen your eyes to return to the text when you have the urge to do so.

The hour two on the clock is vanishing to be replaced by a colossal red ruby.

With three chimes, the green hour of three on the clock lights up. All memories are not good times it is not fair to recall only the good times in life. The majority of teenagers have struggles, growing up and searching to find their place in the world. Recall and locate a teenage struggle. In an instant, close your eyes and concentrate on your teenage years and any struggling times you may have endured. If you come up blank, you were fortunate. Reopen your eyes whenever you desire to continue on this unusual trip around the clock of life. The best time has yet to arrive.

The hour of three on the clock is vanishing being replaced by an unspectacular gem. With four chimes the hour of four starts to blink in a brilliant gold.

Go deeper into self-hypnotic sleep now. From your mind's memory vault extract your first meeting and other times with your true love, whenever these events happened. If you feel you never had a true love than think of a pet you may have once had, a friend, a family memory, or who or whatever comes first to greet you.

Close your eyes in a few seconds to concentrate as you open your heart to that spectacular memory. Bring back as many early memories that you can handle, your wedding day, your first vacation, your first house, your first child, the good times you shared with your loved one. Only reopen your eyes when you are convinced you must continue.

A brilliant diamond replaces the hour of four on the clock. Five chimes announce the hour of five lighting up in blue on the clock. The hour five represents a recent special, happy memory you are going to order up. A recent time of shared joy it can be any place or recent time you recall where you were happy. You may wish to call up several especially happy days. Your child's birthday party, a summer picnic, playing catch with a pet, perhaps a day at an amusement part. Let's see what you can visualize from the memory banks. Shut your eyelids now and be absent for as long as you wish.

Return whenever you are ready. Continue following the text whenever you have the urge to do so.

The hour of five vanishes and is replaced with a bright crystalline jewel. Six chimes announce the hour of six glowing green on the big clock.

Call up the first Christmas Day after you were married. If you never married think of any Christmas Day with friends. A time which had lots of excitement happening. You understand how to do it now. In a jiffy, observe what pops up when you close your eyes. Stay to enjoy this happy memory as long as you so enjoy. Return to the clock of life when you are impelled to do so.

After seven chimes, a black hour of seven on the clock ignites, as the hour six vanishes to be replaced by glittering silver stone.

Normally, most newlyweds or young adults endure hardship of some nature, not necessarily financial, it could be anything, a major setback, called to war, an illness or the death of a loved one. A personalized youthful hardship, perhaps several is what you should now request your imagination to bring forth. You can find at least one. Time on earth would be rather boring if every day was continuous good stuff. Notice that you are experiencing that your eyes are getting sleepy. So very heavy you will soon allow your eyes to rest while you contemplate. Concentrate on a perhaps a long gone personal hardship. Allow the small, minute veins that surround your eyelids to become relaxed and so very tired. So, in a twinkling you will take a restful pause, for your tired eyes.

Simply drop your eyelids and focus on an early adult hardship you have endured memory, remain so as long as it requires then return to the text.

The hour of seven on the clock vanishes into solitary blackish granite stone.

Eight chimes announce the hour of eight that ignites in brilliant bronze.

Children make your life worthwhile; you may have had some children. Certainly you know a favorite child or children. Perhaps, all the children you have ever known are your favorites. Let's find out what the memory banks contain. Select some memories of young children. Maybe at a Halloween or a birthday party memory with young children or any other exciting event, this included children. In a bit, close your eyes and let the memory powers commence the search. Reopen your eyes whenever you are finished reviewing the memories of the children memories your inner brain selected.

Nine chimes signal the hour of nine that is kindling in a shiny topaz stone while the hour of eight on the clock disappears and is replaced by a shiny diamond.

Call up a good day at work. Unquestionably there was one. Work cannot be all that bad, it supported you to achieve whatever you have at this point of time. This may take your recall resources a little time. It is hoped your inner brain does not choose a party with work associates. It is not also hoped that your inner brain does not select the day you retired or got fired. Concentrate on your life of work, career, the important tasks of your life. "Relax...relax...relax, remain calm." Close your eyes; observe whatever memory comes first. Reopen your eyes whenever you have experienced enough of your work time.

The hour of nine vanishes in a cloud of smoke and is replaced by a glowing piece of tin. Ten chimes announce the hour of ten that begins to flash in a brilliant aqua stone.

The hour ten represents hobby time. It could be anything that turns you on. Watching television, movies, golf, any activity that has continuously given you pleasure. Ready, recall your most interesting hobby memory. Take a break, close your eyes gently, and think of a hobby, you really enjoy as a pass time then return to the trip around the clock of life when the urge strikes.

The hour of ten recluses and becomes a resplendent pearl as eleven chimes announce the hour of eleven carved in brown rock eclipsing on the face of the clock.

The hour of eleven, unfortunately represents a sad day. A day, which really shock you up. You may still be trying to recover from it. You will be recalling the very minute of the very day that you were informed that you learned you had a serious illness. It is for your own welfare that you now should recall the terrible memory of that time and the accompanying misery you may have experienced. You may have thought that to forget this event was the best thing you could do. It is! But first you have to face this tragic memory square in the face in the inner brain. To conquer a hurt, you must heal it, and to heal it properly, you must feel it. Facing this hurt will melt away any frozen feelings of remorse and sorrow. Afterward, this frightful time shall be buried forever. This unpleasant memory shall be accepted and forgotten sealed in your memory bank, never to arise again.

Allowing any terror to remain buried mentally alive and active permits the pain to grow larger and repeatedly hurt more. Inviting the painful event to arise, you can consent to the hurt recognize it and embrace it. In doing so, your thinking of this tragedy can be altered. When the pain is recognized and your impending death is dealt with mentally, the soreness reduces. The hurt gradually loses its size and psychological disturbances.

It is natural to grow old. You cannot escape old age.

You are the nature to have ill health. You cannot escape ill health.

You are the nature to die. You cannot escape dying.

All that is dear to you along with everyone you love are of the nature to change.

There is no way to escape being separated from those you love. You cannot keep anything. You come here empty-handed, and You will leave empty-handed.

You cannot escape your fate.

Concentrate strictly on that terrible day. Do not be frightened. A memory cannot hurt you once it is revisited then the entire memory will begin to dissolve. The illness you suffer must and can be accepted. Let's get it over with. Order the terrible memory of that day of doom to be displayed in your conscious mind and be done with it. In a second, close your eyes, dwell on that day and time. After reliving that place and time, return to focus your attention on the text. Do so now.

The hour of eleven vanishes on the clock as it turns into a twinkling butterfly medallion. The hour of twelve is announced with twelve chimes appearing in glowing red bulbs.

The hour of twelve represents "stop."

This space of one hour is set aside for your to come forward, unfolding yourself and preparing to separate from your robot body which up until now has hopefully serviced you well.

Your mind is a tool to guide you inwards, to a calm bliss that waits.

Your mental endowment is commencing to shut down everything you have ever known and become accustomed to. But you always knew it had to happen some day; death happens to all living creatures of life and nature.

The best way to help you prepare for the final click of the concluding minutes on your clock of life. Is to take you there.

Then you shall know there is no need for melancholy regretfully reflections, any boring or sad moments.

In a little while you will close your eyes, allow your tired eyelids to draw down. You shall close your eyes to meditate on any persuasion your inner brain may release the minute of midnight beginning to strike. Summon any spirituality assistance that you have available.

You shall imagine exactly what is going to happen the second after your physical death.

There is no need to rush.

When the hands on the clock comes to the last minute of your clock of life, you may hear a voice directing your transition journey. You just may look around and see those who hover over your body on earth. You are a deceased body. You know that you have properly prepared your loved ones for your departure. Some may be pleased that your physical suffering has finally come to an end. A whispering voice beacons you to come upward and you do so. You will float upward through a tunnel of bright, flashing lights. A funny thought arises, you cannot believe it: "I actually enjoyed the days I spent dying."

You learned how limited your remaining time was with your family, friends and the activities you love, you actually had the courage to make every last moment count.

You cherished your loved ones and friends during this remaining final period of your allotted time.

You expressed your appreciation and love to the ones you cherish.

You have made a difference.

Your presence has been vital and meant so much to those you loved.

You have touched their lives and will always be remembered lovingly.

At the end of the tunnel of brightness, you will be greeted by what you really expect and deserve.

Only you can envision this bounty.

In a little time forward, drop your eyelids over your eyes imagine and dream who and what shall greet you at the end of the tunnel of lights.

The moment you enter into the glory of the unknown. An unknown place beyond all human understanding.

Close your eyes now and imagine making this journey, certainly take as long necessary.

The completion of this Session has arrived.

Reopen your eyes when you wish to be totally reawakened to the time where you are now: "the here and now."

On the count of five you shall return to your world, right now, where you supposed to be at this moment.

Wear a smile because you enjoyed the inner brain trip through yesterdays and tomorrow.

Ready to return and be wide-awake, let's go.

1...coming back.

2...almost there, remain "calm, calm, calm."

3...you are feeling good, happy, experiencing no pain.

4-5...fully awake and feeling great and calmly uplifted.

Preconditioning Program for Self-Hypnosis Session #6
Living with a Permanent Illness or Disability

In the USA there are 250,000 people living with spinal-cord injuries. Among them, the actor Christopher Reeve was paralyzed from the neck down after a fall from a horse in 1995. Doctor Isadore Rosenfeld states that seventy years ago, the majority of similar victims died. Today, thanks to modern medicine and therapy only 20% die before reaching a hospital while 85% of those who live 24 hours are living 10 years later. Mr. Reeve has established an excellent public image of "take it on the chin" attitude for 250,000 North Americans and other millions of worldwide victims inflicted with a similar disability. Mr. Reeve can be called "Superman."

Ray Charles, the icon singer, and gold record/CD maker went totally blind before he was 10 years old. Ray Charles thought, "I am blind. I guess I'll never amount to much."

After many years of poverty and struggle, he began using his inner brain's imagination. "I saw myself as a recording-artist star. It was the image inside my head that pushed me forward and kept me going. I saw myself as a star and so I made up my mind to become one." Ray Charles has supplied living proof that a major handicap does not wipe you off the map. Mr. Charles sets an admirable image for the millions of blind people.

Andrea Bocelli, the world-famous blind opera tenor singer, followed Ray Charles' philosophy of never giving up. He achieved goals beyond his imagination.

Louis Armstrong, the legendary black trumpet player and jazz singer, was captured in a 1945 international press photo after he had become world famous. A crying Louis Armstrong was sitting on his suitcase, outside the also famous Vancouver Hotel, Canada. The hotel had plenty of vacant rooms—but Louis Armstrong was refused a room only because he was black. Mr. Armstrong, was also refused a room by all the other Vancouver hotels. He slept the night in the seat of a rented band bus. At that time, Louis Armstrong was living with a severe race handicap. He was quoted the next day: "I got a simple rule about everybody. If you don't treat me right—shame on you!" Louis Armstrong never gave in to condemn the white man's racial intolerance. The addiction of racial prejudice is a nearly incurable inner brain addiction. Mr. Armstrong set a brave, black race example.

Helen Keller (1880–1968) was blind and deaf. Ms. Keller overcame her handicaps and became world famous for helping many humanitarian causes. She became a glowing light for the many with similar afflictions.

Three of the many well-known statements she made regarding her handicaps are:

"Never bend your head. Always hold it high. Look the world straight in the eye."

"Life is either a daring adventure—or it is nothing."

"I thank God for my handicaps, for, through them, I have found myself, my work, and my God."

Lou Gehrig, a famous baseball player in the 1950s, was the first human diagnosed with a disease that was later named Lou Gehrig's disease, a long suffering and incurable illness. He died at the age of 38.

Mr. Gehrig knew his horrifying fate when he broadcast a final goodbye to the world: "So, I close in saying that I might have had a bad break, but I have an awful lot to live for. Today, I consider myself the luckiest man on the face of the earth."

Oscar-winning actor Charlton Heston spoke on a morning television show, *NBC Today*, interview recently regarding how he felt after being diagnosed with symptoms of Alzheimer's disease. Mr. Heston stated: "Maybe it is good that God gives you something to think about every so often. But life is full of surprises, isn't it? Whatever happens, happens. You take it in stride. You don't have many options there."

These individuals mentioned above discovered: "So, life is tough. I shall be tough. I shall not give in. I shall show them. It is not what I have lost, but what I have left that is important."

Life is a classroom. You often learn more from ten days of agony than from ten years of contentment. You are to learn from the trials, you have been sent. You may be disabled but you remain able.

You can think of what can be right now rather than lament of what might have been. You can accept what is now, forgetting what was before. From the trial of your handicap, you can grow. You can adjust to the seriousness of your loss—you can experience the wonder of remaining alive.

The obstacles you must overcome will never disappear. How you internalized your handicap in an optimist, imaginative inner brain can assist mastering what before you may not have been able to do.

Internalize the fact, that due to circumstances, perhaps out of your control, you are handicapped. If you escaped being a wheel bound paraplegic or a totally paralyzed person be thankful. Any physical handicap is a rugged volcano to be climbed, but there is no other acceptable alternative. There is no other option. There is always the hope of an amazing medical breakthrough. It is happening all the time. Prior to 1921 everybody who got type two diabetics died.

Those who are exceptional religious, like Sister Alphonsus, of Edmonton, forced into a wheelchair due to rheumatoid arthritis discovered her spiritual insight. The Sister accepted the handicap as part of her God's plan to give her time to pray for more people. Despite enduring pain and immobility, the Sister states: "I always loved life and I still do. This catastrophe is but a small bump to eternity."

An eighty-two year-old blind nun with continuing near heart and lung failure for twenty-five years stated: "I have always consulted my Bible for saints to guide my life. But no one in the Bible lived like this. I know my God will not ask more of me than I can bear. I am happy and content to be alive."

Henry David Thoreau, a writer (1817–1862) wrote:

"However mean your life has become, meet it and live it; Do not shun it and call it hard names. It is not so bad as you imagine. The faultfinder will find faults everywhere, even in paradise. Love your life."

You can persuade yourself to throw away any pitiful apathy and think boldly regarding your handicap.

A shattering spiral of stress dwelling in your thoughts on your handicap can become overwhelming. The continual working through of these sorrows within your inner brain that can lead you out of the stress of self-pity.

You can cease giving quarter to negative feelings that intensify and amplify crystallizing the very worst emotions. Negative emotions that can reduce your opportunity of rehabilitation to an acceptable existence.

You can replace any negative stresses or regrets into positive courage.

You can believe in the hope that through the darkness there lies a pathway out.

You can overcome your handicap using inner brain imagination power. No matter whatever shall occur—no matter how terrible fragile your condition may be.

You may have burned to the ground.

You are sitting in the ashes of what is left of what you were.

You can successfully go onward with your handicap. Onward again, then onward again.

You can be philosophical regarding your handicap. Your handicap can be considered a life experience.

You may be riding an emotional roller coaster of self-pity. A ride you certainly don't want to be on. You can "hangith in there" and come through any unpleasant rides with negativity. You can grow a strong belief that your life is worth living with a handicap. The inner brain's imagination can assist you to create this belief into a true fact.

Be assured that your loved ones will never stop loving you because of your handicap.

You can fully trust and "let go." Become an empty vessel ready to be filled, making headway for healing and rehabilitation into a different lifestyle.

You can tell yourself: "If I have to live with this, I can do it well."

Your handicap is not a punishment, it is a reawakening into an unknown world.

In the beginning the awakening will be shattering and humbling. You can discover reasons to celebrate the voyage through the remainder of this unplanned journey.

You can learn that it is possible for you to bear the unbearable. Learning to live in a changed life must be an education to let go of what you have lost. Letting go of your previous benefits is truly the hardest work you may ever do. You cannot divorce yourself from the condition of the "here and now." You can willingly accept your handicap. By doing so, your life will be changed, but not taken away.

Dante, the Middle Ages writer, understood what becoming handicapped means. He wrote in *The Divine Comedy*: "In the middle of this road, we call our life I found myself in overwhelming suffering. I was petrified, alone in dark woods with no clear path through."

From St. John of the Cross's book, *Dark Night of the Soul*: "With no other light or guide, I went through the darkness. With the candle that burned in my heart."

You can master your life, be the true captain of your fate, rather than submit to it.

You can detach and release your handicap, you can abandon all fear. You can rediscover the joy that exists only in fully living in the infinite "here and now" moment. You discover acceptance and roll with the punches as they come.

Never shut off the possibility of learning from your handicap.

This Self-Hypnotic Session is a forceful passage of genuine hope. The inner brain's imaginative visions have been created with the genuine desire to supply you with unquestionable optimism. To carry onward with hope and cheerfulness that will assist you with your handicap. You shall establish a pleasant and acceptable life. A different way of life you want to claim.

Self-Hypnotic Session #6
Living with a Permanent Illness or Disability

Dear reader, many chronic pain suffers develop a pattern of shallow breathing, the breath equivalent of junk food. Good breathing comes from your diaphragm not the top of your chest. Inhale to a count of four, hold for a count of four, exhale for a count of four and hold again for four before taking the next inhaled breath. This breathing exercise is called the foursquare full-breathing cycle. This exercise promotes a deeper breath, slow breathing and the full distribution of the air you breathe. Practice this exercise several times before proceeding. Take the time to reinforce the breathing exercise as frequently as you wish during this Session.

Permitting your body to rest is very important. When your body is at ease and relaxed, your mind becomes calmed. The relaxation of your mind is essential for your body and mind to rest and heal from the negative effects of over-stress and anxiety.

Settle yourself comfortably in a chair or lie down on your back on the floor or on a bed with a pillow under your head.

The time has about come for you to draw down your eyelids and rest your eyes, for as long as you wish. When you do so breathing in and out, become aware of your whole body hanging down. Feel all the spots of your body that are touching the chair floor or the bed you are lying on. Be aware of your heels, the back of your legs, your buttocks, and your back. Be aware of your arms and hands. Relax the back of your head. With each exhaling breath, feel sinking and deeper downward, letting go of any tension. Letting go of all worries, not holding on to anything.

As you breathe in, feel your abdomen rising, and as you breathe out, feel your abdomen falling. For several breaths, just notice the rise and fall of your abdomen. As you breathe in become aware of your two feet. As you breathe out, allow your two feet to relax. Breathing in, send your love to your feet, and breathing out. Smile to your feet.

Breathing in and out, know how wonderful it is to have two feet, that may allow you to walk, to run, to play sports, to dance, to drive, to do so many activities throughout the day. Send your gratitude to your two feet for always being there for you whenever you needed them. Breathing in, become aware of your right and left legs. Breathing out, allow the cells in both legs to relax. Breathe in a smile to your legs, and breathing out, send each leg your love. Appreciate whatever degree of strength and health there is in your legs.

As you breathe in and out, send both legs your tenderness and care. Uncoil and unwind any tension you may be holding in both legs. Breathing in, become aware of your two hands. Breathing out, completely relax all the muscles in your two hands, releasing any tension you may be holding in any fingers. As you breathe in, appreciate how wonderful it is to have two hands. Breathing out, send a smile of love to your two hands. Breathing in and out, concentrate on all the many activities and objects you touch with your hands. Your hands allow you to write, to cook, to drive, to hold the hand of someone else, to hold a baby, to wash your own body, to draw, to play a musical instrument, to type, to build and fix things, to pet an animal, to hold a cup of coffee. So many things are available to you because of your two hands.

Enjoy the fact that you have two hands and allow all the cells in your hands and fingers to be calmer. Breathing in, become aware of your two arms. Breathing out, allow your arms, to fully relax. As you breathe in, send your love to your arms, and as you breathe out, smile to both arms. Take the time to appreciate your arms and whatever strength and health are there in your arms. Send them your gratitude for allowing you to hug someone else, to swing on a swing, to help and serve others, to work hard on any job, cleaning the yard and the house, mowing the lawn, to do so many things throughout every day of your life. Breathing in and out, permit your two arms to let go and be calmer. Embrace your arms with your mindfulness, feel joy and ease in every part of your two arms. Breathing in, become aware of your shoulders. Breathing out, allow any tension in your shoulders to flow out into the floor. As you breathe in, send your love to your shoulders, and as you breathe out, smile with gratitude to them.

Breathing in and out, become aware that you may have allowed a lot of tension of stress to accumulate in your shoulders. With each exhalation allow the tension to leave your shoulders, feeling both shoulders to relax more deeply. Send them your tenderness and care. Knowing that you may have put too much strain on your shoulders. You want to live in a way that will allow your body is always relaxed and at ease. Breathing in, become aware of your heart. Breathing out, allow your heart to rest. With your in breath, send your love to your heart.

Gently instruct your heart to lower it beating rhythm. With an exhaling breath, smile to your heart. As you breathe in and out, get in touch with how wonderful it is to have a heart still beating in your chest. Your heart allows your life to be possible, and it is always beating within, every second, ever minute. It never takes a break. Allow your beating heart to gently slow down. Your heart has been beating since you were a four-week-old fetus in your mother's womb. It is a marvelous organ that allows you to do everything you do throughout the day. Breathe in and know that your heart also loves you. Breathe out and commit to live in a way that will help your heart to function well. With each exhalation, feel your heart calming down to a slow rhythm. Send each cell in your heart a smile for its reliability. Your heart beats with ease and joy. Breathing in, become aware of your stomach and intestines. Breathing out, allow your stomach and intestines to relax. As you breathe in, send them your love and gratitude. As you breathe out, smile tenderly to them. Breathing in and out, realize how essential these organs are to your health.

Give these organs a chance to rest deeply. Each day they digest and assimilate the food you eat, giving you energy and strength. Your stomach and intestines need you to take the time to recognize and appreciate them. As you breathe in, feel your stomach and intestines calming and releasing all tension. As you breathe out, enjoy the fact that you have a good working stomach and intestines.

As your inner brain quiets down, take a few moments to refresh your eyes. As you breathe in and out, know how precious your two eyes are. They allow you to look into the eyes of someone you love, to see a beautiful sunset, to read and write, to move around with ease, to see a bird flying in the sky, to watch a movie. So many things are made possible because of your two eyes. Take the time to appreciate the gift of sight and allow both eyelids to blink several times. You can slowly raise your eyebrows to help release any tension you may be holding around in your eyes. The sight which you value so much, just close down your eyelids, roll your eyes to the back of your head several times for a moment to allow both eyes to relax.

Go into "deep hypnotic sleep now."

At this point you can continue to relax any other spots of your body, simply by directing tenderness and love thoughts to that particular spot.

Now suspend any disbelief.

Summon your awesome, illustrious imagination, the most powerful instrument you possess.

In the South Pacific Ocean there is a place named Blue Lagoon where few people have ever been because of its remote location. The Blue Lagoon is surrounded by high Rocky Mountains that has many channels of cascading waterways running down the mountain delivering bring fresh water from the surrounding sea. A long, narrow outlet sends the waterfalls back out into the Pacific Ocean. The Blue Lagoon's main occupants is a thriving community of dolphins, extremely intelligent creatures, they have bred and lived happily in the blue lagoon for millions of years. Thousands of beautiful dolphins thrive in this closed society. A private dolphin club in the secret Blue Lagoon. The dolphins would never leave the safety and security of the lagoon. There was only one way out, one very long narrow stream of a fast flowing river with dangerous currents that led outside the Blue Lagoon. To swim out the long narrow outlet to the ocean was never considered, because those few that had, never returned. The dolphin tribe called the Pacific Ocean, the Doom Water.

Cyrus was an only child in his dolphin family. Cyrus was a young dolphin who had a delightful existence living with his mother, father and younger brother. The family of dolphins enjoyed every moment of the day speeding and leaping through the Blue Lagoon. On dark moonlight evening's beams of moon glitter sprinkled over the lagoon. And on hot, sunny days of the blazing sun shafts of sunlight filled the waters down into the deep depths of the Lagoon. Strong winds often caused the lagoon to have high towering waves covering the entire lagoon. Cyrus and his friend Creator swam faster on windy days, ever flying over one wave to belly flop onto the next. Cyrus's boy friend Creator would often swim together to the lagoons narrow, long outlet then stop outside at the entrance. After years of being instructed never to leave the Lagoon, there was never a time when they ventured so close faraway into the opening. They began wondering what the waters of Doom River were really like. Every dolphin was trained since the first dawn of thought to never venture out into the unknown Doom River. "Never swim into Doom River because it means to never return. It is a forbidden place of Doom."

Cyrus and Creator's thoughts were very similar to a little girl named Angelica, who lived in Yonkers, New York. She was named Angelica because her father believed she was like a crippled angel from heaven when she was born. Angelica was the only child in her family, eighteen years old and drove a car. Angelica was born a thalidomide baby, her body was deformed, a condition caused by pills her mother's doctor had erroneously recommended during her pregnancy. Angelica had a deformed left arm, a stump, and her right leg was a flipper. Angelica never considered herself as an invalid. Angelica had endured and overcome many years of being stared at, laughed at, shunned, bullied and belittled. But Angelica was stubborn, determined, and an optimist. Angelica hid her arm deformations by always wearing a long sleeve blouse. She wore a wooden leg, cover by wide slacks that concealed her flipper-like right leg. She made friends and eventually made herself a special friend Danielle. Together, they enjoyed a shared fun-time life. Angelica had always been told by her teachers and parents to never smoke cigarettes. To do so was a doom, a toxin poison, an addictive habit that could eventually kill her. Still Angelica saw people smoking cigarettes everywhere, even some of her own relatives. They all seemed so happy and in excellent humor most of the time. How could this product that almost all stores sell, with advertisements displaying people having lots of fun be a poison, she wondered. When her older best friend Danielle started to smoke cigarettes, Angelica scolded her. Danielle replied: "I could do a lot worse things." And on the day that Angelica turned nineteen, the forbidden cigarette that had tempted her imagination since childhood took root in her conscious mind. Angelica went into a grocery store displayed her birth certificate, this was the first day of her lifetime when she could say: "I want to buy a package of cigarettes." She did.

Cyrus and Creator were experiencing a similar yearning, a desire to experiment with danger. Neither really believed what they had been told. They didn't think that leaving the Blue Lagoon throughout Doom River could be as dangerous had been drilled into their heads since as far back as they could remember. Dreaming and thinking about swimming into Doom River leading to the ocean, became their shared desire.

Angelica began smoking cigarettes, every day. She became a chain smoker, and resented any time she could not smoke and smoke more. Soon days of smoking cigarettes accumulated into ten years. Angelica's lungs developed asthma, a serious breathing disease. Her doctor told her she had to stop smoking and stay away from second hand smoke. Angelica tried and tried but she never could and the disease in her lungs thrived and flourished.

On sunny afternoon, Cyrus and Creator could no longer contain their desire to explore further into the entrance of Doom River. They both decided to swim a little ways into the stream of fast moving water. Entering Doom River they were shocked by the fast flowing turbulent rapids, in a few minutes they butted against a coral reef blocking their entrance into the huge ocean on the other side. The reef was no problem, both dolphins leap over the blockage to enter into the warmest water they ever experienced, the sparkling, clear waters of the Pacific Ocean. The view was beautiful there, no more confining mountains. The water was even fresher and more beautiful. They discovered new fish in the sea, which neither had seen before. The ocean's fish tasted better than anything they had never eaten before.

Everything in the ocean was better than being the lagoon. They both thought the warnings they had received about Doom River were ridiculous tales. How wrong their parents had been to believe that there was any doom here in the huge beautiful, fish filled ocean. Both dolphins roamed and leaped out of the water with joy, exploring the ocean for many days and many nights, and each day was better than the last. Each day brought the two dolphin's unbelievable pleasure. They were so pleased they were considering returning to the Blue Lagoon and bring their girlfriends out into this new territory with so many delights. All was absolutely beautiful for the two dolphins until they encountered a herd of killer sharks, all of which came attacking. The two dolphins soon learned the sharks intended to eat them. A shark bit out a part of flesh out of Creator's chest. The herd of sharks' vicious assault alerted both dolphins' instincts with immediate instructions. They had to swim fast and find that long narrow river that would take them back to their home, the Blue Lagoon.

As fast as their tails could wiggle, the two dolphins made speedy headway in that direction with hungry sharks in hot pursuit. They reached the corral reef, Creator leaped high in the air just managing to leap over the coral blockage. Cryus followed, but as he leap out of the water, a trailing shark vaulted up out of waves to bit off one of Cyrus's flippers. The dolphin hurdled high into the air. Cyrus's high jump barely allowed his body the few inches needed, to clear the rocks and drop into the raging rapids of Doom River on the other side of the corral rock.

Angelica began smoking cigarettes continuously making her asthma attacks worse. It became necessary for her to quit her job and stay home attached to an oxygen-producing machine day and night. Angelica could not breath without it, finally the cigarettes had to be abandoned. Smoking one cigarette would cause her to faint and she would have to be rushed to the hospital to survive. Life seemed meaningless now, she could not smoke and she could not breathe without a machine attached to her nostrils. Angelica became very despondent.

Creator and Cyrus had to swim very hard against the currents of Doom River until they both reached their home the Blue Lagoon.

After a month of being back in lagoon, Creator's deep wound finally healed, as did Cyrus's but he could no longer swim. Cyrus could very barely float on top of the water. Cyrus became very despondent.

As time passed, Angelica grew to accept her always near death condition. She knew she had to find some other activity to survive, she emerged herself on the Internet. Angelica found friends, played games on the Internet. Angelica had discovered a challenging pass time. She had discovered an exciting activity that provided her with contentment without the need for a smoke of cigarette.

Cyrus was badly handicapped but his mother, father and brother brought him food and propelled him around the Blue Lagoon.

Eventually, Cyrus began serving a great purpose as a symbol to the young dolphins. What had happened to him was what would happen to any dolphin that ventured outside the Blue Lagoon. Terrifying killers were everywhere. Many times Cyrus told of his harrowing experience in Doom River. Cyrus warned many dolphins, by example to never leave the lagoon and he found peace and contentment in doing so.

Cyrus and Angelica's stories are imaginary, but both represent what happens when one gives in to our temptations; however many endure being handicapped through no fault of their own. You could have been a victim of your disability due to an accident caused by another or any freak accident, perhaps an illness. Like Cyrus and Angelica you can discover contentment and peace with your affliction, providing that you never quit trying to explore and discover exactly where your particular challenge may be. For the remainder of your live your inner brain shall be courageous, strong and ever ready to welcome whatever new opportunities that shall unfold. Your inner brain will guide you to a peaceful acceptance within that shall sustain you. Cryus and Angelica had to search for a way to live with their impairments. So can you.

You may now awaken.

1-2...coming up.
3...You are stronger, courageous and you can accept what before may have been unacceptable.
4...You feel much better.
5...Wide awake and feeling good.

Preconditioning Program for Self-Hypnosis Session #7
Public Speaking Enhancement

You may skip this Session if you really enjoy delivering a speech to an audience of any size. If you are among these fortunate people, you may decide you do not need this Session. Otherwise, you may continue reading.

In every poll taken since the end of World War II, the absolute number one fear of all living humans is delivering a public speech. Having a nest of butterflies invading your stomach, before giving a speech—this is normal, "stage fright." U.S. President John Kennedy's hands often trembled before a public speech, so did his brother's, Bob Kennedy.

A nervous quiver never stopped the Kennedy brothers from being regarded as two of the premier speakers of their time.

Many people in powerful positions carry this secret fear. It may be that they were never pushed into giving a speech by their parents, teachers or they experienced a negative speaking event at one time or another.

There are many excellent books in every library on how to prepare a speech.

Public Speaking for Dummies is very comprehensive and easily accessible.

All of the available self-help speaking instructional books can help you prepare an excellent speech. If you require practice giving a speech phone the Toast Masters Clubs, membership is usually free and the members will enjoy assisting you to deliver a non-stop fifteen-minute speech.

But isn't the element that all the books in the world and practice courses—will never provide you with is the "intestinal fortitude" to stand up, in front of any audience and speak?

That is what this Session can and will accomplish in a very imaginative, unique way.

Two other important ingredients to delivering a good speech are also never mentioned in public speaking books or the Toast Masters Association, the vocal cords and the jaw.

For many people during their workday have little opportunity to speak frequently in front of a crowd during their duties. The vocal cords and the jaw become the most undeveloped muscle in the human body. To eliminate both these deficiencies is really quite simple. No hypnosis trace is required.

Vocal Cords:

Prior to delivering your speech, read out loud for a half an hour. Read slowly in a loud voice, pronouncing each word with proper diction. Many stage actors read or recite long passages before hitting the boards. Many actors follow especially designed vocalizing tapes or CDs—thereby perfecting their vocal instruments the most important possession in their profession. Popular singers and opera stars practice singing the scales or sing a challenging song before performances. These people wish to make sure the talent remains with them. By practicing they are strengthening the projection power of the vocal cords. The performance capability which a profession golfer, piano player or violin player perfects by practicing in a lot of their spare time.

The Jaw:

The jaw is often the most unused tension and heavy stress causing muscle in your body. Few people exercise their jaw properly, especially before a delivering a speech. The special time when that jaw has to be oiled and calmed and relaxed prepared to ready to up and down, smoothly without a hitch or tightness.

The following exercise is easy to do also expels saliva into your throat—avoiding a dried up month. The worse appearance you can have during a speech is chewing gum attempting to steady your nerves and avoid a dry throat.

During hockey payoffs on television, you may have noticed some coaches with their mouths in constant movement. They are always chewing on gum. The coaches believe the rapid chopping on gum will calm their anxiety during the hockey match.

Actually, the constant chewing of gum tightens the jaw causing facial tension trigger spots in front of one's lower two ears.

Some people get (temporal mandibular joint) TMJ headaches resulting from over chewing on anything. The two hinges in front of your ears where the lower jaw attaches to the skull can easily become over tightened.

This following exercise will ease this jaw's hinges.

The Easy Jaw Exercise:

#1: Grasp your forehead with your left palm—place your right palm firmly on the bottom of your jaw.

#2: Place the left hand over your forehead as far back as you can. At the same time, using the palm of your right hand to yank down on the jaw as far down as you can.

#3: With you right palm remaining on a yanked chin, rotate the chin as wide out as you can clockwise, three times. Afterwards, rotate a rotate the chin anticlockwise as wide as you can, three times in the opposite direction.

#4: Hear those bones crack.

#5: Rest your jaw. The jaw tension has been relieved. Now you shall speak easier, no more ringing ears, which is caused by the same jaw tension.

Public speaking does not have to be stressful.

All audiences truly want the speaker to succeed. Most attendees of the audiences harbor a fear of public speaking. The audience is on the speaker's side; they want the speaker to succeed in their delivery. No matter what happens during a speech delivery a negative incident can be used to your advantage. Humor and humility can be combined to be very effective, for example when a speaker creates a major screw up like getting tongue-tied, or perhaps even says something quite stupid during the talk, what can a speaker do, besides faint? The audience does not really care about speaker mistakes. The audience only wants to get something of value out of your entire presentation. A speaker could try saying something like this, "What lies at the bottom of the ocean and shakes all over? Me! A nervous wreck!" This turns the lemons into lemonade and the audience laughs or even applauds encouragement. Speeches often get more interesting when the speaker goes off a prewritten text and talks spontaneously.

Some speaking advice that speakers often forget is:

You do not have to be a brilliant or perfect speaker.

Do not to impart too much information or cover too much territory in a short presentation.

The speaker is there to give and contribute a purpose not to entertain an audience.

It is unrealistic to try pleasing everyone.

Do not emulate other speakers always be yourself it is natural and easier.

A speaker should be personal, revealing, humble and humorous when required.

Speaker should not be fearful of potential negative outcomes, if such does occur the speaker can maneuver the situation to their advantage.

Never try to control the behavior of an audience.

Instead of trusting in a natural ability, the speaker spends too much time over preparing a speech. Over preparing a speech can cause unneeded stress and anxiety.

Do not believe the audience will be as critical of your speech as you might be.

One tiny fear in the conscious mind creates many. Disowning any exaggerated self-imposed fear of speaking in public is the primary priority of this Session.

You will take command of any speaker's platform.

Self-Hypnotic Session # 7
Public Speaking Enhancement

Dear reader, I want you to know totally relaxation. A way of relaxing that can always make you at ease. A system that works best for you, so let's do that. Let yourself be calmed down. Make yourself comfortable now. You shall allow yourself to enter into a deep self-hypnotic trance of self-hypnotic sleep, a state of tranquility.

Allow your breathing to be normalized. Merely breathe in and out at any pace that is comfortable for you at this time. You may notice a slight tiredness creeping into your eyes and all the small veins that connect to your vision. It would be good to allow your eyes to be rested and restored to full vision power before continuing with the text. In a few seconds, you will close your eyes, but prior to taking this refreshing eye rest, stare and concentrate at on "an important word." The word is "calm."

In a moment, close both of your eyes and think only of "calm" for as long as your can, before reopening both eyes to return to the text.

Open your mind think and focus imaginatively of both feet. Concentrate on your feet.

Start wiggling your toes. Wiggle your toes up and down, up and down. Up and down as hard and as fast as you can. The harder and the faster the better for you, it is very important to get warm blood coursing down into your feet. That's it wiggle, wiggle, wiggle. faster, faster, faster.

You are doing a good job. You are beginning to feel the tendons in your feet tighten.

Wiggle, wiggle, faster, faster.

Your toes are becoming slightly stressed this is a normal reaction, you are also noticing that your feet are getting warmer, this too is absolutely normal. Wiggle, wiggle, wiggle, faster, faster. Now you are doing a very good job.

Now relax everywhere. Cease wiggling your toes. Permit your feet to be still. Let you feet completely collapse now. Feel that warm relaxing feeling melting into both feet. Let that warm current of relaxation move up into your ankles. The feet and ankles feel so good just let them completely collapse. Your feet feel simply beautiful. Deep sleep, a deep relaxation trace is moving into your shines and calf muscles. It feels so good to let your calf muscles dangle from the bone, let them to be totally limp. Your knees are smooth and deeply relaxed, deep calmness is moving into your large thigh muscles, it feels so good to let these muscles sink and uncoil. Your pelvis is loose and relaxed, both buttocks are warm and comfortable. Deep calmness, deep relaxation is moving into your waist. Breathe in and let your tummy out. Try this breathing exercise it is called the triangle. Pretend an imaginary triangle is placed outside your body. The top corner is at the base of your head the bottom two corners are stationed outside the right and left leg. As you breathe in imagine circulating the fresh oxygen rhythmically all the way around the triangle clockwise, when you exhale imagine sending the stream of air around in the opposite direction, anticlockwise. Practice this no holding back of the breath circulation breathing exercise several times. You will find it quite easy and relaxing after a few tries.

Your mouth is becoming dry and even quite thirsty. When you swallow, it immediately relieves your thirst and you go deep into self-sleep now. Your body is limp, all over limp like a ragged Ann doll. Calmness begins moving into your arms and hands. Your elbows are loose, your arms are relaxed and comfortable. Now let your wrist and fingers melt into deep calmness. The relaxation is moving into your chest cavity. Your heart is gently slowing down just a little now. This is good for your heart it needs a time to rest. This will alter your breathing cycle, just slightly, when you breathing does change you go a 100 times more into self-hypnotic sleep now. The calmness is swirling into your lower back and spine.

The spine is going into a deep self-hypnotic asleep. Imagine all the stress and any sore spots begin flowing out leaving your back. Flowing out of the back even now, flowing out onto the floor. Deep sleep and absolute calmness is moving from your spine, into the side of both of your shoulder blades, up over you shoulders and into your collarbone. Let all them little knots and tendons there begin uncoiling. Unwinding and relaxing, going into the deep self-hypnotic sleep now. Restfulness is moving up behind your neck and going behind your ears. Let all those little tendons, those little muscles behind your ears just let them go completely. Permit the little places around your ears to go into a deep self-hypnotic sleep now.

Deep sleep continues up the back of your neck, the back of the head, over the top of your head and into your forehead. Your forehead becomes smooth and relaxing feeling tranquility. A sense of ease sweeps through your facial muscles, your nose, cheeks, and chin. It feels soft, warm and sleepy, you jaw is becoming quite heavy. Part your upper and lower teeth. It feels good to take the pressure off your teeth. Breathe in and breathe rhythmically out as you normally do. Each gentle breath allows you take you go 100 times more easily into self-hypnotic asleep. Deep sleep, deep relaxation is moving deeply inside your body, everything inside you is working perfectly and automatically, Drowsiness is seeping into your mind, you haven't a care in the world.

Where you are now there is absolutely nothing that bothers you. You are comfortable and becoming calmer. Imagine that you are as light as a feather. Imagine a feather. Imagine dropping a feather into a very deep rock lined well. On the count of 1 to 5 imagine the feather is floating down the well.

1...the feather is floating downward.

2...the feather is light, the feather strikes some rocks on the sides of the well's wall as it continues to drop and float deeper downwards.

3...Imagine the feather approaching the water at the bottom of the well.

4...See the feather drop onto the placid water's surface.
5...go into self-hypnotic sleep now.

Now you can open up your limitless, most brave imagination.

Now you are going to visit a very wonderful, special location. It is a warm spring day in the woods of a forest. You feel very peaceful walking along the pathway you can see the sun shining through the trees you smell the clean, mountain air. You are walking slightly uphill and your legs are beginning to get tired. It is very pleasant walking through the trees in the forest but your legs and feet are beginning to get very tired.

You are going to your own special place, up on the mountain and you are looking forward to getting there so you can lie down and rest.

Your legs and feet are getting to be very, very tired. They feel so heavy, it will be so nice to lie down and rest.

You are climbing to a special resting station at the peak of a small mountain. It is a small clearing by a pleasant stream winding down from the summit. There is large hammock, with a pillow on one end spread between two trees. See yourself lay down on the hammock. It feels so good to lie down and rock back and forth on the hammock. The hammock is gently swaying just enough to be pleasant. Listen to the gurgling sounds of the stream's water. Birds in the surrounding trees are chirping. Smell the aroma of pine in the clean mountain air. You feel serene, calm and relaxed with the pleasant awareness of yourself being here.

Rocking on the hammock, gently swaying back and forth, back and forth, you feel very positive about everything. Mentally you may have an urge to drift away, but you know that life has a way of always working out and you feel very good about that. You know every day you are becoming more and more calm. You are secure in the conviction that everything will work out the way you want things to go. You are developing stronger and stronger feeling of being stronger mentally. A healthy dynamism recharged storage cell of vigor that will remain within you throughout each day and night. You will begin sleeping better at nighttime because each day you are looking forward to the next day. The inner forces of your imagination are tuning into your desires. You will be a leader. This includes a goal of being an excellent public speaker. You can do this, without consciously thinking of it.

The power is coming closer and closer and with this power there is responsibility.

You know that all things are possible and you can become anything you want to be. The power of your inner brain can direct you to the accomplishment of providing you with latent talent that will make you a brave public speaker.

You can be led to this accomplishment by the power of your imagination.

You know that all things are possible and you can do anything you want to be. Anything at all that you wish.

In a moment, you will direct yourself. You are going to imagine a positive visualization of perceiving you being an excellent calmer speaker.

You are fully composed. You shall be braver than ever unafraid to speak out, in fact, you shall want to speak more than ever to others.

Now every day, you feel more alert, wide awake and energetic you become much less easily tired, much less easily discouraged and filled with negative self-doubt. You abandon any possible depressing fears of public speaking. As a matter of fact, from henceforth, your capable imagination will cause you to become so interested in whatever you are doing, whatever is going on around you, that your mind will become completely distracted away from yourself. You will no longer think at all about yourself. You will no longer dwell upon yourself or any concerns of public speaking. You will become very much less conscious of yourself and much less occupied with yourself and your own feelings. Your nerves shall become stronger and steadier. Your mind will become calmer and clearer. More composed, more placid, more tranquil each day, you will become much less easily worried about yourself when you speak out in public. You shall be at ease and full of confidence whenever you speak out in public. Upon beginning to speak in front of any crowd, normal stage fright will be under your command and turn into a powerful ally to compel you move forward.

You shall be less agitated, much less fearful, and much less apprehensive, and much less easily concerned about your words and not be upset in any way whatsoever.

You will even be able to think more clearly, to concentrate with absolutely continuity. You will be able to give your whole and undivided attention to whatever you are doing to the complete exclusion of everything else. Consequently your memory will improve and you will be able to see things in their true perspective without magnifying any unexpected or future difficulties while public speaking. You shall never allow a negative self-defeating thought of public speaking to get out of proportion in any way.

If fact, every day, in every way, you are now becoming emotionally much calmer, more settled, much less easily disturbed about speaking out with authentic feelings from your heart. Every day you are now developing a good image of yourself. You shall look forward to rending any public speech.

You know that you are a worthwhile person. A person who can speak in public at any time or any place.

Your self-esteem as a public speaker will grow day by day from now on.

Each day you will be much more confident of yourself and much more confident in your speaking ability. Speaking what you have to say each day. You are much more confident in your speaking ability.

You shall now proceed with speaking out at any time, without any fear of previous failure or consequences.

Unnecessary, uncontrolled anxiety or uneasiness shall now swiftly vanish.

Every day you will feel more and more independent, more able to stickup for yourself to stand up on your feet and speak out calmly and relaxed as you do so. To hold your own, no matter how difficult or no matter how trying things may be during any speech that you present. You shall feel an immense feeling of well-being.

A new sensation of safety and security that will guide you and make you the captain of your fate.

You shall become more and more relaxed each day, so you will remain calmed and less tense when you are speaking in the presence of any other person, no matter if they be few or many. No matter if they be friends or strangers.

No matter whether it may be at home, at work, socializing, whenever you are presenting a speech. No matter what the occasion may be, you will be able to meet anyone or multiple persons on equal terms.

You will now feel at easy in any one else's presence, without the slightest feeling of inferiority, without becoming self-conscious, with no concern of being embarrassed or lost and confused in your spoken words. You shall speak out on any matter, without making yourself feeling conspicuous in any way. You will become so deeply interested, deeply absorbed in what you are saying, and doing that you will concentrate entirely on doing this to the complete exclusion of everything else. You will remain perfectly relaxed, perfectly calm and self-confident. You will become much less conscious of yourself.

Your own feelings and concerns shall be totally put out of your mind when ever you make a speech. You will consequently be able to talk and act quite freely with others, without any concern in the slightest.

Even if you begin to become nervously self-absorbed and up tight about yourself, you will automatically shift and move you attention back to the "here and now." You shall concentrate on what you are saying, exactly what you are doing.

You will be able to contain and overcome nervousness, discomfort, and uneasiness. In fact, the moment you begin to give a speech in front of any crowd any trace of nervousness shall disappear completely. And you shall feel more completely relaxed, completely at ease, completely interested in what you are saying or doing.

The present of spectators will no longer bother you in the slightest. You shall never again be confused or conspicuous or self-conscious in any way. Your mind shall become so fully occupied with what you are saying or doing that you shall have no uncontrolled fear in the slightest degree. You shall no longer feel nervous, self-conscious or embarrassed.

During the entire time of rending any speech you will be settled down and be calmer, confident, and self-assured. Every day in every way you are now becoming more confident and self-assured, especially at the time when you are speaking in public.

You know you want to speak in public. Visualize yourself as vivid and detailed as you possibly can, in this self-directing period. Imagine yourself standing on a platform standing in front of hundred individuals in a seated audience. Most normal people have an increased heart beat at the beginning of a speech. When this occurs, press your thumbnail into the third finger of either hand, this is a nerve relaxing acupuncture point. Take two deep breaths and while exhaling think three times to yourself, "I am the captain of my fate. I am the captain of my fate. I am the captain of my fate."

Immediately your heart rate will gently return to its normal rhythm, your mind and entire body shall recognize a refreshing sensation of total calmness being released through all parts of your mind and body. A steady calmness will arrive from the top of your scalp immediately moving throughout your entire being, down to the very tips of your toes.

You want to speak, you want to talk and let the listeners hear your important message. Your relaxed inner brain is prepared to deliver whatever is required.

The purpose of your speech shall be relayed to each listener.

In a moment, you will close yours eyes this period will take you to center stage in front of a large seated audience, a spot you may erroneously think you fear. Until you are there and whisper the code to yourself.

You shall make this experience gyrate into an experience of success.

In a few seconds, when you close both eyes, prepare to direct your imagination into a pretend situation of you speaking in front of an audience of two hundred and fifty people.

If you do not have the words for a speech available in your inner brain at present, your imagination is unlimited. The imagination can create a speech on any subject you wish. The words of most speeches are created from your inner brain's vast imagination.

So in a moment, draw down your eyelids and imagine, and feel yourself being a calm, relaxed, fun to listen to speaker. Imagine and visualize being a speaker to the seated audience for as long as you want. Remember before proceeding, pinch those fingers and think the code three times: "I am the captain of my fate." Take notice of how your heart beat gently calms down before commencing with your speech. Feel the calmness your mind and body has achieved.

Here the audience applause when you finish speaking.

Return to the text when you are convinced you did well.

The visions you have given yourself will be effective because you want a positive change. You now look forward to speaking in public. The imagination will direct the wanted ability to speak to audiences and you shall always be the captain of your fate.

Picture yourself back up the mountain peak swinging on the hammock. You are safe and serene on the mountain peak. You are at the peak of mental and physical health. There is a beautiful panorama of nature all around you in every direction. You feel at one with nature with all of your bodily systems functioning in a natural and healthy way. You oneness with nature makes you feel mentally and physically healthy. See yourself arising from the hammock and walking over to the clear blue magical stream. The stream is flowing down from the mountain peak. With cupped hands take a sip of water from the stream. Swallow the pleasant tasting water, sense the very essence of good health flowing into your body. You can feel the warm glow of new strength coursing throughout your body and mind. You enjoy this magic water, like a sponge you take pleasure soaking the first gulp into your throat. Scoop up and drink more of the magical water. The stream's magic water is supplying your throat with magnificent courage to deliver any speech. Continue to enjoy. You have now gained a new power, look forward with positive enthusiasm to deliver a speech to any audience anywhere, anyplace. Use this skill with care.

You are getting better and better as each moment of each day goes by.

You have enjoyed completing this Session.

On the count of three you will now become fully awake, alive and feeling fantastic.

1... With all these good feeling return to the here and now.

2...Take two deep breaths, pinch the thumb and third finder of either hand, think or say, three times to yourself: "I am the captain of my own fate."

3...You shall convert negative inner nervousness to positive creative vitality.

A strength that will turn you into a sought after speaker, a leader in the world, a planet where good leaders and speakers like you are always short of supply.

Preconditioning program for Self-Hypnotic Session #8
Anti-Cigarette Smoking/Tobacco

If you are not a smoker of anything, you are excused from this Session.

If you are a Canadian smoker, you don't need anyone to preach to you about the possible results of smoking cigarettes. On the front of each package of cigarettes are graphic, colored pictures of brown nicotine stained lungs, hearts, throat or whatever is the organ of the month, each destroyed by cigarette smoking. Children's widowed families, teenagers puffing away, the anti-smoking folks really know how to dish it out.

Canadian packages of cigarettes have warnings plastered on the front cover: "33,000 babies die each year from secondhand cigarette smoke." "Elevated levels of poison carbon monoxide are in your body."

Then surprise time, you open the package and written all over the cigarette container, printed in small print appears a stern lecture on the evils of cigarette smoking.

Who dares write all this anti-smoking propaganda? So what? You have conditioned your inner brain's imagination and the conscious will power to ignore all this as nonsense. Your inner brain, where the imagination resides, may truly enjoy smoking, along with your conscious will power. You take out a cigarette, light it, and wonder who pays for the anti-smoking art and literature.

Then you realize 2/3 of a price of a pack of cigarettes go towards taxes. As a taxpayer, you indirectly pay to chaste yourself.

A new industry is now flourishing in Canada, they have created sleeves that you insert over the purchased packets of cigarettes. A devise designed to absolve guilt when a cigarette is extracted. Smokers like the custom designed sleeves that give smokers "cool" identities. A yellow smiling face with a cigarette in its mouth; a mug brimming over with beer, pictures of marijuana leaves. Printed words: "What is next—sex?" Text on the other side of the sleeve defends the civil rights of smokers.

The Canadian press reports the Montreal manufacturers of the "cool" sleeves cannot keep up with production demands. The sleeves are selling like hot cakes in Quebec, Ontario and British Columbia.

The anti-smoking folk are preparing legislation to outlaw this industry. The tobacco companies advertising geniuses target youth in order to replace older customers who die early due to tobacco-related illness.

In the Canadian, the province of Saskatchewan limits stores that can sell cigarettes. Upcoming legislation in Canada will require all stores allowed to sell tobacco products to be out of sight from public view. Canadian drug stores are already prohibited from selling tobacco productions. A new Canadian government promises further legislation that will prohibit public smoking everywhere. Some Canadian provincial governments already have legislation that makes smoking in the presence of children a chargeable offence.

Soon, you shall have to go to some undeveloped, foreign country to relive the pleasure of smoking anywhere except a residence you own. The anti-smoking cigarettes or any other tobacco product use has become almost a worldwide program. Recently, all the pubs in Ireland were ordered to cease all smoking activities, with no private smoking rooms.

The anti-smoking folks, by governmental approval are certainly controlling the ever-increasing price of a package of cigarettes and other tobacco products.

The anti-smoking folk did not make a joke when they named cigarettes: "coffin nails." Physicians in most countries now state cigarette smoking worsens all diseases. Due to the severe shortage of qualified general practitioner in Canada, many patients seeking a permanent doctor are refused if they admit to smoking.

How many times have you told yourself "I would go nuts without my cigarettes"?

How many times have you been at work, or in an out of residence, perhaps a non-smoking sports auditorium having a nicotine fit, craving a few puffs of cigarette smoke wildly in your brain? How many times have you had to search for an acceptable place to light up.

Her doctor told a fifty-year-old woman she would lose both her legs, if she did not quit smoking. Cigarette smoking was worsening the already badly damaged blood circulation in both her legs. A fifty-two-year-old woman with no legs still smokes to this day. An incurable case of lung cancer often causes even heavier smoking. For some there is one benefit to mention about smoking cigarettes: weight loss. A smoker often forgoes eating for a, several in a row cigarette smoking break. Each cigarette causes your heartbeat to increase. If you are a pack a day person, which is classified as a regular smoker, you body is losing 32 calories a day to keep your heart beating at a faster pulse rate.

Cigarette smoking is a compulsive oral habit. Habits are strong to break, and gentle persistence is necessary to effect change.

Even when the new habit of being an ex-smoking settles in, always be on guard, it is very easy to slide back. One individual's friends held a one-year anniversary of "not smoking" party. The feeling good celebrate decided to prove their will power by smoking—one cigarette. The individual now smokes two packs of cigarettes a day, twice the quantity before giving up smoking.

Perhaps previous attempts where you merely cut back on the amount of cigarettes you smoked—failed. This is normal, when several major irritations occur in any day, by instinct, you return to your regular smoking habit.

Many experts in addiction acknowledge that cigarette smoking is the hardest addiction to conquer, especially if the smoker is a veteran of many years of smoking a pack a day.

Initially, using any treatment overcoming the addiction to cigarettes will be a short-term persistent struggle. Similar to a chronic alcoholic it often takes many people a more than a few attempts before they can finally quit. But the health benefits are almost immediate.

If you make the commitment to quit smoking "cold turkey" it may the very hardest thing you will ever have to do. It will not be an over quickly situation. Regardless of the treatment used expect to be bitchy, irritable, stressed out, out of sorts for at least a week. This Self-Hypnotic Session offers remedies to relieve and assist during the initial non-smoking period.

The Webster's Dictionary's definition of nicotine reads: "Poisonous, oily alkaloid from tobacco, used as an insecticide and tanning agent."

Forsaking the poisonous nicotine can be achieved. It is your prerogative.

Millions of ex-smokers found the courage to confront this challenge then forged ahead successfully. In the last ten years the world's smoking population has decreased by over 50%. The winners were no stronger or courageous than you.

Before entering the Self-Hypnotic Anti-Smoking cigarettes or any other tobacco product, you and you alone—must make a firm commitment that: "I want to give up nicotine—now! I shall fight with all my might the conscious ingrained instincts and inner brain cravings for a cigarette! I shall win because I am stronger—I will no longer contaminate my body with an insecticide!"

You must resolve in your mind that you desire to submit to this vital commitment. A sincere pledge, which is a firmly rooted desire that shall come to materialization.

If you are wavering over to quit cigarettes or not, prior to the Self-Hypnotic Session, then it is best to pass over the Anti-Smoking Session. Return when you really know you want to quit poisoning yourself. It is better to keep smoking than make a half-hearted effort and fail. Make this decision right now! Do you really want to quit smoking? Nobody is going to force you, except yourself, but the trail ahead gets tougher, so if you wish to drop out now and come back then by all means do so. Otherwise continue with the text.

Congratulations! This decision to continue will affect the rest of your life, it will make you, your family and friends feel proud for you. You may even wish to join the anti-smoking lobbyist.

You still may not wish to continue with the text when you read the two important features of this session—two physical exercises you must observe to conquer your cigarette smoking addiction. Perhaps, two of the hardest things you may ever have to do.

A chronic alcoholic requires only seventy-two hours to clear the entire system of alcohol, providing the liver is functioning properly. A chronic cigarette smoker requires 7 days to commence clearing out only a portion of the accumulated nicotine throughout the body. Some experts have stated that a long-term smoker's lungs takes five years after quitting to become completely clean of the poison nicotine. However other experts claim this is not the case, residues of nicotine always remain in the human system. Residues of nicotine have caused terminal diseases in those whom quit smoking 25 years previous.

You probably have brown nicotine engraved on some of your fingers or covering some fingernails. Your teeth are stained yellow with the poison of nicotine. You may cough and spite frequently.

Imagine what your insides look like, not just your lungs, but every single organ. Of course you do not need to imagine if you buy your cigarettes in Canada. Every package of cigarettes sold legally and taxable in Canada display living color actual photos of brown nicotine colored organs.

For seven days, you are not only going to be doing battle with your brain's imagination and willpower but also the strong addictive urge instinct of satisfying the brown substance remaining in your entire system. A poison insecticide which has penetrated every single organ in your body. A poison your entire body has become accustomed to being satisfied.

Nicotine resembles a dangerous dragon that has been allowed to expand into a huge size within your will power and imagination. After this Self-Hypnotic Session the dragon will commence shrinking, in seven days it will be shrived to the size of a deflated balloon. You do have the courage to last one week, seven days to complete a life changing and health-improving miracle.

So there you have it. The Self-Hypnotic Anti-Smoking Session should be repeated daily for 7 days after quitting "cold turkey" perhaps during the Session. Perhaps, you are experiencing one of many attempts to give up cigarettes and seek a permanent cure. Be pleased, you have found the miracle that may avoid much physical pain and save your life.

The seven-day program guarantees that the 4,000 poisonous substances contained in one cigarette are vanishing from your body. After seven days your natural, well-trained urge to smoke a cigarette or other tobacco—will be fading away. You may become an anti-smoker not an ex-smoker. An ex-smoker is maybe an individual who is forced to quit, you are doing it willingly of your own free will.

Smokers daily spend hard-earned money to poison their brain and body with an insecticide. The instinct's ruler: nicotine will soon be compelled to abdicate your inner brain's throne. A self-regulation of non-smoking conduct will be substituted and established.

When a smoking urge enters your conscious brain, a relieving vision from your inner brain's imagination will come forward to do combat the "smoke just one or two puffs" craving. An implanted positive message that will assist you to conquer any urge to relapse to smoke a few puffs of a gigantic, poisonous chemical filled cigarette.

At that time you will remember that smoking is a dirty, disgusting, and very expensive addiction.

You shall know you are absolutely right.

How to survive the seven potential relapse days of the smoking instinct urge?

Drink continuous glasses of water, this will speed up the nicotine washout.

Carry around and chew on raw sunflower seeds that contain an ingredient that staves off addictive nicotine cravings, a pound costs approximately $1.50.

Eating plenty of ice cream. This produces a cooling effect on the mind when doing battle with any addiction.

If at all possible, the Self-Hypnotic Session Anti-Smoking/Tobacco should be repeated for 7 consecutive days to do warfare against the enormous deposits of nicotine that remain in your body. You will decided and pledge to going to war against cigarettes poisonous nicotine. The brown insecticide substance that intensifies the instinct urge to relapse and light up a cigarette. Nobody said this battle was going to be easy, no worthwhile success is every easy.

You are going to give up the "urge to smoke, the nicotine cravings." You are going to stop this habit: "cold turkey." Not forever, but one day at a time. You will not be locked up in a rehab center for 7 days. Each repeat of the Session will go deeper into the inner brain than the one before and make your will power stronger.

Long-term heavy smokers who make a pledge to quit "cold turkey" realize that they are entering perhaps "the hardest thing" they have ever done. To achieve the very maximum of imaginative power to assist you in the hardest battle you may ever do combat in there is one recommendation to be made. The imagination becomes alive and works at its very best during the period just before going to sleep. Thomas Edison told his son that his greatest inventions came into his mind moments before taking one of his several naps every day. Scientists call this period of time the "Alpha State" a period when the imagination begins to assume command. Therefore, future non-smoker, if at all possible do read the Session prior to going to sleep for seven nights or whenever you decide to have a nap.

Cigarettes just kind of subconsciously light themselves, sometimes you may have four burning cigarettes at the same time in an ashtray, unaware of what you are doing by habit.

If cigarettes and a lighter are convenient, without even thinking about it, you could light up. The instinctive for nicotine is so overpowering, you probably would do just that.

To combat this well cultivated murderous urge, you are going to preset your inner brain's imagination, with a physical assertive shock wave.

Two distinct physical acts should be followed, upon completion of the Self-Hypnotic Session. If at this time you continue to smoke prepare to sacrifice your supply of cigarettes. If you have already quit but struggling, have an unwanted newspaper or pieces of paper available, you will be pretending during the Self-Hypnotic Session that these pages are cigarettes.

These actions will confirm your inner brain's ultimate desire to successfully abandon the habit of smoking tobacco or any other tobacco product.

You will have an empty garbage bag with you, when you enter the Self-Hypnotic Session Anti-Smoking Cigarettes or any other tobacco product.

Upon completion of the Self-Hypnotic Session, you shall hand shred any remaining cigarettes you possess (or the unwanted pages) in the opened garbage bag. The cigarette shreds, the cigarette package, your personal lighter or matches along with any other cigarettes in your vicinity must be shredded into the garbage bag.

If you have an uncooperative mate, demand that any cigarettes he or she may have be well hidden and absolutely unattainable.

Personally you shall take the nicotine filled garbage bag, which you have double knotted outside to the nearest outside garbage container. The moment the bag drops into the garbage can, speak out loud:

"At last, I am free. I am no longer a slave of nicotine."

After the 14th days of non-smoking, you will want to write me a letter of thanks.

Now prepare for what may be the hardest thing you ever did. The hardest, of course is never easy. It is at the furthest branch to reach on any fruit tree where the best reward awaits.

Self-Hypnotic Session #8
Anti-Cigarette Smoking/Tobacco

Dear reader: congratulations in your decision to take this opportunity to become a healthy, energetic anti-smoker, one day at a time.

This message is designed especially for you. This is your opportunity to become a non-ex or anti-smoker, a change that will gradually come to assist you during the next week and at that time you will be pleased that the poisonous addiction of smoking tobacco is fading away.

You will begin to realize and believe that becoming an ex-smoker is a wonderful experience. You may want to see yourself as a smoker, who simple does not smoke anymore, or an ex-smoker, or an anti-smoker.

Simple use whatever words or self-image works for you.

Follow the instructions, repeat the positive vision and suggestions message contained in this Session for seven consecutive days.

Here is an important key every time you repeat this text, you will love the feeling that this free newness shall give you, you shall be completely reinforced to achieve being an ex-smoker. These are your code words, during the seven days and nights when the mighty forces of the poison nicotine will come attacking unceasingly, pounding into your brain for just one unwanted, forbidden fix, one or two puffs. You shall press the thumbnail into the third finger of your previous smoking hand; this is an acupuncture nerve spot point.

You will be touching a nerve ending. While doing so, take several deep breaths think or say to yourself: "I am free of nicotine, at last."

Practice is needed. In a few seconds, close your eyes and repeat this statement to yourself. Memorize the words: "I am free of nicotine, at last." Repeat this commitment statement three times with your eyes closed before returning to the text.

"I am free of nicotine, at last."
"I am free of nicotine, at last."
"I am free of nicotine, at last."

You shall develop a new habit that is to live one day at a time, as a healthy energetic non-smoker, ex-smoker or anti-smoker.

You are going to tap into the tremendous imaginary powers of your inner brain for assistance during this time of struggle. Powerful inner brain positive visions that will guide you 24 hours a day.

Researchers tell us the average person uses less than 7% of their mental potential. Well, you are going to surpass that percentage and unleash the ultimate power of self-help that exists within your imagination.

Just believe in the enormous capacity of your inner brain's imagination to build a great calming foundation on which you shall become an ex-smoker and grow stronger in that conviction, and healthier every day.

Since you realize smoking is extremely dangerous to your body and your loved ones there is no time to lose. So let's get to it. Go into self-hypnotic sleep now.

Lie down, or sit down if you must and simply "relax." "Loosen and float downward." Enjoy.

Incidentally while you are experiencing this Session, you will be in complete control at all times, simply sit up or stand up and you shall be wide-awake.

You are simply going to guide yourself to a wonderful sense of inner calmness. A feeling that you shall relish so much that you shall want to do it over and over again. By doing so the ideas and positive visions become part of your natural thinking and feelings.

You shall let your subconscious mind, your inner brain drift into a wonderful sense of relaxation while it accepts proper effective positive suggestions.

Let yourself be comfortable.

Take a normal deep breath in through your nose. Then exhale slowly through your mouth.

Be limp and loose all over, as you drift, dream and float into self-hypnotic sleep, which is very good for you.

Fifteen minutes of self-hypnotic relaxation is equal to 2 or 3 hours of a regular sleep. That is why you shall enjoy it so much.

Take another deep breath. Breathe out slowly.

As you breathe in again notice a beginning inner calmness and relaxation. When you breathe out, think of expiring out any stress, apprehension, tension, or irritation. Let's clear your mind of stress, uncoil any irritations, becoming even calmer.

Take one more deep breath all the way in. As you exhaust, search for any remaining stresses as you exhaust.

Now breathe normally and relax.

Try this breathing exercise technique, visualize and imagine that you have a large deflated balloon in you stomach. Each time you breathe in imagine and visualize that the incoming air inflates the balloon to its full size. Then while exhaling slowly, imagine that the balloon loses all the air and becomes once more deflated. On the next inhale blow a heavy breath of air into the balloon. Imagine blowing the balloon up to its greatest size possible. Feel the inhaled air expand on both sides of your stomach. Now send the air to the very bottom pit of your stomach. Before exhaling send the air upwards blowing the balloon so high you imagine and feel your stomach rising to the ceiling before exhaling. Practice this exercise three times before proceeding with the text.

Allow yourself the use of your magnificent imagination.

Starting with the top of your head, imagine that the top of scalp is now relaxing. Feel the sensation of calmness and relaxation while the feeling flow down through your forehead, your eyelids down through your facial muscles, let these tissues and muscles become calm and relaxed.

The deeper you go into this beautiful relaxation the more calm you become.

Imagine, feel and visualize refreshment of facial relaxation flowing into your lips, your jaws, your tongue and your throat. You want to make sure your jaws are not clenched together but separated. Part your upper and lower teeth; this way there is no room where stress can hide. You may find it more comfortable to allow your lower jaw to hand open a bit loose and limp.

Feel peaceful and calm flow down through your neck muscles. Feel it branch out in through your shoulders down into your back muscles, relax all those muscles.

Imagine you can feel that wonderful sensation just trickling down through your spinal column. Right down to the small of your back. It feels wonderful to relax like this.

And it's so easy, once you know how; you can do it easily and effortlessly.

The relaxing calmness flows down into your arms, your forearms, your wrist, and both hands, to your very tips of each of your fingers.

Some of the sensations that you are developing along the way will help you to relax deeper, soon you shall recognize them.

For example, from time to time you will get vibrating tingling sensations, especially in your fingertips or toes.

Your arms may feel heavier than the rest of your body.

Your legs may feel as heavy as lead but it is a pleasant sensation.

Your eyelids may be fluttering and your eyes may be moving back and forth as they do when you dream.

It is called REM sleep, rapid eye movement.

While becoming drowsy you may find that you are swallowing a bit more often that is fine too.

There are many more sensations to be recognized. Sensations that guide into a deeper self-hypnotic sleep.

Feel the restfulness flow through your lungs; notice that breathing becomes easy, placid and rhythmic. Your heart is automatically slowing down to take a little rest. Your heart has worked so hard. A slowed down rest period will do your heart no harm whatsoever.

Stomach muscles are calming. Abdominal muscles calming and relaxing.

Now the relaxation, followed by a sense of tranquilly goes into through your hip then moves down deep into the thighs.

The blanket of relaxation and calmness pass over your kneecaps, down through your shines. Stillness settles into the calves of your legs, now in through your ankles. Your feet feel the sensation all the way down through into the very tips of your toes.

Your entire body is beautifully relaxed, calm, peaceful, loose as a goose and limp. Kind of like a raggedly Ann doll, and it feels so good.

There is a technique for going deeper into self-hypnotic sleep.

All you have to do is visualize a beautiful scene where you would like to rest. A scene of your choosing. It can be if you like, an ocean scene with waves rolling in along the shore with a warm sun in a beautiful sky. You can just about feel the warmth of the sun on your face, feel the warmth of the sun on your body. If you prefer the mountains, covered with tall green trees, bushes, grass and flowers. You may wish to visualize a lake or a pond, a stream, or a waterfall. Add the moon, perhaps a gentle rainfall or a light snow shower.

You select the scene. Take all the time needed to select the location you prefer.

Feel yourself relaxing in your chosen location, see yourself in this private spot.

Absorb the scene, the peaceful surroundings.

While experiencing this location, let's count from 10 to 1, and the lower you go the locale becomes clearer.

10...Getting drowsier.

9...You do not want to poison your body by smoking cigarettes or other tobacco products.

8...Down deeper into self-hypnotic sleep. Your surroundings are relaxing and calming. This is your private oasis of inner peace.

7...Relax, uncoil, become loose and limp, become calm all over.

6...Go into self-hypnotic sleep now.

5...Down you go.

4...So drowsy and tired, limp and heavy.

3...You are proud that you have made a commitment to stop smoking cigarettes. One day at a time.

2... Your eyes are becoming very drowsy.
Down to a beautiful state of relaxation, right now on the count of 1.
Go into hypnotic sleep now. You are relaxing in the Alpha-Theta level of your mind.
You feel wonderful.
Deeper self-hypnotic sleep develops with every word of the text, with every breath you take.
Allow your imagination to be receptive to powerful, positive visions and suggestions that shall guide you in a most enjoyable and automatic way. Believe right now from this moment on that you have become a calm, healthy non-smoker.
Believe that your body does not want the thousands of poison chemicals in your bloodstream any longer.
Believe that you are going to be free of the dozes of poisonous nicotine in every cigarette, an insecticide, arsenic, cyanide, and tar with thousands of chemicals. The cigarettes manufacturers have blended in a cigarette to addict the young and unsuspecting.
Believe that you shall be free.
In a moment you will let your eyelids close and when you do visualize yourself wherever you purchase your cigarettes or any other tobacco. Imagine your usual routine, waiting perhaps in a line to select your favorite brand of poison. The sales clerk passes your selected brand of cigarettes. You take out the money or a plastic card to pay for the carton or package of poison with your hard-earned cash. Now let's imagine taking a giant mental leap, imagine yourself doing this for one entire year. Imagine yourself purchasing cigarettes during the winter, summer, spring and fall. Whenever, in the early morning, evening or middle of the night. The time has come to close your drowsy eyes. Close your eyes tightly and visualize making these multiple purchases of poison to put into your body.
Take as long as you wish before your eyes to return to the text.
You have made a commitment to stop smoking. You respect and take care of your body, you want to breathe clear, clean fresh air. You want to really taste the food you eat. You want your smoker's cough to vanish along with all the puking and phlegm pulling from lungs

straining to extract from the pit of your brown nicotine stained lungs. You want to breathe freely, not be compelled to live with asthma gasping for your every single breath of air. You no longer want to damage your body. You want to escape while this opportunity remains. You do not want people to say: you endured severe suffering and early death but you brought your death on by yourself. You may suffer and die merely because you could not live without another dirty, disgusting, filthy, expensive puff of a cigarette.

Smoking is expensive and is only going to get much more expensive. Recall your visualization of one year of daily purchasing your personal brand of poison. In a few seconds you will close your eyes again. Take this time to make a guess amount of how much money you would have spend for a year's supply for these packages of poison. Forget the pennies, round the price off to the highest dollar amount. Remember you wasted gasoline driving a car, or wore out shoe heels walking to purchase an ever ready supply of poison.

Allow your sub-conscious mind all the time it needs to figure about how much you spend in one year on cigarettes. After you determine a guess amount spent in a year, give some consideration on what worthwhile purpose you will now spend this hard earned cash. A vacation, a new car, a computer, a child whatever you feel that you want to do with this pile of hard earned cash. Now close your eyes for this prolonged deliberation. Return to the text when you have some idea of how you are going to spend this future saved pile of hard earned cash.

Your nerves can take quitting puffing a cigarette cold turkey. You will make your nerves strong. You can have nerves of iron. You are calm, strong, relaxed and gradually becoming in absolute control of the smoking urges.

Before you could not live a day, an hour, without a cigarette or tobacco. Now you can and shall. Soon you will not even miss the pacifier you placed between the lips of your mouth.

Think about this disgusting addiction to nicotine you are diffusing right now in your conscious will power. Nicotine is truly a poison. About 40mg placed on the tongue will kill anyone in five minutes. There was a continuous smoking contest in China, sponsored by a cigarette manufacturer. One contestant smoked 50 cigarettes in a row and barely lived to tell about it. The winner smoked 100 then fell dead from nicotine poisoning. Nicotine first stimulates, then depresses and paralyzes the cells of the brain, spinal cord, and nervous system. The skeletal muscles and the diaphragm (breathing muscles) are momentarily paralyzed. Respiratory dysfunction and severe lung congestion becomes steadily worsened. Most hospitals are now 100% smoke-free, as they should be, but stand outside and observe another characteristic of nicotine addiction. Patients gather in the parking lot or the garage for a desperately needed puff of cigarette smoke. Some pull chemotherapy IV pumps behind them. You often observe a classic picture of a smoke addict, someone smoking through a hole in their throat called a "stoma." An individual, who continues to smoke despite having nicotine caused, cancerous larynx removed. This is the ultimate power of nicotine addiction.

The addiction you pledge to absolutely quit now.

Perhaps during stressful or fun times you often smoked one cigarette after another. You were free to kill yourself. You were committing suicide, a slow, ever growing habit of death. Yul Brynner, a famous actor, starred in the play and movie, *The King and I*. When Yule developed lung cancer, he paid for television commercials telling the world in his self-destructed body, "Quit, quit smoking. Cigarettes are poisoning you. You are going to end up dead like me." Mr. Brynner was a courageous man who desired to help human beings from killing themselves needlessly from smoking cigarettes. You now desire to follow Mr. Brynner's lifesaving advice. You must not die because of cigarettes. You can endure the cravings of the nicotine blues and fight the urge for one more coffin nail. You know you must. You do not wish to crave poison, insecticide, arsenic and cyanide.

So now you shall act, think and feel like a non-smoker and love every minute of life.

You have made this commitment to yourself and perhaps others.

You will now reinforce this commitment.

Always recall your code words during times of heavy nicotine craving. Think about the hand you used to smoke with. The hand you used to lift the cigarette to your lips with. Just leave those fingers

wherever they are. Pinch your thumbnail and third finger, an acupuncture point of your previous smoke holding hand, take several deep breaths saying to yourself: "I am free of nicotine, at last. I am free of nicotine, at last. I am free of nicotine, at last."
And you are.
If you wish add this statement: "I shall respect my body and no longer shall abuse it."
Repeat these words with conviction in this fashion three or more times. Except this time close your eyes tightly and repeat to yourself, memorize these words, engrave both sentences into the inner brain. Dwell on this pledge statement until you feel prepared to continue with the text.
"I am free of nicotine, at last. I shall respect and protect my body and no longer abuse it."
"I am free of nicotine, at last. I shall respect and protect my body and no longer abuse it."
"I am free of nicotine, at last. I shall respect and protect my body and no longer abuse it."
BELIEVE IN YOUR COMMITMENT TO STOP SMOKING ONE DAY AT A TIME.
Make this commitment on a daily basis until the urge to relapse completely vanishes.
Make it the last thing you think about as you fall to sleep and the first thought as you awaken each day.
Think of the beautiful, relaxing and peaceful thoughts and capture the feelings of those images of you with no cigarette or tobacco in your hand. That hand now has increased possibilities of a longer survival. The hand will be able hold your grandchildren, your great-grandchildren just because of your firm commitment to quit poisoning your body by smoking yourself to death.
You shall find that you feel very good about your cold turkey, stop smoking cigarette commitment. You feel good about yourself.
You feel good about everyone you come in contact with, because you realize your goal of never smoking again is so much easier to maintain when you feel good about yourself.

Take a positive, expectant attitude because a positive optimistic attitude is so important.

Think of the wonderful opportunity that you can now have to provide a smoke free atmosphere for your home, for you, your loved ones, your car, your workplace or wherever.

Whatever your motivation may be to be a non-smoker, whether it be health, children, grandchildren or other loved ones. Perhaps a doctor's warning. You have selected a worthy lifesaving goal.

You will become a successful non-smoker. You shall display a calm, peaceful, exulted confident example for other people. When you see others smoking even at your own table, you will see that as another opportunity to reinforce your attitude of being a happy and energetic non-smoker, as you watch them smoke. And you may feel somewhat awkward, different as you visualize and smell the terrible, disgusting taste of a cigarette. The stinking burning sensations and the death wishing poisons that go into the human body, spreading poisons into the air that others that you love, once were forced to breathe.

You no longer desire that scene.

You no longer wish to pollute your body and the environment that those you love live in.

Forget about cigarettes, a puff of poisonous nicotine is no longer a desire. You want no part of that scene and you have no desire to ever put a cigarette between you lips again.

Instead you sincerely wish to set the example as the person who feels very good about your choice of not smoking any longer. You love being free of nicotine poison. Your nerves will become stronger that steel, your willpower will eventually be strengthened. Develop and maintain a positive, happy expectant attitude. Personal happiness is often not a reality it is an attitude. Continuous happiness is the mental attitude of an optimist.

Think about all the healthy, wonderful reasons to remain a non-smoker and remember nothing can stand in your way with the right attitude, backed by persistence and determination.

By your choice you have become a healthy, ex-smoker. There is never going to be any acceptable reason to put a cigarette between your lips again or any other kind of smoking materials.

By your choice you are going to start respecting and protecting your body.

Smoking is now a thing of the past let the past die, it no longer exists. Cigarette smoking has gone down memory lane. You are pleased, happy, and glad to see the last of the poison nicotine. The nicotine urge to smoke cigarettes will soon vanish.

You do not want all that brown nicotine coating every organ in your body, your teeth and fingertips. You shall no longer have your fingers, teeth and body organs covered with sickening brown poisonous nicotine.

You shall forever see smoking as a disgusting, distasteful and undesirable toxin that will never again harm your body and loved ones. Your clothes, home curtains will have the smell of newness not nicotine.

At last you are free of nicotine. You no longer will abuse your body.

You will soon be breathing and living in clean fresh air.

Every breath you now take will be loaded with life-giving oxygen. Pure breaths of oxygen that is cleansing every muscle, every tissue, every cell of your body.

You shall love this great feeling.

You shall feel better and better every day.

Perhaps, better than you have felt in years.

And you shall help your body to accept these wonderful changes by doing things a little bit differently for the next 7 days.

Limit your coffee and alcohol, which may be reminders of the smoker, you no longer desire to be.

You shall drink lots of water and chew on natural sunflower seeds, eat ice cream which abates relapse cigarette cravings.

Sit in a different chair, when you have a meal or any kind of a drink.

Use a different hand to lift your cup.

Drink your coffee at a different time if you must have coffee, try drinking water or tea as a substitute.

In other words try to change your daily routine, you will find alternate routines enjoyable and a fun to do.

You shall become aware of how you are treating your body and that it is important. Clean out as much of that poison nicotine out of your body as you can by drinking lots of water. The water will cleanse your bloodstream of nicotine, and is very refreshing and helps control your weight. Water is good for your body. You will never put anything into your body that is harmful. You shall always make the right choice. There is no reason to gain any weight unless you want to, by drinking 8-10 glasses of water a day, you can keep your weight under control. You will develop an image of how much you want to weight and what you want to look like. Make it an ideal image and plant that deep into the inner brain. Becoming a non-smoker has nothing to do with body weight.

You are in total control of your mind and body in all aspects of life. Now you have the power to shut out the memory of cigarette smoking these memories will become past ancient history. You were a smoker in the past and now you are a non-smoker and getting healthier every day. The so-called pleasures of smoking are only disguises that were detrimental to your mind, body, and pocketbook. And now, it is over so you shall forget about smoking one day at a time.

You will rise above the smoking habit because you realize that you are far more important than any cigarette. You shall remember this and act that way.

No person, no situation or circumstances can cause you to smoke again. You have the power to say no and make the right decision. Day by day you will feel more and more pleased about your achievement.

Nevertheless, you must address the worst outcome if you do not survive the seven-day program without a few puffs of a cigarette. During this time using any treatment, to maintain your commitment to stop smoking may be the hardest thing you ever have to do. Imagine and visualize your physician saying to you and your family, "You have terminal cancer caused by smoking cigarettes." Most of those who fail to keep their non-smoking commitment eventually are told this bitter news, often at a very early age. To reinforce your pledge to quit smoking the germ of nicotine. Imagine what will be happening to your lungs and body if you fail to keep the non-smoking pledge.

Your lungs and insides may be nicotine brown and sooty from years of previous smoking, if you neglect your pledge, with each puff of a cigarette the film of brown soot shall become thicker, spreading to the bronchial tubes then the larynx. This would be the ultimate of personal stupidity.

On the positive side, you are determined to not break your pledge to quit cigarettes cold turkey, visualize your lungs and insides becoming pink, healthy and slowly becoming perfect, the only way you want your organs and insides to be.

Now using your ex-smoker's hand, press your thumbnail into your third finger together and believe in the words as you repeat: "I am free of nicotine, at last. I am free of nicotine, at last. I am free of nicotine, at last."

Imagine the unbelievable freedom you are going to have.

This mental motivation is becoming realized. The image of you being a non-smoker will materialize.

Imagine your special relaxing place you chose with fresh air, no toxic smoke.

Picture your loved ones there with you. You have won, perhaps the hardest battle of your life.

Now imagine and visualize, your body responding to being an ex-smoker. You feels so good.

"You are free of nicotine at last."

You love being a non-smoker. Each day upon awakening make certain to take a nice deep breath of clean fresh air and think to yourself: "I am an ex-smoker and I love it."

You feel great. You love the freedom.

You now have the freedom to respect and protect your body. If the tempting thought of smoking a few puffs of a cigarette ever crosses your mind cancel it out immediately.

Remember the birds, keep active, move, laugh enjoy and keep busy and active during the next seven days.

Remember that every day that goes by as a non-smoker you are getting healthier and much stronger mentally. You will become more confident as the thought of smoking a few puffs of a cigarette gets weaker and weaker until eventually the desire completely disappears.

Soon, you will be living in a world of non-smokers. You will not be alone. You have joined millions of people who are ex-smokers and are living healthier, happier lives in a smoke free environment. The acrid smell of stale tobacco will no longer coat your skin when you perspire, your clothes will no longer reek with the dank smell of nicotine.

You will become an ex-smoker. Believe it. Believe in yourself.

Embrace the feeling.

Love the feeling.

Smoking a cigarette is no longer a friend or companion.

It has been a silent killer.

You have taken this wonderful opportunity to stop smoking cigarettes or any other tobacco products. Soon the thought of smoking will be forever forgotten. Get on with a brand-new healthy lifestyle.

So now act, talk, walk like a happy healthy non-smoker and remember that you are far more important than any cigarette.

Keep acting that way.

"I am free of nicotine, at last."

Enjoy the freedom. You never relished being a slave to the obnoxious habit of smoking nicotine.

In your everyday life you may find people who will try to discourage you. Someone you care for just might say "Don't be stupid, have a cigarette."

Pay no attention to what a convict of cigarettes might say. Do accept suggestions from people who may encourage you during the rough early cold turkey days.

When you see someone outside huddling in a dry spot, trying to avoid the rain while lighting a cigarette—feel pity for these addicted individuals. Remind yourself, once that was I. I was so stupid, but those days of being a slave to nicotine are now ancient history.

Most important always be true to your commitment to stop poisoning yourself. Your deepest desire is to remain a happy, healthy energetic non-smoker. Feeling so good about yourself, because when you feel good about you, you can do anything. Believe it.

No longer will your heart beat faster constricting the glands while

GO BEYOND STRESS

straining to reject the toxins you puffed into your body when you smoked.

Every time that you dwell on this text, you will love the feelings and you will be completely reinforced when your thumbnail presses into the top of the third finger, especially when you say or think: "I am free of nicotine, at last."

In a moment, on the count from 1-5, you will become fully awake. You will be sleeping better, feel better and looking better. You are now in a New World, a world of non-smokers. Do not ever let that go. It is like an insurance policy on your life and you purchased it the hard way, the only way—cold turkey.

When you awaken each day at the proper time, you will feel wonder relaxed, enjoying your unclogged healthy pink lungs. You will be pleased filled with fresh energetic strength of healthy thinking.

You shall love the feelings. Your lungs will appreciate the pure life-giving oxygen you will soon provide.

One...Two...Three...Four...Five...Awaken. Wide awake and feeling fantastic.

Now you must fulfill the necessary physical requirement to enforce your commitment to quit smoking puffs of a cigarette cold turkey. Gather up all the cigarettes or other smoking materials in your personal possession.

Open the empty garbage bag toss in your lighter or matches. Now, into the garbage bag, shred and ripe into little pieces the complete supply of any remaining available cigarettes or smoking product. If no cigarettes are available then rip up and throw in some pieces of an unwanted newspaper or paper, pretend and imagine the pieces of paper are cigarettes. Tie the garbage bag. Now physically stand, get dressed if necessary and carry this bag of toxic waist (or pretended nicotine) to the nearest outside garbage container. As the bag drops into the garbage can, press your smoker's hand, thumbnail and third finger together, while saying: "I am free of nicotine at last. I am free of nicotine at last. I am free of nicotine at last."

You have made a pledge, keep it never let yourself down.

Reconditioning Program for Session #9
Problem Solving & Creativity

Solving problems, increasing your creative imagination and achieving dreams can become a realistic goal.
Are you having trouble making up your mind about everyday or major life matters?
Encountering challenges or failures that always defy a solution?
"Psycho-Cybernetics" is the principals of Cybernetics applied to the inner brain's imagination. The word "Cybernetics" is derived from a Greek word that means the "Steersman."
A computerized, subconscious function, which can be used to automatically, to solve conundrums (unknown) or major or pesky problems and open the inner brain to expanded creative imagination to resolving situations or invent something new. Thomas Edison, one of history's greatest inventors is reputed to have used and been the first to document Psycho-Cybernetics. Mr. Bell who invented the telephone and a devise to stabilize the world's first fleet of airplanes also utilized this Sessions program.

Self-Hypnotic Session #9 shall provide you with needed answers, provide new ideas and inspirations. A guidance system to automatically steer your mind onto the correct blueprint directions to achieve goals and make proper responses to events. Cybernetics utilizes your imagination with links to the memory system. Psycho-Cybernetics is a highly complex, servo-mechanism-goal striving mechanism. The inner brain's self-propelling guidance system can achieve miracles. This magnificent resource will supply creative solutions for any situation. You were created with a beautiful inner brain creative imagination with the capacity to form and extract images of artistic thoughts that are not present to the senses. The golden key to successful problem solving device dwells within your inner brain's imagination.

The inner brain can combine old ideas with new thoughts to both your inner and conscious brain.

Psycho-Cybernetics is a self-generated goal seeking mechanism which steers its way to a target or goal by use of feedback data utilizing the stored information in the brain's memory bank.

The steering devise automatically corrects any pursuit for an acceptable solution course and has the capability to incubate over a creative challenge or problem when necessary.

The target, a goal or any number of unsolved puzzles, a solution from the inner brain shall materialized. The inner brain's silent work is to reach the objective, then accomplish the assignment. First the blueprint is supplied by the imagination to meet the target with a deadline. When the final solution arrives it is immediately relayed into your conscious thoughts at any place or time. Where the answer is unknown, the steering mechanism of the inner brain will guide the assignment to its completion.

The inner brain along with your nervous systems operates in conjunction with the conscious mind to achieve the assignment.

During a modern sea battle, a self-guided torpedo or an interjection missile relies on the same principal. The target or goal is a known enemy ship or airplane. The object is to reach it.

A propulsion system propels the torpedo in the general direction of a target. A mechanical sensor keep the automatic mechanism informed when it is on the correct course (positive feedback) doing the correct thing and just keeps on doing—what the assigned task.

When negative feedback informs the mechanism that the object is off beam, too far to the right, the corrective mechanism automatically causes the rudder to move in that direction to steer the fired missile back to the left onto an accurate course. If the missile overcorrects and heads too far to the left the mistake is made know through negative feedback and the corrective devise moves the rudder so it will steer the fired missile once again onto the correct path.

The inner brain's Psycho-Cybernetics is a computerized, changeable program that ignores positive feedback. Positive confirmation of success is already known.

The torpedo accomplishes its goal by proceeding forward, making errors, and continually correcting them. Utilizing a series of zigzags it literally corrects it self to reach the target. Your inner brain is wired with similar capabilities of automatic mechanism. It remembers its success, forgets its failures. The system repeats the continuous successful action without any further conscious thought. Achievement becomes an understood, expected completion.

Successful utilization of Psycho-Cybernetics began when you were an infant. You took time to successful move your arm, your fingers to reach for a rattle. When a toddler, you began exploring your entire body. You began to crawl before learning to walk. The first time you tried to stand up and walk, you fell down. These are your earliest experiences of Psycho-Cybernetics accomplishments that soon developed into the mind and body applying your inner brain's growing memory bank into a skillfully performed mechanical habit.

The Psycho-Cybernetics guidance system develops the best course of action from negative feedback data. The inner brain acknowledges errors, which is equivalent to criticism in order to amend and stay on course. The goal-striving servomechanism is far more magnificently designed than any guided missile or computer program conceived by man.

Any goal achievement can be a tough job. Once creativity has created a goal, there is absolutely no substitute for self-motivation. Nothing fortifies an individual as when he must and shall face a painful potential loss in a chosen struggle and does mental combat spite losing odds. No successful route is ever easy. The conscious mind observes and is often deceived by false concepts, values and beliefs. The will power must become a guard to the entrance of the inner brain, protecting and policing the access route to the inner brain. The willpower of the conscious mind screens all incoming data and allows the inner brain to accept only that which is perceived as truth, even though faulty. Even the best-prepared goals entailing great creativity can suddenly turn against you. This Session upholsters the inner brain's ability to perform mental combat when the road to achievement turns rough and hard. Thomas Edison had to create over 500 electric bulbs before his imagination discovered the missing element to make it glow long and brightly.

The word "crisis" comes from a Greek word that means—decisiveness or point of decision. A crisis is a fork in the road. Every crisis situation is two pronged. One fork holds a promise of a better condition, the other a worse condition.

The proper blueprint directions to make a choice in a crisis by using inductive reasoning. The inner brain lacks a will of its own—it is purely a calculating instrument and a computer bank memory of every moment you ever lived.

Henry J. Kaiser, a successful automobile manufacturer and major builder of ships during World War 2, stated: "I imagined each future project intensely with my imagination before anything was begun."

The creative, imaginative, inner brain loves a challenging idea, especially a work problem. Other problems, be it family, financial or whatever outside of your work are often accompanied with anguish and perhaps over stressfulness. Work problems are a pure challenge. Work problems normally contain no heavy emotional attachment. Solving a work problem is often the only place where you can become king of the jungle. A non-emotional attached work problem requires the unhindered creative, imaginary juices to flow. There are many ways to amplify any work inspirations: listening to enjoyable, stimulating back ground music lights up your concentration while relaxing your senses.

Taking a walk anywhere, perhaps only to the wash room, viewing each different scene actually stimulates the inner brain and assists keeping the creative spark alive. To retain creative imagination alive in your inner brain, think merriment, positive thoughts—no fresh idea realistic or not should be "scoffed at." Never allow your conscious brain to make the judgement for any ridiculous creative ideas, merely pass these ideas on to your inner brain.

Slow and belated judgements are sometimes the best judgements.

Allow each of the bubble of ideas to enter into your inner brain then be forgotten. To "dump" a creative imagination "slump" it is best you mentally "walk away." Forget the problem of whatever; detach the inner brain from further concentration with a diversion of thought and effort on to another activity or subject. Detaching completely from the goal allows the inner brain time to ponder a solution.

An original idea must be allowed time to incubate. Rather than chasing after the solution, permit your inner brain to be the creative sleuth to seek a compelling angle to any challenging problem. This unconscious internal mental operation will continue, without your awareness. Imagine further ideas, ideas that are out of the ordinary, ideas that appear ridiculous to your conscious mind. Allow your conscious mind to indulge in fantasies, unconventional, humorous ideas. The gathering of creative ideas stimulates piggybacking and adaptation. This is a vital part of unconscious internal problem solving process a continuous creative imaginative thinking. You may have noticed a "pool player" practicing in their head, checking out several or more angle approaches to the ball, before the stick finally strikes the billiard ball. Enjoy any creative thinking that comes your way—just for the pleasure of the contemplation. You will get a kick from these creative juices, a bigger kick that you get from champagne.

The inner brain can be trained to utilize the "capability of imaginative suggestion" when responding to any unforeseen or implemented problem.

Birds have a success instinct which guide them, where and how to build their nests, migration routes that often cover thousands of miles of endless flying while successfully coping with the prevailing environment. Relatively few wild animals like birds or snakes ever die of starvation. An animal's success or survival instincts are pre-set psycho-cybernetic genetic instructions. Animals like humans share chief objectives: self-preservation, comfort and procreation. You have a survival/success instinct, much more marvelous and much more complex than that of any animal.

Your inner brain's imagination mechanism is not only limited to built-in instincts, you can select your own goals—you have a creative imagination. You are much more than a mere creature, you are a creator.

Napoleon stated: "Imagination rules the world." He certainly tried.

This Self-Hypnotic Session shall guide you to select your "possibility" goals. You create the goal with thoughts of what is desired in terms of an end result. Your inner brain, the most powerful computer on the world commences the calculations and waits to be requested to create a plan of action. A plan of action that shall accumulate the best available happening to achieve what is mentally desired. How do you operate the servomechanism? Triggering it into action, you must allow your self-acting, self-thinking inner brain mechanism to completely take over to create the solution to a conundrum. No longer search in the dark for solutions when you apply the inner brain psycho-cybernetics applications.

Applications that permit your imaginative, your creative inner brain to have access to stored information in a potential, universal mind, the superconscious. You have been engineered for success. You have access to a power even greater than your can imagine, the never fully explored superconscious within the inner brain. You will no longer use hard, iron-powered conscious effort while being distressed by all the multitude of things that are likely to go wrong.

You very simply learn how to relax and allow the psycho-cybernetics endowment take command. The conscious mind can be tamed to give up a perhaps frantic search for a solution and avoid conscious mental striving.

Imagine the situation you really want to resolve, consciously review the pertinent factors, and then pass along this data to the creative inner brain mechanism to take over. Permit this hidden source to work out the best way to achieve a solution.

Most often the solutions your request using the Psycho-Cybernetics application will come at any time, perhaps in the middle of a sound sleep you will be awakened—with your conscious mind containing the solution you sought.

There can be no real satisfaction or happiness in life without obstacles to conquer problems to solve and goals to achieve. Within you right now is a power to achieve anything you never dreamed possible. This power becomes available to you just as soon as you believe you have it. There are many magical switches inside your inner brain that can forcefully transform the worst to the best or the best to the worst. Your ultimate goal to discover and master these mechanisms.

"A wise man will be the master of his mind. A fool will be its slave."
—Publilius Syrus (1st century BC)

Self-Hypnotic Session #9
Problem Solving & Creativity

Dear reader, please get nice and comfortable and let yourself relax. Just close your eyes for a bit and think, "Go into self-hypnotic sleep now."

Allow your breathing in and out to be a steady sort of rhythmic without forcing it. This is the normal way you should always breath. However to continue with the breathing exercises: breathe in, do so to a count of four. When you exhale also do the blowing out to a count of four. Without putting effort into it. Practice this expanded breathing exercise on your own several times. Just let your breathing be nice and steady.

Continue breathing in these splits of four counts and as you do so imagine that the four counts of oxygen are travelling in a sealed square box. On your next breathe in imagine pulling the box of sealed oxygen down under your feet. Then imagine pulling the box of sealed air up over the top of your head. Before exhaling, pull the box down to your mouth. Imagine breathing the boxed air out of your mouth. This is called the boxed air exercise, give this expanding exercise a few tries.

As you are breathing steady, deeper in this manner just decide now that you are going to let yourself go completely. Direct all that inhaled oxygen into your lower back and spine; simply send it down into this part of your body. Practice this on your own for several times. Sense that your lower back and spine are beginning to sink downward. More down with each inhale with each exhale to the count of four. Feel your spine and lower back uncoiling and unwinding.

Allow your conscious mind to wander as you "go into self-hypnotic sleep now."

GO BEYOND STRESS

The mind is getting very drowsy. This tiredness will cause the positive visions to be carried out by the work of the subconscious, so leave it up to your inner mind. Be restful. Let your mind be comfortably calming down into a tranquil, drowsy relaxation. Dismiss any worry, distress, and uncertainty from your mind. Be loose as a goose. You feel tired and you want to go into hypnotic sleep now.

The eyelids feel heavy, very heavy. The head is heavy too. Any is tension flowing away, down through your lower back and spine and out onto the floor.

Stress and anxiety is leaving you literally melting out of your body. Disregard all outside sounds and interruptions. You just go into deep self-hypnotic sleep now. You are so tired that your body is resting more and even more peacefully and comfortably. Your head is feeling drowsy too, freed from all tension. Each muscle on your face are relaxing and calming. Your tongue, chin, neck, feel them tingling, restfully, comfortably as you go still deeper into self-hypnotic sleep now. Your shoulders are heavy with tiredness. You can feel the sensation that your shoulders are sinking down, heavily but so comfortably. You are drowsy, sleepy. Both arms are relaxing now. Feel as each shoulder begins to unhitch as both move down around your neck. Your wrists and hands are heavy drawing your arms down. Be comfortable, feel your arms tingling, tingling comfortably from your shoulders down into both hands right down to the end of each fingertip. You are sleepy. Your whole body is becoming heavy with self-hypnotic. Your chest and ribs are becoming heavy with calm restfulness. Your back is tired, feel numbness moving down your spine and into both legs. "Go into hypnotic sleep now." Your legs are feeling heavy, comfortably, numb from your hips down to your knees, a heavy comfortable sleep. Heavy relaxation continues moving down from the knees to the ankles to then into both feet. Both your legs are calmed and relaxed. Feel each toes tingling to the very tips.

As you breathe easily, you relax more. With every breath you take you sink lower into self-hypnotic sleep. In fact on the count from 10 down to 0, you will go way down and sink much deeper into self-hypnotic sleep.

Visualize, feel and believe that you are at the top of a long well lit stairwell. Just imagine that.

The stairwell contains securely safe comfortable steps and there is a sturdy handrail for you to hang onto as you descend down each step. There are ten steps. With each step you take down you good-naturedly inform the inner brain that you wish to go deep and deeper in to self-hypnotic sleep. As a matter of fact as you descend from step to step you descend 100 times deeper into self-hypnotic sleep. And as you do so you will allow every cell, every fiber in your body to go complete and safely into and enjoyable deep self-hypnotic sleep.

Now step off the 10th step, down to the 9th...into a deeper calmness.

8th step—descending slowly.

7th step—feeling even more drowsy.

6th step—so very drowsy.

5th step—you want to create ideas and solve numerous problems easily.

4th step—you want to achieve important goals.

3rd step—your inner brain will always be there to help you solve puzzles.

2nd step—beautiful self-hypnotic sleep.

1st step—so calm, so completely relaxed.

0—"Go into self-hypnotic sleep now."

Uncover any barriers into you limitless most intelligent imagination.

First you will get rid of the weeds before planting the seeds of new knowledge.

Imagine, visualize and believe that you are assembling all doubts that inhibit your creative skills to solve any problem by creative imagination.

Imagine that you are scooping any unresolved issues up and placing them in a garbage sack. As you tie the top two ends of sack together, the contents turn into a bundle of negative energy. But you are now ready to use this sack of bad energy in a productive and positive way.

You can use this energy sack to accomplish your goals, to create and invent solutions to achieve your dreams. Visualize and imagine that a flash of sparkling multi-colored lights magically transforms the sack. The sack emerges as a brilliant colorful beautiful rainbow. The glow of the rainbow is multi-colored. The rainbow fills the room and envelops your body. Imagine yourself surrounded in a spectrum of colorful irrefutable positive powerful energy. You begin to see many new directions, new ideas for problem solving and the creativity to think of new ideas.

You feel confident, sure of your talents and abilities, eager to set your new directions into motion. You will soon direct and control this new positive energy within your mind. You will use this energy to fuel and encourage brilliant creativity.

Now just pretend that you are walking down a busy street in any city or town. You are full of energy, intent on reaching your destination. You are resolute to quickly reach your destination. But you approach a crosswalk and the light changes from green to red. The traffic is heavy so you must wait for the green light.

Tell yourself the red stoplight is only temporary. Take this opportunity to catch your breath and relax. Take a few deep breaths to calm down while you patiently wait.

Take the time to notice the neighborhood around you. Across the street there is a park that's beautifully landscaped. Notice how cold the air outside is yet the day is still pleasant. See the rainbow of positive energy flowing around your entire body. Reflect on the goals that you hope to achieve. Visualize your hopes in the most positive way. Visualize seeking solutions with the new exciting energy source. The calmer you feel, the more enthusiastic and creative you become. Before you know it, the streetlight has changed to green. You are safe to walk across the road, the restrictions have been lifted, and the obstacles are gone. Continue walking down the street.

In a little while you will reach your destination, where some of your creative ideas and solutions have been waiting for you. You are in no rush whatsoever to arrive at your destination. Visualize reaching the destination. You are pulsating will a positive energy force. You feel confident and very self-assured. Imagine yourself entering the room or place where you usually work out solutions. This is your destination, this is your creative place, you feel excited, and your mind is brimming over with stamina. The imagination is active. Seat yourself in a chair while taking a few deep breaths. In a moment you are going to close your eyes. At that time allow explicit images of any unresolved problems or incomplete creative ideas to surface and appear. Whenever you cogitate on a problem or a goal, you shall feed and register all possible thoughts, negative or positive into your inner brain. Review whatever these conundrums are for as long as you need before you close your eyes. Keep both eyes closed for rest and contemplation for as long as you wish.

Reopen your eyes and no longer think or be even slightly absorbed by the conundrums you reviewed before closing your eyes. At this point completely detach yourself from any quest for solutions. Put a smile on your face, the inner brain is executing its psycho-cybernetics homework. The conscious mind will be informed of a solution at the proper place and time. Your conundrums are in a location in your mind where realistic ideas are clearer. A place where solutions flow endlessly and the correct direction are more obvious. The inner brain duty is to find the correct blueprint for success; perhaps it will ask the conscious mind numerous direct questions during this incubation period. The decided course of action will become obvious to your conscious mind in due time. Also, from now on, whenever you experience a creative block, just imagine it to be a red light. A stop sign that says you must take a pause, a signal to take a calming rest. Imagine the light changing from green to red, signaling you to stop and take a rest for a few moments. You can imagine your creative block to be anything that you choose. A red light that changes or a wall that you can easily push and watch crumble before you, any imagine is perfectly fine. The inner brain is available at any time to think yourself out of trials and difficulties. Worry over trials and difficulties are a misuse of the imagination.

Intuition is a sixth sense. Intuition visualizes the mind ahead in time to perceive or sense outside the range of our five senses: vision, hearing, smell, and taste, body sensations. Intuition opens the doors to the superconsciousness and unknown knowledge. Intuition assists emotionally and other ways to make a decision even when everyone else disagrees.

Your decision remains logical and unchangeable in your mind. An intuition thought comes like a thunder bold from the inner brain. Intuitions and coincidences, premonitions, nighttime dreams are related as a wink, a glimpse into the future. Always listen to the whisper of the inner brain's intuitions during the day. Never disregard a thunder bolt-empathic whisper of intuition, a sense of premonition as merely a stupid thought. By doing so, you just may miss the opportunity of a lifetime.

Creative effort drives the imagination into healthful pathways. The lack of creative effort is often at the bottom of mental unrest and nervous stress.

This is an idea spot for your freewheeling imagination to surface. The powers of the imagination grow by exercise. With old age the memory may wither but the imagination flourishes. Drift with your imagination to seek new directions, new inventions, fresh ideas, send your imagination flowing. This is something like daydreaming, but why not?

The inner springs of the personality, the sense of well-being, the hidden feelings, our state of mind surface at night when you are asleep and dreaming. Therefore you can easily call up your creative energy any time to dream, you inner brain has had almost one third of your life to practice, when you were asleep. Goals are dreams containing a priority deadline. Daydreaming is like hoping the future will work out the way we would like it. Often solitude is creativity's best friend.

If you set goals that are unrealistic, you will be discouraged. Goals are the baby steps to get you up the mountain of attainment. Choose to let your mind glide free, allow your mind to simply drift to attainable goals. Do not be too quick to reject any ideas or goals as too trivial. A fair idea put to use is better than a good idea kept on the polishing wheel. There are always plenty of people who will tell you your plan or idea will not work. Always postpone judgment, not suspend it but postpone the idea until the inner brain has piled up additional data. Have more than one goal, it is better to keep a number of balls in the air. Once one is achieved, you can immediately focus on the next one. You will miss the feeling of emptiness and never say, "Is that all there is?" Whenever you are creative expressive, like a distraction or a sedative, the dreaming takes your mind off such thoughts which could stress you out. Send forth your imagination in search of alternatives, pile them up. Visualize a new twist, modifications, a substitute, a different rearrangement, vice versa arrangements, additions, multiply or minify or magnify, borrow or adapt new systems to your objectives. Define your goals and ideas. Most ideas are step-by stepchildren of other ideas. Search for the spark plug ideas; see if you can make them click. Your goal-striving mechanism will be channeling these possibilities to their fullest use. To do otherwise the mind rusts like the parts on an old automobile that functions at minimum capacity. You do not want to live your life only achieving a series of meaningless maintenance goals, busy-ness without purpose. A stretch goal or idea, which may either add other ideas, or combine into a better idea two or more of the ones already, produced. Swim forward; do not merely thread water. Maintenance goals are needed but if your mind is not being stretched such activities have next to zero value. Do not permit such this tunnel vision; divert your attention to new-fashionable vision-driven ideas and possibilities which always exist. Any goal and its achievement can be stepping-stones to something larger. The process never ends until you die; you are on a much greater journey. As a lamp at night attracts the moths, so a clear, constructive goal attracts money, people, and knowledge. All humans will obey instructions from one who can produce some original realistic ideas.

You literally take solace with a timeless break from analyzing any problems that you may be focusing on too heavily. The tired parts of the mind can be rested and strengthened, not merely by sleeping, but by using other parts of the mind. Take this duration to visualize what the creative imagination comes up with. Close your eyes for better concentration on goals, new ideas, and creative tasks that interest you.

Do this before continuing with the text.

There is a code you should know when you wish the inner brain to activate psycho-cybernetics. Inhale two deep breaths; with two very slow exhales. Afterwards, use the thumbnail of either hand to press into the tip of your middle (third) finger. The tip of the middle finger is an acupressure point that calms the nerves. Hold this finger pressing activity while thinking or saying three times:
"Inner brain at your will, supply the solution."
"Inner brain at your will, supply the solution."
"Inner brain at your will, supply the solution."
    The inner brain will alert your conscious mind to recognize the right opportunities; people and circumstances needed to fulfill your goal. Releasing the inner brain provides the feeling that it is working for you. Picture the end result you desire. Know that you will get what you want. Visualize and believe that it is already yours, feel and imagine the pleasure, the excitement of being there. The limited conscious mind may conspire against the inner brain with preliminary intelligence. Your conscious mind may tell you what you desire cannot be achieved, that is impossible. Do not accept this as the gospel truth. You will get what you want when you believe as though you already have it. Positively acknowledge that what you want is on its way to you and you will be in a state of magnetic attraction, start behaving as if you know it will happen. The subconscious programming of goals and ideas into your imagination will always dominate the conscious mind. Mental loafing at the right time induces inspiration and intuition. Never allow early judgment to sap creative energy. Immediately address the inner brain with the code: "Inner brain at your will supply the solution," detach all concentration entirely from the conundrums you have reviewed and leave it to the inner brain to ask additional questions or supply the course of action needed.
    Always use the willpower of your conscious mind to completely detach from solution hunt. You can accomplish this by doing any other mental or physical work. Do a crossword puzzle, watch television; read a newspaper, whatever. This will compel your conscious will power to disown seeking an immediate solution. Your inner brain may come up with some questions to your conscious mind, answer the questions as

best you can. This will assist your imagination, preparing and using its missile like computerized mechanisms.

Allow the hidden force whatever spans of time that is needed to develop a proper solution. It may even take several days. However if you have a serious deadline to meet and it must be meet, inform the inner brain to speed up the process to meet this commitment. Your inner brain will eventually supply a solution, perhaps at a time that is even inconvenient to you.

Expect some mistakes to occur in any risk situation, no plan of action is absolutely foolproof. It is through mistakes that your awareness expands. Learning by making mistakes makes life exciting, passionate and full of challenges. Every decision you make and every action you initiate is based on your present level of awareness. When you may have to accept a harsh reality, you can improve the future with the utilization of the imagination's emotional creative intelligence. "We know what we are, but not what we may be," so said Shakespeare. The inner brain is the architect and contractor, which will build your life; your imagination supplies the blueprint.

During rough times, the inner brain will lead you on combatively with a self-motivation with next to no fault data screened and policed by the conscious willpower when a goal looks to be turning sour. When the willpower and the imagination are in conflict, the imagination invariably wins by determining the truth.

Two or more heads are better than one but not always. Group brainstorming can often make a positive difference. Positive self-encouragement and mutual encouragement is a major requirement for any brainstorming team. Dare to dream because you live in a universe so magical that even lost dreams may not really be lost.

Take two deep breaths before repeating the code again. Press your thumb into the tip of the third finger of any hand together, saying or thinking three times:

"Inner brain, at your will, supply me with a solution."

"Inner brain, at your will, supply me with a solution."

"Inner brain, at your will, supply me with a solution."

Do this anytime, anyplace. But immediately begin moving your thoughts or body into any other activity. Disown thinking of any resolutions, pretend to yourself that the conundrum already has been solved will be attended to. Perhaps when you least expect it. The solution shall come. At first, you may laugh, and you could think: "You little devil, inner brain, why now, of all times."

This is how the inner brain worked for two famous doctors, Freud and Einstein.

"More important than knowledge is the proper use of the imagination." A statement made by Albert Einstein.

So it shall work for you.

Always remember your body is the most complex piece of machinery that exists. Your mind is the most remarkable computer that will ever be created. Both are a never to be repeated mystery.

That's the program.

The time has come to become fully awake on the count from 5 to 1, feeling loose as a goose, feeling fantastic.

5...coming up.

4...feeling great and prepared to be a problem solver, not a problem maker.

3...wide-awake and feeling fantastic.

2-1...you are marvelous and you will be provided with solutions to attain any goal that comes your way.

**Preconditioning Program of Self-Hypnotic Session #10
Career Dissatisfaction—Motivation for Change**

The Confucian epigram advises: "Choose a job you love, and you will never have to work a day in your life."

If you believe you have achieved the career goal already in your life you should pass over this Session.

There are few luckier than those who believe them self to be so successful. Those who have this belief would perceive any further success as "pure gravy."

However, if you ponder about your job: "Is that all there is?" as

Groucho Marx did, when he stated: "My highest desire during my last position was—retirement."

Groucho also stated: "As long as you work for somebody else, it's best not to quit at quitting time."

To some going to work every day can be spelt "SUX."

Read on, if you have this attitude towards your work, tasks or career.

Being involved in work that you are properly orientated for is a great therapy for stress, anxiety, depression and grief relief.

Nonetheless, work of any nature is often one of the best tranquilizers for a troubled mind.

The majority of jobs are often named: careers. Money is often the greatest motivation to get a good job.

But how do you stay motivated once you have a job?

Remember how happy you were on the day you got that distasteful job, only do it for the money job?

Remember when you were at your best? Would you like to be there again.

Career Success is described as:

S-ense of direction
U-nderstanding
C-ourage
C-harity
E-steem
S-elf-Confidence
S-elf-Acceptance

Career Failure is described as:

F-rustration, futility
A-ggressiveness (misdirected)
I-nsecurity
L-oneliness (lack of oneness)
U-ncertainty
R-esentment
E-mptiness

Have you committed yourself to a job mistake? If you do not move out of a mistake job, you are committing another mistake.

Have your original skills become rusty, obsolete, nearly forgotten or unused?

Some working people die at forty but are buried at eighty. If you have a lack of self-esteem, perhaps you are not doing anything worthwhile. Consistent happiness and joy springs up from doing something worthwhile.

A lack of self-worth can be challenged and improved. A lost enthusiasm for your job develops if your efforts are not worthwhile. A happy, joyful mind is not derived from being wealthy, or having a life of ease, or from receiving the praise of other humans.

Always proceed as if success is inevitable. Your success may come from not knowing your limitations. If you do not learn from your mistakes, you might as well not have made them.

This Session is designed to upholster and reinforce and increase self-esteem.

"You can because you think you can" Virgil (70–19BC).

Sometimes it takes losing a job to awaken someone up from a living death. In losing a job, one has the opportunity to be reborn.

Everyone has a primitive mission: a survival ticket through growth. You may need to return to school. Your inner brain's imagination is similar to a sixteen-speed bike. You have numerous inner brain gears for which you have never had a need or even thought of using.

Courage upholsters activity, the employing of imaginative powers to smash through self-defeating, negative thoughts, like: "I can not do it."

Take action, even when you are afraid and unsure of yourself. Always act as if you are feeling the opposite of uncertainty, believe in this, and it can become, a fact.

Magic can occur when an unshakable optimistic person uses their imagination. When considering a career change do not concentrate only the usual type of employment. Look into something different, perhaps doing work you have never considered possible.

Due to a need for money or fear of change, one may be stuck in a dead-end job, where the chief goal is to put in the remaining years to be pensioned off. Are you counting the years, days and hours before you get a pension to retire? Have you traded all you have to offer, for money and security?

You are either growing or stagnating. When you locate something you do well and enjoy doing it, this is fulfillment. When you stop growing, stagnation gradually sets in. Unrewarding servitude at any wage eventually ends up being lacking in fulfillment.

One can erroneously think that a lifetime of weekends would be superb. After 30 years or more of going to work, your body and brain is far from conditioned to be idle for long. Premature retirement is often regretted three months later.

It is not because things are difficult that you do not dare.

It is because you never dare that they are difficult.

When one then complains about a job, one should not postpone changing it.

No one enjoys living in a rut. You have a finite number of heartbeats, a finite amount of time. You still have enough heartbeats and enough time to do any task or challenging work that is important to you.

Robert Kennedy stated: "Only those who dare to fail greatly can ever achieve greatly."

If one does not control his or her own destiny, someone else will. You do not want to go to the graveyard with your best songs still unsung.

The way to make an excellent impression at work is to never try. Never be overly concerned what others think about you. Do not consciously try to always be over pleasing to other people. If you are constantly and consciously monitoring your every act, or manner, at work, you could become inhibited and self-conscious. Never allow yourself to question consciously what your boss, or how any other person is judging you.

Merely set the best example that you can.

All that you will be is the result of what you have imagined you thought you could be. When you rule your mind, you rule your world. When you choose your thoughts, you choose results.

Losing your job or getting fired normally causes enormous self-doubt and emotional distress.

If you got fired or lost your job for whatever reason, adjustment to the conditions of the "here and now" must be accomplished. Humiliation and diminution of self-esteem often accompanies a stressful episode from loss of employment. To conquer such wounds, one must heal them but before healing can be achieved one must feel the hurt and accept the pain. Healing and renewal of self-esteem can be achieved during this Session.

One should not make themselves depressed by whining and complaining. The domino effect of one negative thought triggering multitudes of others: feeling sorry for yourself, blaming others, or unfair situations. Make the most of every failure. Fall forward. Carry onward. Fear to act can be the thief of your hopes.

Rejection after a job interview can become a frequent downer.

Looking for your dream job often entails an ongoing handling of rejection. Rejection hurts. Get used to it. Your life will go on, and tomorrow is another day, another opportunity. Congratulate yourself. When the chips are down, you are conducting an active, imaginative, and hopeful job search.

Be pleased with yourself for actually trying the very best you can achieve. Rather than being idle, just loafing watching television, goofing off, waiting for something special to simply drop into your lap. You are doing your very best enduring the job rejection interview cycle. Hard-won victories are the sweetest of success.

You can be assured to a positive work future by actively doing something to ensure that it is realized. It is what you do with your time of life that makes you, who you are. You may succeed with just one more blow.

"Don't let the fear of striking out hold you back" (Babe Ruth 1895–1948). Babe Ruth a famous baseball player, held the all-time record for home runs and strikeouts.

No person ever became successful except through many mistakes.

"Go out on the limb—that is where the fruit is " (Will Roger 1879–1935).

This Session is brimming with forceful, personal motivation to assist in the search for meaningful work. This Session will help anyone on the quest for employment. Your job search will become fruition. Link the inner brain's imaginative exuberance to lively enthusiasm to finding work with purpose.

Remember when you were at your best. You will be there again.

One never says: "I'm ready to take this job. Hire me."

The first step for people attacking the goal of finding suitable work is to loft the imagination on two things:

What talents can you offer and what you want to do.

Imagine what you want as much as you imagine what the person who may hire you wants.

There is no such thing as a passionate job. There are passionate people. The source of any passion brought to work comes from within you. Passion is the enthusiastic attitude you bring to a job and everyone you meet. You can achieve anything you want if you want it passionately enough. Passion is robust enthusiasm that will assist you going after a desired work achievement or dream job. Other people may advise you to give up, when you are uncertain where the current pathway is taking you.

"You can because you think you can" (Virgil 70–19BC).

Science has proven that the human brain can hold 500 times the information found in a set of Encyclopedia Britannica.

Imagination is more important than knowledge. - Albert Einstein

The man who has no imagination has no wings. -Muhammad Ali

One doesn't discover new lands without consenting to lose sight of the shore.

Wonder is the beginning of wisdom.

Franklin Rosevelt thought up the name United Nations in the shower.

Self-Hypnotic Session #10
Career Dissatisfaction—Motivation for Change

Dear reader: Relax please. Make your legs, arms, and hands comfortable as long as they are not touching.

Begin this relaxation by taking several deep breaths. Breathe in...let yourself go...again...breathe in again...and let yourself go. Continue to breathe evenly, deeply and rhythmically. As you breathe evenly and deeply in this manner, send the inhaled air to expand your rib cage to its full extent before exhaling.

Imagine a drop of lubrication is magically being secreted into each inhaled breath. This lubricant is miraculous calming oil. Imagine spreading this lotion along with the inhaled oxygen all over inside your rib cage. Imagine the oil and oxygen being pushed downward to the bottom of the stomach. With each following inhale of oxygen and calming oil begins spreading stillness throughout each part of your entire body. Do this for as long as it is comfortable.

In a short time, you may begin to feel a kind of weakness in your legs and your feet. A tingling kind of sensation that is moving slowly, entering both your arms. Feel it move into your hands. The same sensation of mellowness then settles into the chest and back. This weak kind of feeling is calm relaxation. Feel lose as a goose, breathe evenly and deeply, feel your head and mind calming and relaxing even more with every breath that you take. Continue to relax, uncoil and unwind. Go into self-hypnotic sleep now.

Soon, you are going to count to nine. As you are count to nine you will become much calmer. A more tired, drowsy sensation will be spread into each part of your body. You shall just seem to let go completely and sink down pleasantly into a deeper form of relaxation that is similar to sleep. On the count of ten, you will sink down pleasantly into a deep form of ease similar to the feeling you experience only seconds before regular nighttime sleep.

1-2…and already your eyes are getting very heavy, sleepy and tired. All the small muscles and veins around your eyes are relaxing, as this heavy, sleepy, tired begins to make you very sleepy.

This relaxed and calm feeling can trigger all sorts of body responses. Your head is getting heavier while your entire body feels like a puppet whose strings have been dropped. This comfortable sensation expands moving towards your chest with a heavy, sleepy, tired calmness feeling. The heavy, sleepy, tired, relaxing feeling goes down into your neck then enters both shoulders. And your neck and shoulders muscles are getting heavier. Letting go completely, with every breath that you take.

3-4…This heavy, sleepy, tired relaxed feeling is going down into your arms and hands. Your arms, hands and each finger are getting heavier. The muscles in your arms and hands are calmer. Letting go as your arms and hands continue to become heavier and heavier with every breath that you take.

5-6…and now this heavy, sleepy, drowsiness is spreading down into your legs and your feet, and your legs and your feet are getting heavier. The muscles in both legs are relaxing, letting go completely now, as your legs and feet continue to become heavier with every breath that you take now. Deep hypnotic sleep is covering you with a blanket of peace and tranquility. Go into self-hypnotic sleep now.

7-8…and now this heavy, sleepy, tired, relaxed feeling is flowing throughout every part of your body. Calming you all over, as you prepare to completely let go.

Sink down pleasantly into a much deeper form of lulling self-hypnotic sleep…relaxed…calmed down and going into self-hypnotic sleep now.

9…and down you go now.

You are getting so good at being able to relax, that you are going to count to five to go ever into a deeper hypnotic sleep. Lower than you have ever been before.

A self-hypnotic rest much deeper than you are now. A 1000 time lower than you have ever been before.

1-2…and your eyes are getting even heavier now, sleepy and tired. Every tiny muscle surrounding your eyes could use a rest. Momentarily, you shall close your eyes to rest as long as you wish. Allow your eyelids to drop over your eyes, review the sparkling patterns that your eyes view when your eyelids are closed.

In a second when you close your eyes imagine letting go sinking deeper into body rest. When you do close both eyelids close them tighter and tighter. Perhaps, close your two eyes so tightly, it feels almost as if the lids of each eye are stuck together. You may have to call upon extra energy to resume with the text when you reopen your eyes. Take as much eye rest as you need before returning to the text. Tightly shut down both eyelids now.

3…Be comfortable. Any tension, aches, cramps, stiffness or pains that may have been in your body leave now draining from your body down onto the floor. Feel any tension, aches or pains that may have been bothering you flows away.

5…Both legs and feet are frozen and stiff. Frozen with calmness and you do not feel like moving them. You may try, but you do not want to move them.

Go deeper than ever before into self-hypnotic sleep now.

There is no need to bother trying to listen to your conscious mind. Your subconscious mind, the mighty inner brain is at the forefront now.

You will want to follow all the ideas that are suggested since this will be for your benefit. Any outside sounds seem to become quieter, more distant, as if fading away into the distance. The outside sounds shall disappear completely, and nothing will disturb you or bother you.

Enter into your inner brain's imagination to that peaceful and special place. A location that Nostradamus stated in 1700 was absolutely limitless. He was a seer who through quatrains of verse made prophecies on a multitude of world events for hundreds of years. Prophecies that are continuing to this day to be proven true and accurate.

You can imagine this special place and perhaps you can even feel it. It can be any place where you know you shall be comfortable, calm and relaxed. You may prefer, a beach, or in front of a blazing fireplace on a cold winter evening. Go to wherever you can imagine a special place where you are relaxing. You are alone and there is no one there to disturb you. This is one of the most pleasant places in world for you.

Feel the calmness flow through you with a sense of well-being. Enjoy these positive feelings, you shall keep them with you long after this Session is completed, for the rest of this day, evening and tomorrow. Each and every time that you choose to do this kind of calming relaxation you enjoy it more. Regardless of any uncertainties, stress, anxiety and tension that may surround your life in the "here and now." You can be peaceful, calm, and relaxed. The tension and stresses bounce off and away from you.

Let any feelings you have buried come to the surface. Examine those feelings. Decide which ones you want to keep and which ones you want to discard.

Keep the ones you need right now, and cast away the others. It is normal to feel sad or depressed sometimes. It is your way of being good to yourself.

Visualize a huge blackboard. Review the chalk writing on the board. Negative labels written on the board are all the negative words you may have given yourself in the past. Unarguable bad words that you or others placed on your talents or character. Negative labels like maybe: "lazy," "good for nothing," "mean mouthed." Bitter words that wounded and failed to reflect the wonderful, strong, and excellent qualities you truly do have. Visualize any bad labels on the blackboard of the inner brain. Contemplate for a minute or so on each negative label and try and remember where the label came from.

Believe that whatever negative labels you pondered on where not a true reflection of the real you.

Pick up the caulk eraser sitting on the edge of the blackboard.

Erase all the negative labels from the board, just erase each one, and wipe the bad labels completely off the board.

The bad labels have no meaning for you, no meaning at all. The blackboard is blank and you can write anything you want to write on the inner brain's blackboard.

Imagine picking up the chalk sitting of the edge of the board and you write the words that truly describes yourself.
Write confident—valuable—important—capable—and skilled. Write any other positive words that you know describe yourself.

In a few seconds, you will be shutting your eyes to visualize and contemplate on the positive labels you have written on the blackboard. Take as long as you wish before reopening your eyes. Shut both eyes now.

Begin to imagine yourself standing tall, proud of who you are. You are fine. The way you look, act and think are fine. Your thoughts contribute to making you the magnificent person you really are. Visualize yourself experiencing a new and healthy energy. Reflect on all the positive aspects of your creativity, your intelligence, and your many other worthwhile talents. People see you as a good friend, a good worker, they see you as a good person. Imagine yourself as a positive and very worthwhile person.

Imagine yourself speaking to other-workers, very certain of your abilities, very certain. You are convinced of your accuracy, your talents, your appeal, your conversation with others is genuinely articulate, your spoken words flow easily. People are interested in what you have to say. People notice you and regard you as a wonderful person, just imagine projecting yourself in the most positive way, assertive and self-assured. You will always approach obstacles with a positive attitude such as:

"I shall do it." "I have the energy." "I am just right for the job." "I can take charge of this." "I can solve this." You are confident, capable, and talented and you even have sex appeal. You are kind to yourself. You no longer have time for negative labels, thoughts or feelings. You fill your mind with positive ideas, productive work goals. Consider your life at work as an adventure. Think, imagine and believe that nothing holds you back from reaching a work goal and becoming the successful person that you can be.

Imagine a perfect, kind of day, a day that you awaken to, and just know it is going to be the kind of day where everything is just absolutely right, everything just falls into place. You are feeling good, calm, relaxed, at peace with yourself and you feel self-confident. You are comfortable and protected within the boundaries that you have created. You are comfortable and secure. You may choose to expand your comfortable zone space. Just imagine yourself pushing back any barricades you may have created. Expand your horizons expand your work goals, reaching forward. Be excited as you reach higher and higher for work objectives. You can feel comfortable within expanded boundaries. You feel safe, secure and pleased that you have the control and power within you to change, to eliminate any limitations and be the successful person you desire to be. Your feelings are so good, you will hopefully look forward to any risks you may venture into.

Imagine the work goal or project that you would like to accomplish. Whatever your uncompleted work goal is. Think of what you really want. In a few seconds, close your eyes, and concentrate on what your work goals really are. Contemplate on realistic work goals. Take as long as you wish before you reopen your eyes to refocus on the text. Shut both eyes now.

Henceforth you will:

Act as if you can, you can draw the career, task or work you desire.

Act as if you know you can.

Act as if you can make a difference.

Act as if you are becoming what you desire.

Act as if you can win, even though some people you know expect you to fail.

Act in boldness, the bridge to the job or work goal you desire will eventually be revealed.

Act with a knowing that you can make your work goals happen.

Act and believe that you can achieve doing the work you want to do.

Act with a confidence attitude. Self-confidence is an essential nutrient for great changes in your life.

You can succeed because you think you can.

A creative mind requires constant nurturing. Creative intuitive ideas come to the person who does not fear the insecurity of looking beyond the obvious. The creative powers normally require a breaking of routine, a conscious break in mental or physical activity to allow the inner brain full uses of its resources. Creative guidance often comes through intuition, an impelling urge. Sudden impulses to act, do something, contact someone or go somewhere. Trust and act on this "out of the blue" guidance. Permit your inner brain to take full charge. Always listen to, accept and do exactly what your intuition tells you. If intuitively you know to leave something alone, leave it alone. You may feel you should do some things you really do not want to do until you see the final conclusion of doing so.

Visualize putting minor goals aside and just focus on one goal or project at a time. This may be to finding, a search for any opportunity, seeking advancement at work, secure a better paying job (money will not buy happiness but poverty can buy misery) start a part-time business, or make your hobby your work. Whatever practical work desires you may have, imagine putting energy into this desired work. See yourself doing this work. Imagine fresh challenges that are more exciting than the old ones. Concentrate on building new ideas developed from the old.

Conjecture taking this special day of your desired work success and placing it just a little bit in the future. A day or two, a week, a month, just a little in the future.

Visualize that you have moved ahead towards whatever desired work changes you sincerely wished to happen.

Assume these work goals have been achieved and are now in your past.

Visualize and believe you have succeeded. Wear a smile on your face, your imagination has supplied the needed work solutions. You desire to be successful in your work goals, see it, feel it. The successful materialization of your efforts will happen just as you imagined.

You should reward yourself any way you please once you achieve your desired work goal. Imagine, believe and know that you are worthy of all the good things life has to offer. Reaching your desired work goals will be very beneficial for you. Imagine the continuing work goals in your life, see them as positive events, positive for you, your family, friends, and the people you work with.

Reflect for a moment on other positive work goals you may have already reached. These achievements were good for you and all those around you. Now see yourself becoming more successful. You are most often happy. You are extremely sensitive to others, you are helpful and your success is positive for all. You will be comfortable in your success. You use your success in the most positive and worthwhile ways. Your mind is clear, you see yourself for the intelligent, creative and beautiful person that you are. You have many choices, many options, and whatever you choose to do, whatever direction you take, know it will be positive for you. Your desired work success is a positive event for you and all those who touch your life. Every choice you make and any path you take is absolutely right for now. Imagine yourself clearly, in the near future with many positive work directions and choices. Bring this successful image into the present. See yourself resolving work problems. See yourself confident and successful with many wonderful and positive paths to choose.

You know you will continue being successful. You shall continue to make choices that enhance your life.

That is the program. Believe that you shall accomplish your work goals.

The time has come to awaken. To achieve this become fully alert and feeling very good on the count down from 5 to 1.

5...Reawaken and be teeming of pep and energy.

4...You possess the self-esteem to achieve work goals, to take on challenges and risks.

3...Enjoy and do not abuse the power or responsibilities that accompany work success.

2...Always be sensitive to the needs of any superior worker or coworker.

1...That's it, feeling wonderful. Refreshed and very confident in the work that you shall do.

Preconditioning Program of Session #11
Spiritual Depth

You may be convinced in the "Darwinism" theory that the human race evolved from a tadpole. You may believe the human race is no more than a mere accident, an evolutionary quirk. Do you believe that all the humans and animals that have passed over the earth were a mere freak of nature? You could believe the human race is little more than a highly intellectual ant colony. If so, you may prefer to skip this Session. The very deepest of a self-hypnosis trace called "somnambulism" will never change atheism.

If you still wish to continue reading but lack any feeling or need for an all-knowing intelligence connected spiritually to the superconsciousness. Then you can be granted a higher power anyway. Any illuminating light bulb, shall be your higher power. Perhaps a lighted bulb you are reading by. Two hundred years ago, an illuminating bulb would have been considered a higher power to many.

Most of the acknowledged great thinkers: being philosophers, theologians, mystics or scientists have numerous disagreements on many subjects but there is one subject on which most agree and that there is only one mind in the universe. The one universal mind is the origin of human thought the superconscious.

Your chosen name for the divine is not important.

The superconscious is beyond human imagination.

The superconscious wears many masks and has many names.

The superconscious never looks at labels or names, only humans do that.

No human brain can begin to grasp the superconscious entirety. Truly believing in a spiritual connection leads one onto the next imponderable question, which no human will ever comprehend: What created the superconscious?

A religious belief in immortality denies the finality of death. This belief places faith in the realm of the sacred.

A religion is a set of ideas and beliefs that satisfies the spiritual needs of many humans. Since the beginning of time there have been numerous religious sects.

The sects have supplied a wide variety of deities, including humans. Humans have always dwelled in a state of yearning for a divine connection.

Your inner brain is receptive to being absorbed into the domain of a living spiritual light within. This Session can create a balancing of body, mind and spirit. This Session for some may be a mind-expanding program. A great force, a powerhouse in which a tremendous electric dynamo awaits to guide you at the turn of the switch. The very same force, which sustains the sun, clouds, planets and sea, dwells within the inner brain. Consent to the inner brain supporting your every step towards enlightenment, towards a rejuvenation of a fatigued spiritual dimension. One can become so busy and obsessed with physical senses to lose touch with the superconscious, except in emergencies. The spiritual connection to the inner brain can become so debilitated until it is dead-ended. The superconscious higher intelligence knows your proper place and your highest purpose. Conceivably you have heard its words, mere words have immense creative power but fear and stress may have caused you to shrink from following the correct direction. Always be open to the superconscious: ask, listen and trust the higher source of wisdom. Instinctive intuition is the voice of the superconscious, that first immediate thought before your conscious mind starts censoring everything. When you go against your "gut feelings," you are going against the urge of your spirit.

The highest spiritual powers are available as an advisor to direct you and can change your life. You can taste the ecstasy of a rarefied superconscious relationship. In this Session your inner brain can experience a life-changing enlightenment by contacting the superconscious. Until you can you may remain unconscious of the wisdom of this endowment. A preoccupation with the physical body and mind can cause one to lose the vision of the higher realm of the inner brain's spiritual power. Just as placing one's faith in people who have no faith can cause one to lose their faith.

A fountain of true satisfaction can spring from the Spirit within. If you seek mental peace by not improving your spiritual disposition your search shall be fruitless and you will multiply any sorrow or grief. The Spirit within is a pathfinder to authoritative inner brain guidance. It provides the foundation on which to live your life. Your supreme purpose on earth is to create authentic power by aligning your personality with your Spirit. If you direct yourself away from the Soul inside, everything flows away from you. Activities become burdensome chores, one focuses only on self-concerns. Without Spiritual direction the mind can easily slip into stress and imagined fears. Your Spirit has a wonderful predetermined marvelous plan for your life, an overwhelming positive future.

The foundation builders of the world's major religions attempted to explore all there were to know regarding their Spirit and superconscious.

The major religious founders are Jesus Christ, John Smith, Abraham, Moses, Noah, an ancient Hindus, Buddha, Mohammed, and Zoroastrian. Men who had very diversified lives. Each man did have two very similar experiences while living on earth.

Each lived through extended trials. Mohammed hides himself in a cave, wailing day and night. Jesus Christ endured forty days in the desert with no food or water. Noah took a long boat ride. John Smith was driven out of every town, his group settled in. The believers finally found a headquarters in Salt Lake City. Abraham was instructed to sacrifice his only son. Moses traveled for 40 years to seek the Holy Land. He was never allowed to stand on it. The original Hindu denied himself earthly pleasures, including the eating of meat. Buddha took up extreme asceticism.

But what did each man have in common? Spiritual Enlightenment with the superconscious.

The emotional waters of your Spirit or Soul are very deep. Immersing with the Spirit can be calming as a deeply restful smooth flowing brook or a raging sea with waves of stress, anxiety and fear. You are a Soul temporarily situated in a magnificent robot body.

Your deepest emotions, perhaps buried, desires to know a divine supreme being Everyone is usually interested in experiencing a consummate spiritual dimension.

Unfortunately, strong believing people in different religions never cease to fight. It is as if each religion is a different branch of the military.

Religious faith is often arrogant, believing they and only they have all the answers to the unknown. Most religious faiths do not willingly accept any other religions.

Religions have become dogmatic, institutionalized and authoritarian, intolerant and in some ways absolutely ugly. Each religion has a stern set of man-made rules of various conduct and belief, some beliefs that are repugnant to many individuals. Nonetheless, divine belief is increasing worldwide, although church attendance is in a steep decline. One has the liberty to take only what is wanted from any religion, be it: Salvation Army, Mennonite, Roman Catholic, Protestant, Jewish Hebrew, Buddhism, Hinduism, Islam, Mormon, Jehovah Witness, or any of the others, including the New Age philosophies. A personalized religious faith. A belief that concentrations on seeing the good instead of the bad in any religion. The search for spirituality enlightenment can be successful. Spiritual growth unfolds much in the same way an eagle rises from the ground toward the sky. The eagle never flies straight upward. The eagle circles, passing over the same territory again and again, but each time the view is from a superior vantage view. The Spirit, like the eagle waits for the suitable time to swoop down. It may be during a period of personal dissatisfaction. One may be experiencing a spiritual frenzy or the empty fulfillment when one asks: Is this all there is?

Having the faith that a Spiritual eagle watches, guides and protects you is structured in most beliefs.

Authentic faith is humble and realizes that all of religion's various doors lead to the same destiny.

The superconscious looks at your inner brain and comprehends the state of belief. A mind can be filled with unrepentant evil or a holy devotion to the incomparable overseer.

Some faith is needed to day, as humans experience a dissatisfaction decrease in happiness in the midst of increasing comforts. Happiness never depends upon who you are or what you have; your joy depends solely upon what you think. You are under the influence of a cosmic guidance system and every day you can receive little nudges to keep you on your chosen path. As the Spirit's Inner Light dawns, brilliant sparks melt any negative mental captivity. Now and then, you may lose touch with your inner Spiritual's wisdom because you have become more than necessary solidly focused and frenzied by worldly concerns.

However, if you are out alone driving a boat on a wavy sea when unexpectedly the boat strikes a protruding rock and sinks. You may be left in a towering wave filled ocean and have nothing to grab to keep abreast of the waves. You could expect to drown. Yet, if you trust yourself and let go, you can float. A "lost at sea" emergency is similar to needing faith, a vital ingredient to gain serenity of mind. An emergency when you reach out for the unknown luminous place within yourself. A dwelling place within, where dissatisfaction and fear can be transformed into useful energy. A place internal where physical pain is transformed into strength. The only place where the fear of dying is melted away by an inner spiritual assurance.

The purpose of this Session is to unlock the inner brain doors much wider to reveal an avenue for Soul illumination. A communication with the superconscious is never an empty illusion.

Albert Schweitzer stated: "No explanation of evil in the world could ever satisfy me, but I never let myself get lost in brooding over it. I have confidence in the power of truth and of the soul within. I believe in the future of mankind."

The superconscious unfolds itself, as a lotus with countless petals. Any of the wonders you purse are within yourself.

Celebrate when the glowing Spirit's flame spring forth beaming sunshine at its brightest, allowing the real you to shine through. The lamp that lit the world can light your life.

You can live in peace, radiate peace and spread peace to others.

Spiritual reconciliation begins within you.

If you are spiritually starved or bankrupt, or experiencing inner mental battles this may indicate that you seek a Spiritual reawakening.

The "I" that is me—you cannot see.
You see only the form that you think is I.
This form that you see, will not always be.
But the "I" that is me—lives eternally.
I have faith in the sun—even when it does not shine.
I have faith in love—even when it is not shown.
I believe in the Spirit—even when I cannot feel its presence.

You were created with a majestic, magical inner brain with the capacity to form thought and images of things not present to your senses.

The expectation of this Session is not to persuade you to join any religion. The anticipation is that you shall identify and take pleasure from a richer understanding of the Spiritual connection to the superconscious.

The superconscious contains a sense of something beyond the tangible things of the outer world. There is much more than meets the eye.

Self-Hypnotic Session #11
Spiritual Depth

Dear reader: settle down, take a load off. Decelerate every activity of the mind or body. Never feel guilty of taking precious time as you do this. Focus your attention on the tip of your nostrils. Feel the breath flowing in and out past the tip of the nostril. You want you to begin this relaxation by taking a few deep breaths in this fashion. Breathe in...then let yourself go...breathe in...then let yourself go, continue to breathe evenly and deeply in this manner.

Your breathing is now harmonizing controlling the inhaled oxygen. Upon your next inhale of breath pull the breath down into the pit of the stomach and hold it there for a very long length of time. So long of a time that to continue doing so becomes intolerable.

Continue with this breath regulating exercise for several additional breaths.

Discontinue this breathing exercise and start a new one. The hardest working part in the body is the beating heart. For the remainder of this Session imagine sending relief to this magnificent organ that has been with you longer than any other part of your body, unless you had a heart transplant. Imagine looking into your own heart. In fact your heart supplied the powerhouse that was needed to construct your entire body. Appreciate your heart's good job during the remainder of this Session. Imagine that every breath in of air is directed solely into your heart. The heart will slow down and take a well-deserved rest.

At the same time your inner brain will go on a little vacation.

You are beginning to feel a kind of weakness in your legs and your feet. A weak kind sensation of relaxing feeling. A deep calmness of drowsiness is spreads up into your arms and your hands. This calm feeling is moving throughout your entire body.

This weak kind of feeling is definitely relaxation, and as you continue to breathe evenly and deeply, you will feel your every part of your body relaxing more with every breath that you take that is directed to your heart.

While you continue to "relax...calmer...relax," you are going to count to ten. When counting to ten imagine yourself as a feather being dropped by an airplane pilot flying high above the clouds.

A black and white feather that the pilot is going to release into the sky through an open window. When he does you commence to very slowly flutter and glide down through the clouds in the sky.

And while you are imagining yourself as the falling feather, you will be even more be dropping into a heavy, sleepy, tired, relaxed feeling in various parts of your body.

When you reach the number of ten, you will just seem to let go completely and sink down pleasantly into deep self-hypnotic sleep.

Become and visualize that you are that gliding through white clouds and the sky.

You are a white and black feather.

A feather is light and soft, you float down slowly through the clouded sky. Your eyes are getting very heavy, sleepy and tired. Each of the muscles around your eyes are becoming more relaxed. A patch of clear blue sky passes by. The brightness of the sun encases both your eyes and the tiny muscles around your eyes.

Momentarily you can leave yourself as the feather. Simply let it descend down on its own. You want to close your eyes for a rest. Some people find it easier to recollect their thoughts if they shut their eyes, and eye rest is always beneficial at any time. When you have shut your eyes imagine and visualize a spinning automobile tire right in front of your closed eyes. Watch the spinning tire spin for as long as you wish. After a while, you will see that the spinning tire is slowly beginning to float away. The spinning tire goes further away, further and further, until it is a mere speck, before disappearing. For sound effects you can hear the noise of the tire spinning and this sound turns to a whisper when you see the tire disappearing. Test your imagination for coloration. Imagine that the tire has an orange hubcap? The spinning tire with an orange hubcap is waiting. Close your eyes and observe the spinning tire for as long as u wish.

Return to the image of you being a feather falling downward in the sky. Be that white and black feather.

3...Now the tired, relaxed feeling is going into your head. Your head is getting heavier along with the very weak feeling of pure calmness. As a feather flows downward a comfortably, placid restfulness moves into the chest with a heavy, sleepy, tired relaxing feeling. The sleepy, drowsy, relaxed feeling expands into the neck and shoulders. And your neck and shoulders are getting heavier "relax...be calm...relax..."

Feel the muscles in your neck and shoulders calming, decelerating. Letting go completely as the neck and shoulders continue to become heavier with every inhaled breath dispatched to your heart.

4...Realize that you can live in peace, radiate peace and spread peace to others.

A heavy, sleepy, tired relaxed feeling is going down into your arms and hands. Your arms and hands are getting heavier, and all the muscles in your arms and hands are relaxing. Letting go completely now as your arms and hands continue to become heavier with every breath that you convey to your heart.

The feather, which you are, is coming close to earth now. Weightlessly dropping through a huge snow white cloud. Sudden the feather's speed of downward travel is being aided by a strong northerly gale.

5-6...And now this heavy, sleepy, tired, relaxed feeling is moving downward into your legs and your feet, and your legs and your feet are getting heavier. The muscles clinging to both legs are calming. Faster than ever, you continue to tumble quickly down through a clear blue sky.

7-8...A calm, sleepy, tired, relaxed feeling is flowing throughout every part of your body. Relaxing and calming you all over. You are prepared to let go completely and sink down pleasantly into a much deeper form of self-hypnotic rest much better that bed time sleep.

The very same feeling that you automatically have after you say a prayer each night. The seconds before you drop down into bedtime sleep. This is when the inner brain begins to thrive, as it prepares to take over the dream machine. An inner brain made the dream that Cesar's wife had the night before the day he was knifed to death by his chosen few. The same form of dream that Pontius Pilate's wife had the night before he ruled cruelly over Jesus Christ. This is the place where the intuition also resides.

You as a falling feather you are about to hit bottom.

9-10…The feather lands on earth dropping gently landing on the very top of hay pile in a farmer's field.

Take a very deep breath and recall the oxygen being absorbed into your heart. "Go into self-hypnotic sleep now."

While you continue relaxing there is no need for you to bother trying to listen to your conscious mind. Your subconscious mind, inner brain is at the forefront and will register then carry out everything that you suggest. It will be for your benefit.

Outside sounds just seem to become quieter, and more distant, as if fading away further into the distance. When the outside sounds disappear completely, this is so nothing will disturb or bother you now.

Imagine and visualize that peaceful and special place. You can imagine this special place and perhaps you can even feel it. You are at, a beach, or in front of a blazing fireplace, wherever, a special location that you enjoy.

You are alone and there is no one to disturb you. This is the most peaceful place in world for you.

Imagine yourself there and feel that a calming feeling flow through you. This sense of well-being, positive feelings you want to keep them with you long after this Session is completed, for the rest of this day and evening, tomorrow.

Allow these positive feelings to grow stronger. Each and every time that you choose to do this kind of relaxation you will be able to relax even deeper.

Regardless of the stress, anxiety, fear or tension that may surround your life in the "here and now," you can remain more calm, more relaxed and allow the tension and stresses to bounce off and away from you, just bounce off and away.

And now go very deep into self-hypnotic sleep. You are about to embark on an unusual pleasant voyage.

You are nearing graduation time, the promised finally Session of serenity and peace of mind. But before you graduate you must have an encounter with the Soul that lives within. This is a trip you may have already taken. But since it is part of this course's graduation process, you feel compelled to repeat the experience. Who knows how far anyone can advance spiritually?

Now, suspend all disbelief. Every thought or idea that has ever been pumped into your head regarding the silent, unknown superconscious.

You are going to call upon one of the greatest powers you have. The visionary powers dwelling within your inner brain.

Imagine, believe and visualize that you are approaching the mode of transportation, a mere elevator.

The elevator door opens, you walk in and discover the biggest empty elevator floor in the world. The floor of the elevator could hold thousands of people but nobody else is on with you.

This is your beginning of a search for your Soul. A Spirituality that never takes you on wild gooses chasing, attempting to make you pursuit for perfection or high virtue. See yourself enter the elevator then press the button that is marked "Spiritual and Dream Department." You realize your inner brain is the great dream manufacturer, a subconscious deluxe appointed sphere you have spent mostly eight hours or more of each day of your life in when you have bed rest. For eight hours or so every day you have been sleeping. When you were an infant and growing up you spent much more time there, it is a dwelling foolishly named: "Dreamland."

Every living creature lives a third of their life in Dreamland except hibernating bears, they over do it. If you have a pet, a dog a gold fish they sleep more than 8 hours a day. But all creatures have dreams, some have total recall when becoming awake, some do not. Many talk in their sleep, but wake up with a blank memory of doing so. Forget these mysterious dreams, you are going to greet the dream maker, the mighty inner brain.

Realize you will always be exactly who you are, as the elevator's gray steel doors swish closed and begins the descent.

Going down deeper until the elevator stops and the two steel doors automatically open.

You notice the elevator has stopped on floor number nine a red lit, automated sign above the two elevator doors lights up: "Motivation Department." Some men and women step into the elevator behind you. They are joining you for a spiritual rebuilding.

The elevator's two steel doors close and down, you go, way down deeper downward in the elevator's deep well. The elevator stops again and the two doors whoosh open. You look up at the red automated location sign, it reads: "Problem Department."

More women and men move into the elevator space behind you. Like animals herding and crowing into and around a near dry pond of expectancy all in need of rest, proper nourishment and revitalizing.

The elevator's two steel gray doors close and the elevator again begins descending bottomward.

Down lower into the shaft you travel, you feel like a feather again. Speedily drifting down the elevator's well.

The elevator makes another stop. The doors open. Men, women and children of all ages greet you. These people have brown marks on their fingers and lips, most of them are coughing or clearing their throat, and some are even spitting on the floor. You look up at floor location sign, it reads, "Anti-Smoking Department."

The elevator's two steel door close although there were a lot of people joining you the elevator is not the least bit crowded. Elevator music starts to play, a harp is thumbing one of your favorite tunes, "I shall survive." The two doors close and the elevator begins to plunge downward.

When the elevator stops at the next floor down you look up to see the lighted floor station: "Public Speaking Department."

A lot of people join the others on the elevator, and they are all talking to each other with a very supreme self-confident attitude.

The elevator doors hiss shut and again dives downward. This special elevator travels swiftly down the shaft.

Again the elevator stops and the doors whiz open.

On this floor an especially large crowd of all ages, creeds and nationalities join in behind you. Some are on crutches, some are in beds, and a smiling child lying in a bed is being wheeled in looks up at you. The child in the bed smiles at you, see yourself smiling back to the child before looking up to see what floor you are on. The lighted location sign reads: "Illness or Disability Department."

The elevator's two doors slam closed while the crowd moves to the back of the elevator. The elevator begins to move again steadily even further downward.

At the next stop the elevator doors again open.

Many couples holding hands smiling and laughing greet you. A woman says to you, "What a time!"

You wonder what she is talking about as you observe the floor's location. This is "Marital Harmony Department."

The elevator doors close together again and the loaded elevator descends down deeply once again to stop at the next level.

When the elevator's two doors open and there is a huge crowd of all types now entering. You notice many with trembling hands, blurry eyes, and walking in an awkward fashion. Staring up you see that the floor you are on. It's the "Alcoholic and Illegal Drug Department."

The elevator is really starting to crowd up now, so you move closer to the floor's button column on the wall besides the elevator doors.

The elevator sinks then stops again.

An immense crowd joins you in the elevator. You look down at the lighted location sign. This is the "Depression and Worrywart Department." A crowd of every age and everyone is laughing and telling each other a joke.

The elevator is now fully crowded with people of every type. The elevator doors tightly close as the elevator begins to drop deeper, and deeper until it does drop to the very bottom of the well.

You look down to see the floor number 1 and the floor location. The sign reveals "Spirituality Department: Halfway to Heaven." This is your floor, this is your destination.

You may be wondering what lies beyond. This floor contains the crypts of memory banks of every second of every moment you have ever been alive.

You shall not allow any educated ignorance, spiritual emptiness to allow your conscious thoughts to not trust in the process in what is about to happen. It has worked for million of years, for billions of others.

Do not to pretend to know more than you know. No person has ever fully known the ultimate secrets of human existence or the inner brain. Allow this knowledge to give you renewed interest for any small part of yourself you can now discover.

It shall not be unpleasant.

Your Spirit can unravel worries, stress, and even future concerns. Your long-term future is not merely dust in the wind. You know you are exactly where you are and who you are, because you are supposed to be here. There is much beyond normal comprehension in everyone's spiritual intelligence.

Slowly and mannerly, the entire crowd exits the elevator following you to enter into a huge well-lit auditorium. You and those that followed assemble around raised steel hand railings that fill the room. You may feel like you are in Disney Land not halfway to Heaven. When everyone is settled the lights go out. A circular screen surrounds everyone as the auditorium lights slowly dim.

Around the parameter of the wall a circular theater begins showing a movie. A new film of the highlights of your earthly existence and only you can see it.

Stand holding on the waist high railing in front of you and watch your life's "Recollection Movie."

St. Augustine invented the Recollection Movie series, more or less, in the years 354 through 430. To participate in the Recollection Movie you must engender a passive attitude. Recollection is an exercise of the abstraction. A mental recollecting and gathering together of memory thoughts and visualizing these reminiscences in the mind. One must do their best to shut off the mind from external thoughts to assist producing a Spiritual solitude. St. Augustine documented and achieved this state of a Soul's recall concentration thousands of years ago, just as you can, right now.

Soon you will close you eyes, concentrating on recalling any highlight scenes of your life experiences, good or bad.

After you have seen enough reopen your eyes to return to the text. Close your eyes now for as long as you wish.

Well hopefully you enjoyed most of the movie. There may have been some scenes you were so sorry to have relived. You may sincerely regret some things and if need be you can make a mental note to undo some things or say at least that you are sorry. There were some people you could have helped more, some you loved, but never told them. But overall you enjoyed the Memory Recall Movie.

Realize that every life eventually becomes a recollection of good or bad memories.

As quick as the screen appeared it disappears. The screen is replaced by hundreds of doors, each door has a large, blue lighted sign over top of each entrance. The signs surrounding the wall of the circular auditorium are the list of names of each person in the audience in alphabetical order.

You search for your name, it takes little time to find it. You see your lighted sign, your door. Your whole name is glistening brightly over a door.

Cautiously, you approach the door. You want to read the yellow typed card taped to the door. You approach closer to the door then you read the card. Typed on the card are the words: "Invitation to meet the Spirit." You have been craving for such a meeting. You turn the door's handle, enter the room and close the door behind you.

Sweet smells greet you. The fragrance of burning incenses.

This is a mystifying place, a holy dwelling.

In the room is an opening. It is a cave. This is the holy grotto where the Spirit resides.

Seize this opportunity for spiritual growth. Rid yourself of Spiritual stressors, conceivably no forgiveness towards yourself or others, bitterness and grudges for any reason or an enormous guilty conscience.

You can delegate and unburden yourself during this time of connecting to the Spirit.

From inside the hole in the rock a voice speaks, "Fear not. Come on in. Find peace. A peace that passeth all understanding."

On the Sea of Tranquility on the moon, a wonderfully peaceful place where no other humans have been before two astronauts placed a plaque which reads: "We come in peace for all mankind."

The fruit of human nature is discord, bickering, internal moral battling and violence but the fruit of the Spirit is love, joy, peace, long-suffering, gentleness, goodness, faith, meekness, courage and caring. Your Soul is immortal and shall live forever.

The superconscious is capable of creating unbelievable miracles. The love for the superconscious and others is like the positive and negative poles of a battery, unless the Your Soul makes a trustworthy connection there will be a breach in the wires designed for reciprocal communication. You can attain such communication beyond anyone's imagination. You can get through.

Imagine and see yourself proceeding to enter the candle lit subterranean passage.

Unexpectedly, you encounter lighted turns and twisting corridors. But you remain unafraid.

What do you do when you meet the Spirit?

You close your eyes and pray. Soon you will close your eyes. Pray any prayer you know. If you don't know a prayer, you may wish to pray for help to get through one more day. You might want to say a soul stirring prayer that usually works well. Repeat it many times "I believe in the Spirit. Let there be peace on earth, and let it begin with me."

You have been lead to this divine encounter.

Now you are on your own.

To believe in the Spirit is to let go. Grant the Spiritual forces to take over.

When you pray, whatever prayer you like, wait for a whispering message that you will hear just before you decide to reopen your eyes.

There is no time limit whatsoever. Take as long as your soul needs.

Close your eyes now and pray.

After your decision to open both eyes, yawn then stretch your body to become delightfully fully awaken.

If not already you shall become gradually spiritually awaken.

Our universe operates with exact precision which simply could not just happen. The universe has an architect. We are not alone under the vast mosaic surrounding our world.

Be young at heart and full of the Spirit and life will get more exciting with every day.

Preconditioning of Session #12
State of the Brain—Serenity

You may have health you may have riches, yet no one can be happy until attaining internal sereneness. When the dullness of pleasure drives you to the pleasure of dullness, serenity comes closer.

Serenity is a calm time when your mind and body cease making demands.

A time, the mind is emotionally freed from toxic thoughts of present stress, worry or other concerns.

A time when you can overcome the minds endless obsessive chatter.

A time when you know how to enjoy what you have, while being able to lose all desire for things beyond your reach.

A time when Spiritual storms are diminishing.

At this time you shall enter the calm known only in the "here and now."

Although it usually goes against the grain of human mentality, you can just be, and enjoy the delight of just being.

Do not resist the "present and now" moment. Always attempt to live in this realm moment by moment. Let go of every moment of the past die, good or bad—you don't need negativity. Forget and let go of the future, it may not ever materialize. Soon you will be taking a few brief but beautiful holidays in paradise while still residing on earth. That sounds stupid and impossible, doesn't it? Hang in there.

Forgetting yourself is the passport needed for a passport to enlightenment and transition.

Recognize neither defeat nor victory. Neither has the power to change the mind's satisfaction of wholeness by just being.

Serenity is not to do what you do not feel like doing.

Serenity is to live comfortably in your own presence.

Serenity is when you realize that there is nothing that you desperately need.

Serenity does not consist in having what you want, but wanting what you have.

Serenity is when you stop looking for more of what you want.

Serenity is when you permit your ego to become oblivious.

Serenity ignores praise or blame, excellent health or poor heath, pleasure or sorrow.

Serenity is to calm be like an immense oak tree in the midst of a furious storm.

Serenity arrives when you agree surrender to a present moment—by relinquishing and resisting any distracting serious or serious thought, without reservation.

Visualize an hourglass, the many grains of sand dropping one by one, imagine of each passing grain of sand as your ever flowing conscious thoughts—imagine turning the hourglass side ways. The flowing thoughts as the flowing pieces of sand will cease.

The objective of this Session is to demonstrate the definition of inertia while being alive in the "here and now."

Saint Francis of Assisi (1182–1226) was the greatest Christian theologian of the Middle Ages, who addressed humankind's fundamental questions with extraordinary range and depth. During his lifetime of 44 years, he wrote the following immortal text.

> God grant me
> SERENITY
> to accept the things
> I cannot change
> Courage
> to change the things I can
> and the

Wisdom
to know the difference.
"All is well."
Wellness has been and will always be.
It is your true nature.
You cannot lose it, yet some times you may forget it.
Even if you do forget it—"all remains well."

Especially during any time of the day, including the moments of physical and emotional distress which some how, unknown to you is for the best, "all remains well."

Especially during future moments that shall challenge you—pause to hear the wellspring of knowledge from your inner brain that believes and knows that "all is well."

Welcome home! For eternally, you will realize "all is well."

Smile! Laugh! Enjoy every "here and now" moment.

Self-Hypnotic Session #12
State of the Brain—Serenity

Dear reader, place yourself in a relaxing position. Be alone and be in silence.

When your muscles are tense, they absorb mental and physical energy. To decelerate this distracting electrical energy, stretch out your entire body. This will make all your muscles loosen up a little bit. Be loose as a goose. Take two deep breaths saying "let go" to yourself. Feel yourself letting go of all your concerns, anxieties or positive or negative thoughts. The inner brain enjoys helping you in this process. Once it knows what you are trying to achieve, it will create a habit pattern, which will enable you to easily reach the state of inner calm. Gradually the habit of relaxing and letting go will be self-acting and will be achieved automatically without any effort on your part.

The breathing exercise for this Session is the famous humming invocation sound of "Ommmmm."

The "Ommmmmm" is a chant with humming rhythm emulating from the bottom of the throat. Every type of yoga, most eastern religions and philosophies utilize the "Ommmmmm" technique to establish a calming breath disposition. Breathe in deeply and when exhaling hum "Ommmmmm." Do this several times now and when ever the text requests a few "Ommmmmms."

Stress triggers a set of biochemical responses. Physical relaxation triggers a set of biochemical responses that are opposite of those caused by stress. By tensing and relaxing groups of muscles, you can counteract the physical effects of mind stress and body tensions. Be relaxed as best you can and start this positive response by tightening each muscle from the top of your head include all facial muscles and the tongue. Make these areas as tight as you can and hold the tightness for a count of five. On the count of five, release the tightness in these muscles, let go. Relax these muscles.

Tense your upper arms and shoulders count to five then let go. Let the tension roll down both arms and out through your hands and fingertips. The upper arms, forearms, hands, fingers, and fingertips are calming. Now tense up the neck muscles. Feel the tension in your neck; it is often the tensest part in your entire body. Tighten all the muscles in the neck count to five. Now let go let the muscles in the front of your neck go. Let the tension drain away. Tip your head forward a bit, as gravity seems to pull it down, as the head seems to tug you downward. Now make a frown with your forehead. Tighten those muscles in the forehead. Hold that tightness in the forehead for a count of five then let go. Allow your forehead to relax there is no trick to it, just let those muscles go limp. Tighten your chest, stomach and both legs. Hold these muscles and area as tightly as you can for a count of five. Now let go. The entire body is loose as a goose. It really is not much of a task to just think of calming down and becoming loosened all over. Breathe in deeply and while exhaling hum out loud: "Ommmmmm." Do this three times before proceeding with the text.

And as you do so your body will gradually and steadily become more relaxed. A blanket of peace, serenity, and calm is spreading down from the top of your scalp down over your forehead, down into your mouth and parted lips. Both shoulders and arms relax as the blanket of peace rolls over these parts of your body. Gradually a vague drowsiness and limp dullness and deep sleep covers the area when the blanket comes in touch. Feel the blanket covering sinking into the chest, stomach and both legs.

Your eyes will become rather tired; your eyelids will get very heavy, resting more comfortably. Vague numbness and dullness as the blanket of calm becomes heavier making you drowsier, Your head is getting heavy too. All tension is flowing away to leave you completely and as the blanket gently greets the heart. The heart is beginning to slow down for a little rest. Feel the blanket of fortifying relaxation fall heavier onto the stomach, buttocks, thighs down deeper into both legs, calf muscles into both ankles, and feet then the blanket covers the top of your toes and heels.

Breathe in deeply and then while exhaling hum aloud "Ommmmmm. Do this three times before proceeding with the text.

Go into self-hypnotic sleep now. Go to sleep covered beneath the soft, warm blanket of restfulness.

Now 1...you are going deeper into self-hypnotic sleep...
2...you are sinking into a deeper sleep...
3...deep sleep...
4...5...going deeper still...
6...the blanket of serenity feels so very good...
7...letting go completely...going down 8...a very deep and sound and restful sleep...
9...down you go.
10...Go into self-hypnotic sleep now.

The Herculean imaginative power that you possess is going to take you on an incredible tour. Your imagination the greatest friend or the greatest enemy you can have. Your imagination has more power to heal than any pill or device ever invented. Whatever good or bad changes that comes your way every response starts in the imagination of your inner brain.

Visualize, imagine and see the huge Great Pyramids of Egypt. The pyramid is an ancient, timeless mystery. Carved and fashioned with numberless blocks of rock rising to a magnificent height in the middle of the Egyptian desert. Over four thousands of years ago, literally millions of slaves and workers moved millions of giant sized limestone carried from thousands of miles away. It took centuries of human toil to stack and assembly the stones into huge structures. Over many years since construction, the pyramids have been robbed and studied. Within each pyramid is contained a labyrinth of shafts that leads to hundreds of room-sized chambers, often filled with gold and silver treasure, or tombs often empty and barren. Catacombs filled with living deadly snakes. Vaults where huge knifes come swooping down when the entrance is opened. Mausoleums, which have false a floor, which open wide to an almost mile long shaft that drops to the bottom of the pyramid. Spooky crypts have a variety other death traps to discourage grave poachers. Tomb explorers to this day, continue to fine new shafts. An international television broadcast on October 21, 2002, allowed a world audience to witness a new drill into one of the shafts in the pyramid of Khufu in Giza, Egypt, completed in the year 2570BC. A discovered tunnel led to an empty chamber with a gate with brass knob-handles, but it was a room that no one had entered for thousands of years. To this day, the pyramids of Egypt remain a mystery. New shafts will be discovered for time eternal, but no one will ever solve the pyramid's original enigma. The mystery of the pyramids is much like you. You are housed in a magnificent mystery. What makes you a mystery is not your mind or body, science has some kind of answer for how each of your organs work. What make you a mystery are not your mind or body but your heart.

The heart is the powerhouse of energy that began beating strongly only a few short weeks after your conception. It was the heart that ignited the energy to build your body and brain. It sustains you until this very day, still beating 100 times or so every single minute. This is where the Soul dwells, this is where you obtain your original ability to think and love. The Spirit communicates through the inner brain. You may have experienced differing feelings in a variety of situations: this is a bad thing to do or is this a good thing to do. Intuition guidance supplies the proper response.

The inner brain can transport you back to any time. Even that very time you were in your mother's womb. Memories since your heart had its first beat have been retained in the inner brain.

Mia Farrow, the young nineteen-year-old actress who married Frank Sinatra who was 46, writes in her memoirs that she can remember every minute of her natal birth and beyond. Since Mia Farrow is famous, her remarks became well known. However, many people have similar memories. But few are never documented. Believe that you could hear and sometimes see what was going on through your mother's ears and eyes. For many this is a very big imaginative thought. But guess what? It is absolutely true. Many people have been transported there. A fetus is not a mere tissue. A fetus with a beating heart has all its five senses, the second its heart commences the first beat. When you were merely fetus, you had not experienced any of lives harsh realities; you only felt some of the negativity or positive responses your mother experienced due to the circumstances of her daily life. You may have been jolted around in the womb. During the time, you were fetus in your mother's womb you were growing…growing fast and quickly. To grow in anything one must be calm, relaxed, comfortable, serene and relatively content. During this natal period you enjoyed a serenity you have never truly known since the moment you were born. The first thing you did seconds after your birth was cry, and if you didn't the physician or whoever delivered you, gave you a smack on the rear to make you cry. This proves to the physician so far, you are normal. During your early years you frequently cried when you were a toddler. Baby tears may not have disappeared until you were around five or six years old. Even after the age of seven or eight you may have moaned or cried when anything didn't go your way. There is nothing wrong with spreading a few tears. There is nothing harmful about crying in the least. Sometimes crying is extremely beneficial, in many ways. There is no doubt your greatest time of serenity on this world was in the womb. So guess what? That is exactly where you shall visit.

Detach from any skepticism.

To make an effort not to think about earthy things, it is indispensable to close your eyes for a while and put a hold on the inner brain and conscious mind thinking process.

You are going to that in a little while, but first breathe in deeply and while exhaling hum aloud: "Ommmmmm." Do this three times before proceeding with the text.

To inspire a passive attitude which is the when the inner brain is able to transcendence earthly things and abstract oneself from body and mind. The mind is a wanderer, thought always buzzing obstructing entry to the deepest silence of emptiness in the mind. Once completed you will proceed to reach the liberation of the eternal, the forgetting of everything.

Imagine a huge white cloud with spots of blue sky breaking through at the top and bottom of the sphere in the sky. This is the magical thick puffy snow-white cloud of "Complete Forgetfulness," it is not unknown to you. This is the previously invisible cloud that automatically embraces your thoughts moments before to drop off into bedtime sleep. Believe that the Cloud of Complete Forgetfulness is dropping from the sky to surround your body. The cloud of Complete Forgetfulness momentarily stops overhead before it sinks downward. The cloud's mist covers your entire body. Magically a cool fog begins freeing your mind allowing it to temporarily forget any thoughts in your head. The magic spray from the cloud will conceal any thought of every kind and hide them deep into the cloud of Complete Forgetfulness. A state of self-forgetfulness with no backward or forward thought.

The magic cloud's spray settles and calms you. Enjoy the soundless serene descending with the loss of outward senses, a state of perfect solitude. Do not be concerned with how well you are doing just experience being unaware of yourself. Let all awareness of yourself be gone. You are at the moment deaf and dumb forbidding any wandering thoughts to intrude the solitude. A very simple way of ridding yourself of various distracting thoughts is say "no" to them; this is a means of maintaining a passive attitude. Simply shut the mind off and say "no" to any intruding good or bad or disbelieving thoughts.

Soon in a moment or so when you close your eyes imagine a turtle when it is threatened by any unwanted element it simply pulls itself into its shell. A hard outer protection covering of peaceful impassivity. An absolutely safe domain where it is warm, safe with a calming quiet. When you shut both eyes pull yourself into a sheltered shell where all earthy thoughts are momentarily relieved and completely forgotten.

Imagine cool refreshing water is washing over your eyes, relaxing each eyeball and both eyelids. Remain in the calming turtle shell for as long as you wish before continuing with the text. Please close your eyes now, return to the text when all internal self produced thought has vanished.

Call upon the great power of the spirit and inner brain. Allow your spirit to direct your inner brain to a place and time you wish to be returned.

Recall the duration of experiences that were accumulated in your mother's womb. The mysterious incubation chamber where you existed as a living, heart-beating, brain developing human in an atmosphere of peace, complacent relaxation and serenity. A time when you never heard or thought of something called stress. You were compelled to spend a lot of months in your mother's womb. If you were born prematurely, it does not matter; you will be there. Your inner brain can recall the memories and the inner brain is all geared up and ready to go.

Recall memories of when your brain was functioning and recording in your mother's womb.

You could think thoughts while the inner brain was busy for eight months, more or less directing and constructing the body and mind which you have grown into today.

Most of the time in the womb is allotted to allow your body to gain weight.

Let's apply all the available creative imaginative powers of the inner brain.

Just quickly skip past all of your lifetime of memories even to day. Do this with one gigantic leap of imagination.

Temporarily push every thought and memory under the mist dropping from the snow-white cloud of Complete Forgetfulness that hovers above.

The imagination can do anything.

Have no doubts that you have done that. As you enter a bright room with a wooden-deck. Descending from the deck is a well-lit wooden stairwell.

Approaching the staircase you feel like a like a baby bird taking its first solo flight. Spreading your arms you discover you can actually float and fly just like a little bird. Begin to float down the wooden staircase. Enjoy the feeling of flying and floating going down the wooden staircase. You notice that the air is getting cooler as you go down.

Down you go floating and flying deeper down the stairwell's tunnel.

Now imagine and believe the stairwell's tunnel has become your mother's womb.

Your inner brain will now locate the exact moment that your heart sounded the very first burst of energy with a singular beat.

Let's count the months of your growth.

Month 1: A glow of igniting energy creates your beating heart. Soon, the glow of energy commences construction of your body. The first 30 days is passing while your heart is beating rapidly, very rapidly.

Month 2: Each tiny part of your body are sprouting. A microscopic molecule, your brain is having the most laborious period of its entire lifetime's existence. Feel your heart and hear its beating, beating, beating.

Month 3: Amazing progress, face, arms, legs, fingers, toes, there are all there. You are calm and serene with no tension as you expand and grow bigger and bigger.

Month 4: Construction and growth are going along well. You float and experience tranquility at its best encased in a loving fluid of love provided by the superconscious for your protection during this period.

Month 5: You feel just fine. Your eyes are opening. You look around but see nothing.

Month 6: Your brain and body are in a state of fetus bliss. The brain knows the construction work is almost done. A lot of feeding of energy is constantly being pumped into your stomach by a tube attached to your mother's energy source. The nourishment will make you bigger and better.

Month 7: All the creation work is done now. You rest and eat, eat, eat, while happily relaxing. You got a lot of eating to do and you love eating because it makes you stronger. You weigh all of four pounds.

Month 8 and one half a month: You simply delight in being continually fed by the connecting cord from your mother. This is nonjudgmental serenity. This is the "here and now" mindfulness.

You have all these attributes then and now. In a moment you will close both eyes.

When you do recall the sensations of what your fetus body felt like. The temperature of the fluid, something touching you, perhaps you are a twin or could it be a bump against the moving wall of your mother's womb. Pleasant memories of floating inside a protective ⅰ ble of warm fluid. Remember what the nourishment tasted like; remember any sights that you saw when as a fetus when you opened your eyes inside the womb. Remember what you were feeling, the emotions in your mind, those remembrances voluntarily bring some of these prebirth recollections back in vivid detail with visual aspects. Scan the setting so that you see every detail of any memory recall, the shades, textures, colors, the sounds, soft sounds, louder sounds, all the sound.

Enjoy the positive pure serenity of just being.

Return to the text after you visualize being born out of your mother's womb.

Now draw both lids over your eyes.

Hopefully you enjoyed serenity; you can now bring this no worldly care joy into your every day.

Set the sails of your ship, you have another excursion lined up. An ocean voyage to Samoa, a lush Polynesian isle. You will lodge in a remote nearly deserted village, which has gentle breezes, waving palms and warm tropical plants and forests. A sandy beach surrounds the small island with clear blue ocean waves breaking on the shore.

Before landing on Samoa's white sanded beach a little body rest is needed. Breathe in deeply and while exhaling hum aloud: "Ommmmmm." Do this three times before proceeding to the text.

Again, engage your potent imagination.

See yourself enjoying being on the far-flung South Seas Island of Samoa, you are in a thatched hut called a felas, located near the seashore. Sleeping on a matted floor you are awakening after a pleasant refreshing afternoon nap. You massage your eyes and rise to stand on your feet. The brief nap included a dream that you begin to ponder.

See yourself walking out of the thatched hut, dressed only in a bathing suit. You notice the warm temperature outside is around 80 degrees. You decide to forget the dream and enjoy the sunshine by effortlessly leaning against a moss-covered tree trunk near the ocean's beach. Standing alone in this secluded section of the beach, you notice you are surrounded by rich green foliage that contains banana plants with ripe fruit. You see a flock of colorful chirping parrots resting on the immense green branches of the plants. Make a mental note that you wish to pick and eat a bunch of bananas later.

But right now you have decided to go for an invigorating swim in the booming surf of the ocean.

Joy is a manifestation of harmony and you are truly enjoying this paradise.

Visualize yourself dashing out into the magically surf of the island's ocean. You dive headfirst into a tremendous wave. You feel the essence of health flowing in your body. You can feel the warm glow of health, contentment, true peace and serenity coursing rapidly throughout your body as you surface to the top of the sea and begin swimming.

Entirely you are enjoying this wondrous, magically surf like a sponge each cell is soaking in some miraculous water.

The sea's water is giving your mind and body the power to cure anything that is not right, if there is no peace, it shall give you peace, the peace of serenity. The very same nonjudgmental serenity, you enjoyed in your mother's womb at eight and a half months prior to your birth. Now as then you had a very special, consecrated shield to protect you from all harm and negative experiences. Above an enlightened filled sun appears brilliantly out from behind a large sphere shaped white cloud, the Cloud of Forgetfulness. You notice the misty cloud is fading in the sky burning to smog under the heat of the sun. The sun's rays turn the mist from the cloud into a sky covered with enchanting multi-colored rainbows. The sun burns away any internal fog so that you can see yourself clearly now. The warmth and brightness of the sun melts away any negative or selfish thoughts. The light of the sun is so strong that you will see all humans as a neighbor, regardless of their creed, nationality or religion. As you swim out further out in the high waves of the ocean's warm water, think about all the reasons you have for being mental healthy. Think all the good things that have happened in your life. The loved ones who have been with you throughout your lifetime. You have so much to be thankful for. The pleasure has far out measured any pain. You enjoy these thoughts and the search for serenity.

But now the time has come to turn your swimming direction towards the shore.

Once you reach the beach you walk back to the banana tree. You spot a bunch of large yellow bananas on the top of the plant. Eating three of the bananas makes you feel tired.

So weary you lie down in the hot sand for a little repose.

You cannot remember being been so serene, contented or happy.

As a matter of fact, you could be so happy, you feel that you may want to cry, cry true tears of joy. A person with no tears has no heart. This rare occurrence does not happen that often. Just close your eyes, for as long as it takes to muster a tear. Open the faucets, let the tears come…let everything go…let tears of joy flow.

This is the final Session in this series; you have graduated with full honor.

On the count of 3 you will awaken, return from the beach of Samoa. You will feel refreshed, serene and full of good sensations.

1…Come on back now.

2…You are coming up.

3…Be fully awake. Be Calm in Nonjudgmental Serenity.

You have so much to live for, don't you? You know.

Dedication

Dear Reader:

In most all books the dedication is the first page, the author thought the last page for the Sessions was more appropriate. I thank you, reader for your interest and curiosity of this book. May you live to see the world of your goals, dreams and fantasies be realized in your lifetime. Dedicated to: The Suffers on this world, there are people who have no teeth, people who do not have curing drugs for their illness.

On this world, there are people who eat dog food, people who do not eat daily—simply because they have no money.

On this world, there are people who cannot move one bone and must lie in a bed until they die.

On this world, there are grieving people: with broken hearts and souls.

On this world, there are people who allowed powerful addictions to have gain possession poisoning, their mind and body.

On this world, there are people in real prisons, caged like animals.

On this world, there are people who live daily in fear of hidden exploding bombs.

On this world, there are people who have erected imaginary prisons in their inner brains. On this world there are people who lack a key to access serenity in abundance.

It is to those who suffer that this book is sincerely dedicated by the author.

Sterling Titles on Happy Living

Joyful Living

Happiness is a state of mind and a positive outlook can help you achieve it. These books present to you the secrets of joyful living. They will comfort you and guide you through life's various encounters and help you live a better life.

The Art of Happy Living
R K Jain
ISBN 1 84557 647 0
Rs. 99

Happy Living
K Ravindran
ISBN 1 84557 664 0
Rs. 99

Born to be Happy
Prasanna Rao Bandela
ISBN 1 84557 442 7
Rs. 199

The Art of Peaceful Living
Acharya R. Kaushal
ISBN 1 84557 517 2
Rs. 75

Destination Happiness
J. P. Vaswani
ISBN 978 81 207 3146 2
Rs. 250

Joy of Living
Prasanna Rao Bandela
ISBN 978 81 207 3565 1
Rs. 200

for complete Catalogue visit www.sterlingpublishers.com

Secrets of Better Living

Before managing others we first need to manage ourselves – our fears, attitude, anger... These books will inspire and touch your heart and fulfill your desire for peace and tranquillity.

Management Moment by Moment
J.P. Vaswani
ISBN 978 81 207 4068 6
Rs. 75

Managing Stress
Sumita Roy
ISBN 1 84557 437
Rs. 99

You Can Make a Difference
J.P. Vaswani
ISBN 81 207 3153 0
Rs. 100

Swallow Irritation before Irritation Swallows you
J.P. Vaswani
ISBN 81 207 3152 2
Rs. 125

It's All a Matter of Attitude!
J.P. Vaswani
ISBN 81 207 3150 6
Rs. 100

Kill Fear before Fear Kills You
J.P. Vaswani
ISBN 81 207 3151 4
Rs. 100

for complete Catalogue visit www.sterlingpublishers.com

Healing the Mind and Soul

Modern-day living has become extremely stressful. Uncover the cause and change the course of illness by using alternative systems of healing. These books will help you regain good health and well-being.

Reiki & Hypnosis for Success and Self-realisation
Sumeet Sharma
ISBN 81 207 2108 X
Rs. 75

Speaking of Mind Therapy to Cure Diseases
P C Ganesan
ISBN 1 84557 310 2
Rs. 75

Mind Probe Hypnosis: The Finest Tool to Explore the Human Mind
Irene Hickman
ISBN 81 207 2076 8
Rs. 90

Clinical Hypnotherapy: A Transpersonal Approach
Dr Allen Chips
ISBN 81 207 2888 7
Rs. 295

Healing Mind, Body & Soul
Alan Bryson
ISBN 81 207 2205 1
Rs. 200

Hypno Kinesiology: A Holistic Approach to Healing
Carl Carpenter
ISBN 81 207 2490 9
Rs. 99

for complete Catalogue visit www.sterlingpublishers.com